THE FACE OF THE CENTURY
100 YEARS OF MAKEUP AND STYLE

BY KATE DE CASTELBAJAC

EDITED BY NAN RICHARDSON AND CATHERINE CHERMAYEFF

RIZZOLI
NEW YORK

CONTENTS

Half-title page: Top left: Raymond Meier.
Top right: Erwin Blumenfeld. Bottom left: Edward
Steichen. Bottom right: Ruzzie Green.

Preceding page: **FASHION PHOTOGRAPH FOR**
HARPER'S BAZAAR, **CIRCA 1939.** *Photograph by*
Louise Dahl-Wolfe.

Opposite: **BACKSTAGE BEAUTY,** *HARPER'S*
BAZAAR, **1994.** *Photograph by Michel Arnaud.*

Photograph by
Raymond Meier, 1993.

INTRODUCTION

THE BEGINNINGS OF MAKEUP CAN BE TRACED TO THE BEGINNINGS OF HUMAN TIME. THE FIRST USE OF COSMETICS CAME ABOUT 1.5 MILLION YEARS AGO, WHEN HOMO ERECTUS MIGRATED NORTHWARD FROM TROPICAL CLIMES, DRESSED IN A LOOSE CLOAK OF ANIMAL SKINS, GLISTENING IN A RED BODY SUIT OF OCHRE, LIMONITE, AND BLACK MANGANESE OXIDE—THE FIRST MAKEUP, WHOSE HEALING AND PROTECTIVE POWERS KEPT HIM SAFE FROM RAIN, WIND, AND INSECTS.

Cosmetic use quickly evolved from purely functional purposes to more symbolic applications: as an indication of rank, as religious ritual, as adornment, and as a sign of sexual maturity. Body marking became a part of establishing the cultural order of the community. Beauty was the negation of nature for these early makeup artists, and great lengths were taken to disguise real features beneath color and form. Later in time, Western peoples chose to interpret the function of the mask as a more subtle animalism, or, conversely, as an almost "natural" enhancement of anatomy. The illusion of perfectibility became the goal. Cleopatra's fellow Egyptians made good use of kohl (which had positive side benefits of preventing eye infections and cutting sun glare), Greeks brushed their lashes with black incense, Romans stained their cheeks with wine and painted their face and arms with chalk, the Elizabethans used white lead to obtain their fashionable pallor and the Fairy Queen herself painted and powdered with essences—such as cochineal, saffron and Arabian gum—pillaged from her far-flung empire.

When Catherine de Medici married the future Henry II of France in the sixteenth century she brought from Italy a "medicinal secret." To freshen the complexion, she recommended, visit the royal gardens at dawn and gather peach blossoms still fresh with dew, then by moonlight crush those blossoms with almond oil. (This recipe was perhaps not as much a *succès fou* as her other innovation: ice cream with hot chocolate sauce.) By 1770 the backlash against cosmetics in England had escalated to the point that a law was passed threatening women "of whatever social rank" with trial for witchcraft if they seduced their husbands into matrimony through the use of cosmetics. By the advent of the nineteenth century, the Victorians introduced a fetish for cleanliness, heralding soap as the basis for all skin care, and claiming for it the side benefit of moral advancement. But alone and unseen at their dressing tables, the Victorians improved on nature surreptitiously as they carmined their cheeks, enameled their faces, took belladonna to make their eyes bright, and arsenic to improve their complexions. In the east the Japanese word for makeup—*kesho*—originally referred to colored powder worn on the face and hands for ritual and theatrical purposes. By the Kamakura Era in the end of the twelfth century, eyebrow plucking and painting (with a dye made out of iron, sake, green tea, sugar, and an insect-web fixative) were among the fashionable makeup rituals.

All these points in time are sign and symbol of makeup's force of attractions. Just as the skin markings of primitive man evoked interior and exterior demons, needs, and natural forces, the makeup of the occidental woman in the twentieth century underscores the individuality, fragility, and choice of identity that characterize modern life. The qualms we feel before the painted face result from the fact that it is at once close to us, yet remote. A mirror of our secret hopes and fears, it is as often an indecent representation of an alter-ego. Charles Baudelaire, in his essay "In Praise of Makeup," wrote: "symptom of the craving for the ideal, that craving soars irresistibly to the top of our thoughts, leaving far below it the accumulation of the gross, the mundane, and the despicable that are fundamental to everyday life. Fashion," he went on, "is a sublime deformation of nature." Yet there have always been—and there are today—legions who believe that makeup only touches perfection when it passes unnoticed. As we exit this century the opposite view seems to prevail, allowing makeup to astonish by its candor.

Our second skin in its many and varied forms, makeup serves as erotic flag, as social history, as political battlefield, as fashion, and as morality. As the symbol of psychological and philosophical search for that most nebulous and elusive definition—the meaning of beauty—makeup portrays nothing less than the face of the century.

Kate de Castelbajac

Boston, 1995

A Fine Disarray **1900-**

1919

THE SPIRIT OF THE NEW CENTURY WAS EMBODIED BY THE GIGANTESQUE STATUE THAT STOOD AT THE ENTRANCE OF THE EXPOSITION UNIVERSELLE OF 1901 IN PARIS, GREETING MILLIONS OF VISITORS. SURROUNDED BY ELECTRIC LIGHT BULBS, DRESSED IN STRAIGHT SKIRT AND LARGE HAT, SHE INCARNATED AN IMAGE OF BRISK LUXURY, OF WOMAN AS ORNAMENT AND ELEGANCE, BUT AS MORAL BEACON AND FORCE AS WELL.

By 1900, two generations of women had suffered the drab restrictions imposed by Queen Victoria's heavy moral hand; the world was ready for a return to lighter pleasures. Dancing at the Moulin Rouge, dinners at Maxim's, drinking champagne out of slippers: from balls to receptions, spas to châteaux, amusement parks to dance halls, the growth of consumerism for pleasure informed the era. The Belle Époque captured the last vestiges of grand society, but it also marked the beginning of widespread democratization, along with radical social reform and feminist agitation, making the century's last hurrah contrast sharply with the severe Victorian boudoir society that preceded it.

Aesthetic values, heretofore socially dictated, evolved apace. Feminine beauty, once idealized as fragile, pure, and powdered, became more provocative, flirtatious, covertly sexual. This transition from romanticism to reality, from Gibson girl to coquette, is traced in the way women enhanced their features. Paralleling this social and moral revolution, as its sign and insignia in all levels of society, to greater or lesser degrees, turn-of-the-century women began to use makeup freely and boldly.

Preceding pages (detail) and right:
LES DEMOISELLES D'AVIGNON,
PABLO PICASSO, PARIS, 1907.
Oil on canvas, 8' x 7'8". The
Museum of Modern Art, New York.

Opposite: **JAPANESE PRINT,**
CIRCA 1900. © *Bettmann Archive.*

COVER ILLUSTRATION,
ANONYMOUS, AMERICAN
VOGUE, 1910.

While cosmetics were widely used in the 1890s in France and England in imitation of Queen Alexandra (who wore makeup, however, only at evening functions), in the United States the return to paint lagged by a decade. Except for a dash of flowery cologne and a discreet touch of powder, no lady was suspected of making herself up. Steaming the complexion or washing with soap and water were all that were deemed necessary. Yet by 1900 rouge was in sufficient demand that several brands were advertised in the Sears and Roebuck catalog, and by 1908 makeup was sufficiently accepted that one etiquette writer ruled it permissible to use rouge sticks and powder puffs for dining out at lunch—but not at dinner.

The expense, unavailability, and unsure quality of commercial cosmetic products made it necessary for women in the nineteenth century to concoct their own beauty remedies at home. Recipes for cosmetics and lotions were handed down from mother to daughter. Skin whitening agents such as bismuth, eye salves made out of walnut leaves, burnt match sticks for lashes, and dyes used to paint blue veins on cheeks, neck, and bosom for the truly transparent look were in vogue. Lavender water was the popular perfume: Yardley's version for those who could afford it; Phulnana and Shem-el Nessir for the masses. Cold cream (said to have been invented by Greek physician Galen in the second century B.C.) was ubiquitous, as was Vaseline. And as hygiene became a cause célèbre in social reform, the virtues of soap were extolled everywhere.

Literature detailing the fabrication of these beauty secrets abounded. *Le Cabinet de Toilette*, by the Baronne Staffe, and *Le Bréviaire de la Femme* of the Comtesse de Tramar are two such historic documents. The countess suggested that makeup should be invisible: "Cream, then wipe the face, then take a powder made of the white of pearl, then apply rouge with a rabbit's foot. Make a paste of cloves to put on the eyelids and eyebrows, wiping it with a finger." To lengthen eyelashes, she suggested a harem secret: China ink mixed with rose water. A recipe for the flesh-colored Poudre d'Amour, an early foundation from the Marquise de Fontenoy, was a veritable grocery list of ingredients: cornstarch, six juicy carrots, and half a beetroot, dried and sifted through silk. Spanish ladies, reported Sheila Rothman in *Woman's Proper Place* (1978), were in the habit of sleeping in gloves lined with a hand-beautifying pomade of soap, salad oil, and mutton tallow mixed with wine and musk.

> # EXCEPT FOR A DASH OF FLOWERY COLOGNE AND A DISCREET TOUCH OF POWDER, NO LADY WAS SUSPECTED OF MAKING HERSELF UP. STEAMING THE COMPLEXION AND SOAP AND WATER WERE ALL THAT WERE DEEMED NECESSARY

The Subtle Arts That Make Fair Women Fairer

VOGUE

November 15

Price 25 Cents

FRENCH ROUGE BOXES, CIRCA 1900.
Courtesy A. Bourjois & Cie.

Among the simplest face whiteners were powdered milk of magnesia, rice powder, French chalk, and Venetian talc; many contained lead, arsenic salts, and bismuth. Though the homemade powder was labor-intensive, it was superior to commercially made products that contained fillers such as potatoes and nuts. Other powders turned the face a dirty gray when exposed to gas, candle, or coal fumes. Around 1866, this side effect was cured when Henry Tetlow discovered that zinc oxide, when dried and ground, was a nonreactive, nontoxic base for face powder (and one of America's first contributions to the cosmetics industry). No prepared rouge was entirely safe for the skin; those for sale often contained white lead and other dangerous substances.

A beauty specialist, writing in the 1905 *Ladies Home Journal*, suggested applying India ink to the eyelashes and the eyebrows to intensify them. Further suggestions included burning a cork and using the charred black residue to shade the eyelid.

Technological advances were working their subtle and inexorable changes in the social fabric. As the typewriter became more popular and inexpensive, women gradually replaced men as clerks and typists. Most often, these new white-collar female employees were either from middle-class families or from those aspiring to the bourgeoisie. Similarly, the growth of large department stores and the new consumer class generated an increasing demand for female salesclerks. These women were most often young, coming from backgrounds close to those of the customers they served. Educated daughters of the middle and upper classes, meanwhile, filled the ranks as teachers, while also moving slowly into the professions of medicine and law and the brand-new field of social work. In every instance, class and race determined what occupation a woman might aspire to.

Technology was also at work revolutionizing the home life of urban women, liberating them from much of the drudgery of household tasks. The construction of city water supply pipes eliminated the endless parade of buckets from the well to the kitchen; the widespread installation of hot-water heaters ended the procession of hot water from the stove to the washtub. The new, electricity-powered appliances for washing, sewing, and vacuuming also helped free women from previously onerous household chores.

While the golden age of women's colleges and universities began in the late part of the nineteenth century, institutions for women continued to come into existence during this period, providing new access to higher education. Finally, the era witnessed the establishment, expansion, and vigorous pursuit of the activities of women's clubs and societies.

Increasing urbanism meant freedom for women. Men's

workplaces were typically too distant from residences to allow the family to lunch together. In consequence, daytime socializing among women, once confined to the parlor, now more frequently took place in public restaurants. Department stores, as well as commercial tea parlors, offered ladies' luncheons, and soon the traditional social venues of the sewing circle, the husking bee, and the afternoon visit were things of the past.

In 1910, a *New York World* reporter sat at a café window at Forty-second Street to investigate women's new appearance and behavior, recording her observations: "Although she saw only one woman smoking, she was impressed by the amount of cosmetics women wore. Eyelids can't be painted too blue nor lashes too heavily beaded." Proving that women did not wear the new cosmetics only for leisure activities, activist Lillian Wald noted in her 1915 book, *The House on Henry Street*, that even many of the poor young women who frequented her settlement house wore makeup. Wald saw a practical motive for it: "As for the paint—many girls thought it wise to use it, for employers did not like to have jaded-looking girls working for them."

While the middle class was finding a foothold in an upstart society of their own, the doors of established families closed against them. In America, Mrs. William Astor drew an impregnable social line around the four hundred eligible families (the number that would conveniently fit in her ballroom), reigning as the undisputed queen in a court that encouraged lavishness in both dress and toilette.

By 1910, the mania for makeup that began in the theater had run the course from socialite to saleswoman. Every restaurant, hotel, and store of any importance kept a supply of cosmetics in their dressing rooms or bathrooms for use by female patrons. Most of the exclusive beauty shops manufactured and sold their own preparations, and most beauty parlors, even modest ones, employed a cosmetic specialist or artist to demonstrate makeup techniques to clients. Even the handbags sold during this period had sets of specially fitted cosmetic accessories, complete with powder puff or rouge box, reported Elizabeth Reid in a 1910 article in the American magazine *Woman Beautiful*.

The nineteenth century was marked by exceptional prosperity and progress. The Industrial Revolution, the absence of world wars, and the effects of urbanization contributed to the productivity of the period. "The city has become the central feature in modern civilization and to an ever increasing extent the dominant one," wrote municipal reformer Frederic C. Howe in 1906. "Man has entered on an urban age."

As Edward Richardson stated in an article on "The Future

THE FIRST TOILET, CIRCA 1873.
Lithograph by Currier and Ives.
© *Bettmann Archive.*

Have a beautiful skin

Follow these simple directions

You must give Nature the aid she needs in keeping the skin pores active. This means washing your face and washing it thoroughly, regularly, every day.

Cold cream alone won't do—you mustn't depend upon it entirely for cleanliness. It catches dust and helps fill up the tiny pores instead of cleansing them.

You needn't be afraid of the effect of soap on the skin—not if your soap is right. Use Palmolive and make washing a daily beauty treatment.

Palmolive is the mildest of soaps and the gentlest of cleansers. Palm and Olive oils —ingredients of Palmolive—were ancient Egyptian cosmetics. Cleopatra used them as beautifiers as well as cleansers.

Use your two hands

This mild, gentle soap produces a profuse creamy lather which you should apply to your face with your two hands.

Massage it softly into your skin, so as not to roughen its delicate, sensitive texture. Then just as gently rinse it away.

It carries with it all dangerous, clogging accumulations—the dust and oil secretions, the remains of the day's rouge and powder. It leaves your skin healthfully, thoroughly clean.

Keep that school-girl complexion

A fine and fresh complexion

The gentle washing and rinsing stimulates minute glands and capillaries to beneficial action. This keeps your complexion fine and fresh and encourages natural, becoming color.

Be liberal with Palmolive Cold Cream if your skin is dry. Apply it before washing and again after, and your skin will be beautifully smooth.

Why Palmolive isn't 50 cents a cake

If made in small quantity it would be. We can't make it better.

The gigantic demand for Palmolive keeps the price moderate It keeps the Palmolive factories working day and night, which reduces manufacturing cost.

It permits the purchase of the costly oils, imported from overseas, in such vast volume that the price is much reduced.

Thus Palmolive is popular priced—no more than ordinary toilet soaps.

It is for sale by leading dealers everywhere and supplied in guest-room size by America's popular hotels.

THE PALMOLIVE COMPANY
Milwaukee, U. S. A.

THE PALMOLIVE COMPANY OF CANADA, LIMITED
Toronto, Ontario

PALMOLIVE

of Cosmetics," "With the passing of formal magic, and with the diminution of religious rites which has accompanied both Protestantism and the spiritual indifference resulting from too close an adherence to the data of nineteenth century science, the mysticism of perfume has given way in our cities to a more civilized, though perhaps less cultured interest in the practical uses of creams, powders, pigments, and soaps, exalted the bathroom above the temple and placed washing before purification."

The new conditions of city life were not always salubrious for the skin, however. Dust and dirt from factories and streets, a lack of exercise and fresh air, and a rhythm of life that became increasingly frenetic diminished the benefits of the technical revolution. These factors pushed women to defend their youthful looks—and, regardless of their social station, to therefore seek out beauty products as never before.

The new urban rich displayed their apartments, their houses, and their boudoirs with great pride, more interested in the effect of their wealth than in qualities of good taste. The *nouveau riche* needed a salon à la Louis XIV, a dining room in Renaissance style, a boudoir in Rococo, and a *fumoir* (smoking room) in oriental. Women's wardrobes, like their furniture, were as ostentatious as possible. Couturiers like Worth, Poiret, Paquin, and Lanvin offered highly individual creations, often elaborately embroidered, that reflected their customers' taste for display. Madeleine Vionnet's body-sculpting bias-cut dresses coexisted with Raoul Dufy's and Paul Iribe's colorful decoration in splendid dissonance. Although the intricacies of the toilette had been greatly modified during the past decades, the increase in women's activities infringed on the time formerly given over to daily beauty regimens. Mornings were spent at lectures and musical performances, middays at exclusive luncheons, and afternoons were spent shopping, playing cards, or attending charity bazaars, five o'clocks, and debutante receptions. A busy day was followed by a mad dash home to dress before dinner and the opera; there was less time to devote to a regimen of beauty.

A new tolerance for artificiality was coming into fashion. The latest trend from Paris was for hennaed hair, which quickly supplanted in popularity the golden tints obtained from the use of peroxide, since henna's hue was more generally acceptable to all women. In 1907 the first synthetic hair color was fabricated by a young French chemist named Éugene Schueller and baptized Aureole. (A few years later this same chemist created a fledgling

BY 1910, THE MANIA FOR MAKEUP THAT BEGAN IN THE THEATER HAD RUN THE COURSE FROM SOCIALITE TO SALESWOMAN

PALMOLIVE SOAP
ADVERTISEMENT, 1920.
Illustration © Culver Pictures.

Opposite: **THEDA BARA, AN OBSCURE STAGE ACTRESS TURNED SILENT-FILM STAR, WHOSE NAME BECAME SYNONYMOUS WITH ALL THAT WAS DARING AND LUXURIOUSLY SINFUL, CIRCA 1917.**
Photograph © Culver Pictures.

Above: **VASLAV NIJINSKY IN** *LA DANSE SIAMOISE* **FROM THE BALLET** *LES ORIENTALES*, 1910. *Photograph by Druet.* © *Culver Pictures.*

business called L'Oréal.) Dyed hair required adjustments in skin tone in order to achieve a harmonious ensemble, and women were forced to rely on the blending powers of powder and rouge. Some finesse was needed in its application, but it was no longer necessary to conceal the flattering effects of makeup. Paint was out of the pot. Two worlds, haute monde and demimonde, now met; makeup was the common ground.

In Paris, there were more than a hundred thousand prostitutes, numerous brothels, and two hundred "houses of rendezvous." Employees were recruited from the ranks of *petites mains*, girls who worked for the fashion industry, and included washers, seamstresses, or clerks who wanted to improve their meager salaries. With these new opportunities, however, came the danger of pregnancy or even worse—the *pied de Venus*, venereal disease.

The Belle Époque ushered in two seemingly disparate but oddly compatible ideologies: the glorification of the "woman's sphere," introduced by suffragettes, and the celebration of the female body by the proponents of "Sapphism." Love, beauty, sensuality, and education were the cornerstones of the latter movement. The Sapphists called themselves the Bonheur-des-Dames ("the happiness of women"), and included Renée Vivien and Natalie Barney. In Barney's Paris salon, she gave parties for her female (and some chosen male) friends, such as Colette Willy and Winaretta Singer (the celebrated American heiress), where lightly clad dancers ran around the garden "encircling the temple of friendship." These women dreamed of creating a universe of equality, far from the aggression and hatred of male hegemony.

Central to their Sapphist ideology was the feminist myth of antiquity's Great Mother, a custodian of goodness and equilibrium in society that men later destroyed with their violence. This myth claimed women had lost status because their most sacred function, motherhood, was not honored as were money and social position at this time. While certain feminists of the Belle Époque embraced this ideology, transforming the myth into a *raison d'être*, others emphasized equality under the law. Both groups, however, wanted the same freedom—to partake equally in society through electoral power.

Feminism exploded in the early twentieth century, galvanizing a universal belief in women's moral superiority and bringing women out of the home into reform work. One corollary of that belief was the somewhat Darwinian identification of beauty with the "natural woman," which was opposed by the notion that every woman could be beautiful. Feminists and beauty experts argued that spiritual qualities were more important to creating and maintaining the appearance of beauty than were physical attributes. It was argued that beauty was potentially available to any woman, if she followed a proper ethical path. The conviction of woman's moral superiority waned in the 1920s, but the possibility that every woman might be beautiful, once raised, did not disappear.

Physical appearance, dress, hair, and makeup use was therefore an early, and vocal, concern of feminism. When Elizabeth Cady Stanton, Charlotte Perkins Gilman, and Inez Milholland marched at the head of the 1912 New York City Suffragette rally wearing makeup, a wave of fashionable women followed. Elizabeth Arden was among them. She, too, aspired to be seen as a member of the socially prominent caste: women who didn't need to work and instead devoted their time to humanitarian causes. It was, in fact, the prominent women of the decade who championed bold makeup, along with the freedom of appearance.

By 1910, most advertisements selling cosmetics still stressed the natural look to the middle class. These ads insinuated the moral directive of makeup, stressing that respect for oneself and for the heritage of beauty was the duty of all women—and the rigors involved in maintaining it were an ethical obligation.

Side by side with feminist themes in beauty literature of the period were equally antifeminist opinions. One was the notion that to prevent wrinkling and aging, women must remain calm and serene, avoiding all mental and emotional exertion. Another familiar old canard was that beauty was important not only as a measure of healthy living, but to make certain that women did not lose their husbands to more attractive or younger rivals. A peculiarly twentieth-century rationale was also added: makeup as a path to achieving job security. Harriet Hubbard Ayer, for example, claimed that she took up her career as a beauty expert particularly to help the advance of professional women in a business world of men.

With its democratically available powders and lotions, its cosmetics and hair dyes, the commercial culture of beauty soon became the major means to beauty for all women. British novelist Elinor Glyn noted that women of all ages regularly frequented beauty shops. "It is difficult to exaggerate the importance of the influence of the beauty parlor on American life," she remarked. Yet Glyn was not troubled by the fact that modern beauty culture was in part based on the manipulation of women. She believed that the beauty parlor had been a positive force, arguing that it had "aroused a greater feeling of self respect and hope amongst all classes."

Nonetheless, rigid codes in clothing, makeup, and coiffure at the turn of the century permitted one to distinguish at a glance to which social level a woman belonged: the grande dame of society; the "honest" woman; the demimondaine or actress; the woman who

THE CLASSIC GIBSON IDEAL,
HERE ESPOUSED BY A
GROUP OF CHORUS GIRLS,
CIRCA 1915.
Photograph © Culver Pictures.

Opposite: SUFFRAGETTE PARADE
ON FIFTH AVENUE, NEW YORK,
1912.
Photograph © Bettmann Archive.

worked, and the woman who had no need to. Skin color provided an essential indication of social status—a tan or reddened skin always betrayed the laboring class. In France, other signs of status included the traditional bonnet worn by farm women to hide their hair, which was often cropped and sold to be made into a chignon for urban belles. Blue-collar workers in France wore simple chignons, adding a bit of rice powder imported from China to their hair for special effect.

While the Parisienne, either demimondaine or society lady, had always understood the art of makeup, in England, until just before the war, only prostitutes wore powder, rouge, lipstick, and eyebrow pencil on the street or during daylight hours. A true lady powdered herself (very discreetly) only for the evening.

THE RELATIVE EXPENSE, UNAVAILABILITY, AND UNSURE QUALITY OF COMMERCIAL COSMETIC PRODUCTS MADE IT NECESSARY FOR WOMEN IN THE NINETEENTH CENTURY TO CONCOCT THEIR OWN BEAUTY REMEDIES AT HOME

A gauge of the cultural differences between France and England was the celebrity of three French courtesans of the time. Liane de Pougy, Émilienne d'Alençon and the Belle Otero reigned in the demimonde, and in the hearts of the *beaux dandies* of Paris. Having left the gutter for the opera box, they made heads turn, particularly those of kings. These *grandes cocottes* boasted of many lovers, both male and female, and conducted lively rivalries measured by their fabulous jewels and luxurious wardrobes.

Another star, Cleo de Mérode (who was a dancer and not a courtesan), distinguished herself not only by her extraordinary beauty but also by her exceptional coiffure. Of authentically noble birth, Mérode was one of the most photographed women of her time. When the fashion was for a chignon high on the head, she wore an exotic, over-the-ear style that emphasized her charms yet hid her obtruding ears.

Accounts of courtesan life were hungrily followed in the pages of *Le Figaro* and *La Revue* and pictures showing the details of their latest ensembles, hair, and makeup started trends. Far from being shunned, the courtesans were feted: Cartier created jewelry for them, and the size of a new motorcar's interior was advertised as measuring the circumference of the Belle Otero's hat.

The makeup style of these beauties was learned from the theater. During the latter part of the nineteenth century, stage lighting was crudely accomplished with gas lights and thus demanded crude makeup. Black pencils in tubes, Crayons d'Italie, were used to underline the eyelids and to darken brows and lashes. Prepared chalk and carmine (a reddening agent) were applied on the face.

For men, the illusion of a beard was achieved by burning rough brown paper and rubbing the ashes on the chin and cheeks. The charred end of a match or stick was used to hide wrinkles, and different shades of wool, stuck on with fishlime or solution of shellac, were used to simulate beards and mustaches.

The invention of the incandescent electric lamp transformed the stage from a dimly lit space to a dramatic setting in which the acting, lighting, costuming, staging, and makeup were united in a total artistic endeavor. Makeup changed accordingly. Greasepaint was invented by C. Herbert of Berlin, Germany, and Carl Badius, a member of the Leipziger Stadt-Theater, was considered one of the greatest artists in character makeup in Germany.

Yet makeup's most elaborate expression came with the passion for orientalism that was sweeping Europe at this time. *Mille et une nuits* (Thousand and One Nights) by Joseph Charles Mardrus was the theme song that inspired dance, music, opera, fashion, painting, and cinema. In Paris, Sergei Diaghilev's Ballets Russes began its revolutionary performances in 1910, continuing until after the war. The ballet, which expressed the culture and the flamboyance of the Russian world, enlisted the most prominent painters of the period to create the backdrops, costumes, and choreography. The divine Anna Pavlova was the first principal dancer, with Nijinsky as her male counterpart.

Before this decade, the attitude toward color preserved the Victorian taste for the uniformly pastel. The sensitive palette was revolutionized by the arrival of the Ballets Russes. Cecil Beaton summarized: "It was almost impossible to estimate the effect this theatrical troupe had on Western European fashions. Bright colors had been inadmissible for over a century. The most distinctive shades were the heavy ochres and crimsons which were acceptable wear for wives of opulent Victorian manufacturers ...[but] when the crimson curtain rose to reveal Bakst's fantastic setting for the pas de deux from Fokine's *Blue Bird*, the vast stage was decorated only in two colors—and the most startling colors: orange like wings against a brilliant expanse of butcher blue. Against this overscaled scene, two diminutive figures appeared like insects. Lopokova, dressed in a lilac and emerald green tutu, was partnered by Idzikowsky in his suit and tights of blinding blue and brilliant tangerine. An entirely new world had opened to me. I had never before seen anything equal to the impression of excitement."

Ballet makeup, too, was radically different from the cream-and-roses and baby-blue eye shading of musical comedy, giving no impression of mere prettiness. In the midst of a matte, almond-toned pallor, the eyes were clearly outlined, elongated, and slanted upward at the corners, following the line of the swept-up brows above them; the lashes were heavily beaded like the stamens of flowers. The mouth was faintly and thinly outlined with black, exaggerated in size, painted a deep scarlet, and touched with Vaseline to make the lips shine.

Bronislawa Nijinska, the sister of the great dancer and a minor dancer in the troupe, described the makeup Léon Bakst created for the most scandalous of presentations, *L'Après-midi d'un faune*: "Eyelids were painted *gorge de pigeon*, while the bottom and the nails of the feet were tinted in a rose-colored ochre. Nijinsky was given the appearance of an animal with fur by painting his thin, nearly nude, leotard with large brown spots. The face makeup was extremely sophisticated, and the ears were elongated in points with wax. The obliqueness of the eyes, and the thickness of the mouth were reinforced by painted lines. A wig of golden tresses was mounted on two horns which were put on the head, giving the impression of an intelligent animal who could have been human."

The Ballets Russes directly inspired the rage for bright, strong colors in cosmetics, scents, and decor. Even publicity adopted an orientalist bent, and names for makeup swerved east. Helena Rubinstein recalled in her autobiography that: "the electric combinations of purple and gold excited me beyond measure. Warm, passionate colors, they were as far removed from my virginal whites and noncommittal greens as anything could be. After the ballet, I went back to the salon and tore down my white brocade curtains. I gave orders for them to be replaced with the brilliant color schemes I had fallen in love with the night before."

Top and center: **FRENCH POWDER BOXES, CIRCA 1900.**

Bottom: **YARDLEY & CO., LTD., 8 OLD BOND STREET, LONDON, 1910.** *Courtesy Yardley of London.*

As the orientalist trend gained adherents, makeup formerly seen only at costume balls was now visible at evening gatherings and afternoon teas. American *Vogue* documented the beauty habits of far-flung cultures, reporting in 1911 that "Turkish and Circassian women used henna for penciling the eyes. Among the Arabs of the desert, the women blackened the edge of their eyelids with a black powder, and drew a line around the eye with it to make the organ appear large. Indeed, large black eyes are the standard of beauty among nearly all eastern women."

Another article cited the medicinal as well as beautifying properties of kohl, or *kajal*, and reported that joined eyebrows were a sign of beauty for the Mussulmans, but were not appreciated by Hindus (or in Iceland, Denmark, Germany, and Greece). In Bohemia, in fact, they were considered to be the mark of a vampire. The article then informed readers that Near-eastern women scrubbed their skin with a stone, washed their hair with the yolks of eggs, and used the whites of those same eggs to efface crow's-feet wrinkles near the eyes.

Modern commercial beauty culture was greatly aided by the development of the beauty parlor. Beauty parlors began mainly as haircutting and wig making salons, and in 1880, one F. Goering of Baltimore, who featured himself as an importer of human hair, was part of the wave of business people who helped to legitimize what became the most characteristic institution of modern beauty. While such establishments already existed in Paris, Mary Cob opened the first London shop after she established a branch on New York's Twenty-third Street. It was the first of its kind in America. While in Victorian times face and body paint was identified with promiscuity, hair, almost in compensation, became enormously important in the general definition of beauty. A woman of fashion required masses of hair arranged in intricate displays.

The prototype of the beauty salon as we know it was also a manicure parlor. In early manicures, metal knives and acids were used to cut the cuticle. Formerly a torturous process, the manicure was revolutionized by a Madame "Doctor" Sitts of Paris, who used softer instruments, including the orange stick, still popular a century later. Advertisements in *Harper's Bazaar* and *Vogue* showed that beauty as a business was in the process of formation. The business of manicuring was imported from Paris to the United States in 1870 by Harriet Hubbard Ayer, after she visited Madame Sitts. As late as 1874 there were no more than two manicurists in the nation; but by 1884, beauty writer Emily Faithful commented on the surprising number of established manicurists.

A prohibition against the employment of men as manicurists meant that women often began their careers as beauty specialists in manicuring salons. By the 1890s, Rikers Manicure Parlor in New York City occupied several floors of a downtown building and included separate departments for hairdressing, electric scalp treatment, hair dyeing, facial massage, chiropody, and manicuring. The profession became so elite that some manicurists opened their own beauty parlors, where hairdressing and other beauty services were subsidiary to the central emphasis on hands.

If the early cosmetics firms primarily marketed creams and lotions, they were followed by a generation of business women who, although they often developed their own lines of cosmetic products, were based in shops where they applied these creams and lotions directly to their customers' faces. Elizabeth

Arden and Helena Rubinstein were the most prominent of these women. They generally focused on the rejuvenation of the skin and, in so doing, were influenced by major developments in the field of dermatology and by a new group of physicians calling themselves "professors." These professors set up colleges, schools, and institutes where they practiced new techniques in facial restructuring. Accounts of what went on in these dermatological institutes came mainly from muckrakers who considered the techniques dangerous and their practitioners charlatans.

Claiming to represent new specializations within the medical profession, their techniques involved dubious procedures, like face peeling. First done in 1886, and popularly called "skinning," it involved the application of acid and electricity to remove the upper layers of skin to eliminate scarring or simply to give a youthful appearance. As actors and actresses of the period reached middle age, they flocked to face skinning parlors, reported a *Ladies' Home Journal* article in 1908. Paraffin was also injected under the skin to round out gaunt cheeks and sagging eyelids, and surgical techniques were available to reshape noses, as were rudimentary face lifts to eliminate wrinkles. These early plastic surgeons could also tie ears back, and tone down high cheekbones.

The services of beauty specialists were not necessarily ineffective. Their creams contained oils and bleaches that could soften and whiten the skin to attain the translucent quality that many women sought. Before the renewed popularity of makeup, cosmeticians were limited in the number of services they offered; massage, first advocated by S. Weil Mitchell, was added to make beautification rituals more attractive to clients. By the 1880s, electrolysis, an effective technique for removing facial hair, had been developed. By the 1890s, facial massage became the most important part of a treatment. Shrewd beauty shop owners realized the psychological aspect of the services they performed, and even at this early date, decor was purposely luxurious, with thick carpets and gilded, lacquered furniture.

The development of the beauty business was greatly affected by the talents of several figures who, through a combination of business acumen, zealous preaching, and scientific interest, became central to the industry that would develop after the first World War. One of these figures was Helena Rubinstein. Born in 1870 in Krakow, Poland, the oldest of eight sisters, Rubinstein received a traditional Eastern European education and a motto along with it: "Outer charm and inner beauty will give you the power to control your life, and hold the love of the man you will marry." After studying medicine, Rubinstein realized she hated the sight of blood, and decided upon another career. After a move

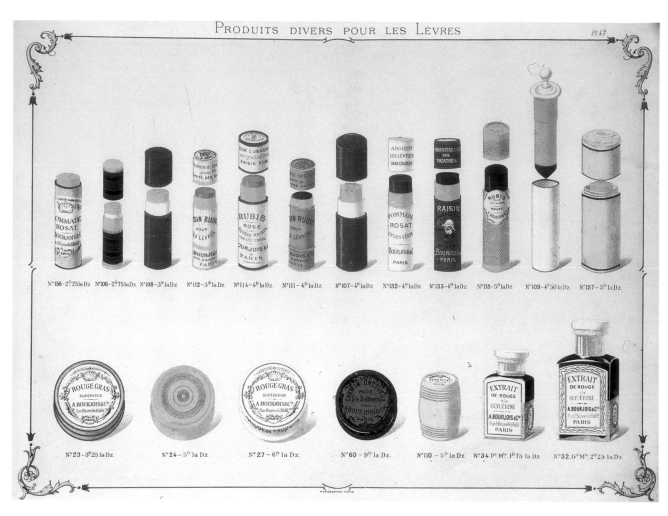

N° 156 – 2f 25 la Dz.   N° 106 – 2f 75 la Dz.   N° 108 – 3f la Dz.   N° 112 – 3f la Dz.   N° 114 – 4f la Dz.   N° 111 – 4f la Dz.   N° 107 – 4f la Dz.   N° 132 – 4f la Dz.   N° 133 – 4f la Dz.   N° 115 – 5f la Dz.   N° 109 – 4f 50 la Dz.   N° 157 – 5f la Dz.

N° 23 – 3f 25 la Dz.   N° 24 – 5f la Dz.   N° 27 – 6f la Dz.   N° 60 – 9f la Dz.   N° 110 – 5f la Dz.   N° 34 – Pt Mn 1f 75 la Dz.   N° 32 – Gd Mn 2f 25 la Dz.

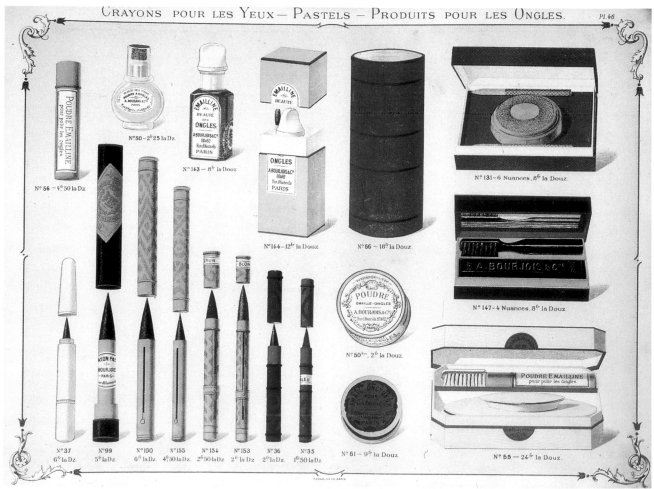

N° 56 – 4f 50 la Dz.   N° 50 – 2f 25 la Dz.   N° 143 – 8f la Douz.   N° 144 – 12f la Douz.   N° 66 – 18f la Douz.   N° 131 – 6 Nuances, 8f la Douz.

N° 147 – 4 Nuances, 8f la Douz.

N° 50 bis, 2f la Douz.

N° 61 – 9f la Douz.

N° 37 – 6f la Dz.   N° 99 – 5f la Dz.   N° 100 – 6f la Dz.   N° 155 – 4f 50 la Dz.   N° 154 – 2f 50 la Dz.   N° 153 – 2f la Dz.   N° 36 – 2f la Dz.   N° 35 – 1f 50 la Dz.

N° 55 – 24f la Douz.

from Krakow to Australia, she noticed the deplorable state of Australian women's skin and offered for sale a cream she had devised for her personal use in Poland.

Rubinstein was not just a purveyor but a believer in makeup. She was influenced by theatrical makeup style, but she sought a natural look; she was also particularly effective at creating products. "Women of good families knew very little about the application of cosmetics," according to Rubinstein, who experimented privately on her own face. She discovered a method of slenderizing the nose by blending red and mauve dots at the corners of the nostrils and adding shadow on the eyelids and over the temples to enhance the size of the eyes. She put a touch of red on her cheeks and, with a hare's foot dusted with terra-cotta powder, touched the lobes of her ears and the tip of her chin.

In the process of all this painting, Rubinstein realized that better ingredients in makeup would enhance their appearance and stability on the skin, and she also quickly gave her allegiance to the color that is still associated with her—pink. "I detested the chalk-white 'rice powder' then in vogue. It had originated in China, and it made every woman look as though her face had been whitewashed. Color was the only answer. A rosy, pink-tinted face powder seemed the most logical start, and for fair-skinned blondes a shade of rachel." Rubinstein's next innovation was to introduce perfumes into her preparations, making them immediately identifiable through subtle fragrances.

NONETHELESS, RIGID CODES IN CLOTHING, MAKE-UP, AND COIFFURE AT THE TURN OF THE CENTURY PERMITTED ONE TO DISTINGUISH AT A GLANCE TO WHICH SOCIAL LEVEL A WOMAN BELONGED

Another milestone in makeup occurred in 1886 as the California Perfume Company (later Avon Products) was created by an enterprising former book salesman named David H. McConnell. McConnell had noticed that the small samples of perfume he gave to customers (in heliotrope, white rose, violet, and other scents) were more popular than the Bibles he was selling, so he began to manufacture a line of beauty products sold directly from the factory to the consumer through agents. McConnell's business grew rapidly, especially in remote rural areas where access to department stores was limited.

Photographs began to appear in fashion magazines when Condé Nast bought *Vogue*. He continued using illustrators such as Lepape, Vertes, and Benito, but he was certain that the future of the magazine concerned reproductions that reflected a truer image. Contacting Baron Adolf de Meyer, the renowned European photographer, he employed him in 1913 to help forge the link between the worlds of fashion, art, and commerce.

De Meyer had established his reputation as a photographer in Paris and London, photographing the members of the Ballets Russes. Although he worked for *Vogue*, de Meyer was not primarily interested in fashion photography, since the fashion industry as such did not exist in New York. Haute couture was centered in Paris, and most of the clothing de Meyer photographed belonged to the wearers themselves. De Meyer instead sought to create an icon of feminine beauty, full of softness, luxury, high romance, lush textures, and silvery fabrics. His sittings took place in his own studio, which was furnished with lacquered screens and Empire pieces imported from Europe. His women were objects of admiration, mysteriously feminine and luminous. Through the work of de Meyer, *Vogue* presented a world born of the Belle Époque of Europe. Protected from care, swaddled in furs and satins, his models did no work, played no sports; they existed to be admired. The new woman seeking emancipation was consciously absent in his vision.

The beauty industry during the early 1900s featured publicity that assured the reader of its products' ability to re-create the woman glorified by de Meyer's photography. As yet, no real controls existed, and no governmental restraints were exercised to limit the outlandish claims made by manufacturers. In the U.S., it was reported in 1916, there were 559 manufacturers of cosmetics, which spent a total of 845,494 dollars on advertising in more than thirty national magazines. (By 1945, as a point of reference, the number of manufacturers was only three and a half times larger but the advertising dollar had been multiplied more than forty-three times.)

In January of 1914, *Good Housekeeping* magazine contained seventeen ads for toilet articles. Included in that fairly typical and representative array were Ivory Soap, Klein's Glycerin Hungarian Soap, LaBlanche Face Powder, Luxor Face Cream, MHP Aluminum Hot Water Bottles, Packer's Tar Soap, Pompeiian Massage Cream, prophylactic toothbrushes, Sanitex Hairbrushes, rose glycerin soap, Cello Metal Hot Water Bottles, Creme de Keridor, Daggett and Ramsdell's Perfect Cold Cream, Dioxogen, and Dr. J. Parker Pray's Toilet Preparations. Products sold by correspondence comprised the majority of the ads published. It was possible to obtain plasters against wrinkles in the form of bands that were impregnated with an unguent, or a rubber mask that was covered with pomade. A double chin could be dealt with by ordering a *mentonière gamesh* (chin strap) copyrighted by Madame Adair of New Bond Street, London. To reduce the width of the nose, an apparatus could be ordered that pinched the nostrils

throughout the night, or so said the French magazine *La Vie Heureuse* in 1908. Other remedies available by mail order in France were Oriental Pills from Ratier, which claimed they would increase the size and elasticity of the bust. For the face, there was Antirides de Camélia, and Mouche Pompadour.

The awareness of the need for trademarks grew slowly, keeping pace with advertising, along with the establishment of brand names and growth in distribution. In the U.S., the first trademark law passed in 1870, but was transformed ten years later. Ten thousand trademarks were registered in 1906, jumping from the 1,221 registered in 1871.

Prior to 1900, manufacturers turned profits by coining a wide variety of brand names for their (very similar) products. They avoided patents, since those required that the product formula be made public. Once formulas were known, consumers could recognize that some were dangerous—and others useless. A trade name, however, registered with the Patent Office, and indicating the brand but not the product ingredients, benefited manufacturers by maintaining secrecy, while they enjoyed government protection of their names. The Pure Food and Drug Act of 1906 established initial controls on promotion, while essentially leaving the nostrum producers free to mix whatever concoctions they desired.

The cosmetics industry now aspired to more rigorous goals. After a millennium of empiricism, it was encouraged by the new interest in scientific investigation to study, scrutinize, and analyze its products. The era's formidable progress in research combined scientific advances with new insights. In the field of pharmaceuticals and extension cosmetics, Berthelot, a French chemist, showed it was possible to synthesize organic bodies, beginning with mineral substances, launching into a science of colorants. Solvay also modified the technique of making soap in 1862 through the use of soda, an inexpensive and readily available ingredient. Soap quickly became the basis of all modern hygiene.

Biochemistry emerged as a new branch of chemistry. It led to the isolation of vitamins in 1912, enabling scientists to understand the nature of hormones and endocrine secretions and thus to synthetically create them. Identification with these impressive advances in science and technology helped legitimize the beauty industry, which put them to use.

Electrical appliances were employed at beauty parlors expressly for their medical overtones. The technique for treating wrinkles in the early 1900s, for example, began with a thorough cleansing of the face with distilled water. Then cream was smoothed in and wiped off and a cooling lotion applied. This care was followed by the application of "wrinkle remover," a thick white paste painted on the neck and face and left to dry for half an hour. Once the paste was taken off, face cream was again smoothed in, and the subject was set under a red "hot" light, to be certain the cream fully penetrated the skin. A vibrating massage followed, then the client was cleaned up and released.

Hair care, too, was changed by technological advances. Marcelling, a process invented by the French-born Marcel Grateau in 1870, required an electric curling iron and a skilled operator to produce best results. Soon after, Alexandre Godefrey revolutionized the salon by inventing a low-blast hair dryer. In 1906, Charles Nestle, an exclusive London hairdresser, created the permanent-wave machine (which did not, however, come into widespread use until the 1920s).

In 1916, only twenty million of the hundred million inhabitants in the United States were users of toiletries, a mere fifth of the population, at a per capita expenditure of fifty cents. Prior to World War I the perfume and cosmetics business was small. From 1910 to 1916 some important names in cosmetics emerged: Richard Hyudnut, Colgate and Company, Swansdown Powder, Geo. Borgfeldy's imported brushes, F. M. Prindle's imported Violet and Veolay lines, Roger & Gallet, Houbigant, Lentheric, and LaBlanche.

**ANN ANDREWS IN HORSEHAIR
BRAID HAT,
AMERICAN *VOGUE*, 1919.**
Photograph by Baron Adolf de Meyer.

The final watershed for makeup, marking the beginning of a new era, was undoubtedly the First World War. Recruitment of women for war work deprived the upper and middle classes of domestic staff, and nursing and charitable work began to be embraced by society women. Social life in consequence became simpler and more restrained. In the span of a decade, corsets gave way to suspender belts; pajamas superseded nightgowns.

The chemical factories of Germany, France, and the United States, which had retooled to produce mustard gas and other weapons in wartime, were converted to peacetime pursuits after the war. Among their new products were cosmetics. One more sign of the new century in Russia was the appointment of Madame Molotov (wife of the general who gave the incendiary bomb its "cocktail" name) to head the new Bolshevik department of women's affairs, which produced and sold perfumes with names like Red Star Rising and Polar Express to millions of Russian women. The world had changed, and beauty along with it.

PRODUCTS

THE FASHIONABLE WOMAN MAINTAINED WHAT AMOUNTED TO A PRIVATE SALON IN THE EARLY DECADES OF THE TWENTIETH CENTURY. BASIC ITEMS ON HER DRESSING TABLE INCLUDED TOILETTE VINEGAR TO SCENT BATH WATER, VIOLET WATER, A GENERAL TONIC, AND SKIN ASTRINGENT, WHICH PREPARED THE SKIN FOR POWDER. CREAMS AND LOTIONS ABOUNDED, AS DID FRECKLE REMOVERS, BLACKHEAD, MUSCLE, AND WRINKLE PASTES, REDUCING JELLIES, PORE CREAMS, NIGHT CREAMS, SKIN NUTRIENTS, SKIN BEAUTIFIERS, AND SKIN REJUVENATORS.

FACE POWDER WAS AN AVOWED NECESSITY FOR THE AVERAGE WOMAN. IT FOUND A HOME IN BAROQUE BOXES; TINY, ROUND, OR OBLONG CONFECTIONS OF GOLD LACE OR GAUDY FLOWERED SATIN; OR IN LARGE GLASS CONTAINERS. THERE WERE FOUR BASIC POWDER SHADES: WHITE, CREAM, PINK, AND RACHEL (OLIVE); THOUGH VIOLET AND GREEN WERE RECENT INNOVATIONS. LIQUID POWDERS WERE MOST FASHIONABLE. A CHAMOIS SKIN OR SWANSDOWN POWDER PUFF WERE SOLD WITH THE POWDER; A RABBIT'S FOOT WAS CONSIDERED EVEN MORE EFFICIENT. WOMEN POWDERED AT THE LUNCH TABLE (BUT NOT AT THE DINNER TABLE), USING COATED PAPERS IN BOOKLETS OR IN COMPRESSED CAKES.

AN "ILLUSION CREAM," SAID TO CONCEAL DEFECTS OF THE COMPLEXION UNDER AN IMPERCEPTIBLE COATING, WAS SOLD AS A FLESH-TINTED LIQUID. ROUGE WAS CONSIDERED ACCEPTABLE, BUT ONLY WHEN USED BY MARRIED WOMEN. LIPSTICK, OR ITS LIQUID CREAM OR SALVE VARIANTS, WERE INFREQUENT SELLERS, AND WERE SELDOM USED OPENLY. MANICURE ITEMS CONSISTED OF PINK PASTE POLISH, WHITE CAKE, AND BUFFER. EYE MAKEUP WAS SELDOM USED, ALTHOUGH EYE CREAMS, MASCARA, AND EYEBROW PENCILS WERE AVAILABLE IN STORES, REPORTED *TOILET REQUISITES*.

AT LEAST ONE ARTICLE FROM THE TIME, IN *VOGUE*, URGED THE USE OF COLORED CRAYONS IN FIVE SHADES—BLACK, BROWN, CHESTNUT, BLONDE, AND BLUE—USED IN THE THEATER TO DEEPEN THE SHADE OF THE EYELASHES. THE CRAYON NEEDED TO BE WARMED FOR BETTER SPREADING AND WAS PACKAGED WITH AN EYEBROW BRUSH AND A CORK.

THE DANGERS OF SOME OF THE NEW COSMETICS WERE EVIDENT IN A *LADIES HOME JOURNAL* REPORT IN 1905. A YOUNG GIRL IN ENGLAND, DISSATISFIED WITH THE PALENESS OF HER COMPLEXION, ENTRUSTED HERSELF TO A BEAUTY DOCTOR WHO CLAIMED TO POSSESS A TONIC TO ADD ROSINESS. THE FLUID WAS INJECTED, AND IT SPREAD OVER THE ENTIRE FACE AND NECK. A REACTION OCCURRED, PERMANENTLY RUINING HER COMPLEXION.

THE DIVISION BETWEEN THE CLASSES WAS ERASED IN ONE ODD TURN-OF-THE-CENTURY FASCINATION FOR THAT MOST INDELIBLE OF BODY MAKEUP, THE TATTOO. MONARCHS SUCH AS THE KING OF DENMARK WERE TATTOOED, AS WAS QUEEN ALEXANDRA OF ENGLAND. GEORGE BURCHETT, THE MOST FAMOUS TATTOOIST IN BRITAIN, WAS WELL KNOWN FOR HIS CORONATION TATTOOS IN 1910. HE WAS ALSO KNOWN AS A BEAUTY DOCTOR IN HIS OWN RIGHT; FOR HIS PROCEDURE TO GIVE SKIN A "NATURAL LOOK" HE INJECTED DYE INTO THE LIPS AND CHEEKS—PROBABLY THE SAME PROCEDURE THE *JOURNAL* HAD INVEIGHED AGAINST IN 1905.

Opposite: **MAGAZINE COVER ILLUSTRATION BY FABIANO FOR** *LE RIRE,* **1907.**

★ Nouvelle Série. N° 234. — 27 Juillet 1907.

20 centimes.

UN AN
Paris et Départements, 10 fr.
Étranger, 14 fr.

SIX MOIS
France, 5.50 — Étranger, 7.50

RÉDACTION
122, rue Réaumur, 122
PARIS

VENTE ET ABONNEMENTS
9, rue Saint-Joseph, 9

Le Rire

JOURNAL HUMORISTIQUE PARAISSANT LE SAMEDI

—·- Si j'étais homme, je ne voudrais pas épouser une autre femme que moi !

Dessin de FABIANO.

Breaking

The Taboos *1920s*

NEVER HAD STYLE BEEN SO ANARCHIC AS IN THE PERIOD FOLLOWING THE FIRST WORLD WAR. ARTIFICE AND EXCESS COL-ORED THE DECADE, WHICH WAS HELD IN BALANCE BETWEEN ASSERTIVE MAS-CULINITY AND FEMININE SOPHISTICA-TION. THE 1920s WOMAN RACED INTO THE MODERN AGE WITH THE GRACE OF CON-TRADICTION; SHE MOLTED ELEGANTLY, DISCOVERING HER LEGS AND HER ARMS, CUTTING HER HAIR, PAINTING HER FACE, AND FORCING HER BODY INTO NEW ANDROGYNY WITH PILLS AND DIETS.

Preceding page (detail):
LOUISE BROOKS, ARCHETYPE OF THE FREE WOMAN IN G.W. PABST'S FILM *LULU*, *MOTION PICTURE* **MAGAZINE COVER, CIRCA 1929.**

Opposite: **JOAN CRAWFORD IN ELABORATE ORGANZA HEADDRESS FROM THE MGM FILM** *OUR DANCING DAUGHTERS*, **1928.**

Right: *DAINAH LA MÉTISSE* **FILM POSTER, CIRCA 1925.**

The made-up face of the twenties woman represented a reaction to the demure appearance of Gibson girl prewar femininity, but at the same time its frankly exposed look suggested vulnerability. Darkly rimmed eyes, brightly colored cheeks, and "bee-stung" lips acces-sorized an attitude, dressed a style, as the 1920s face revolution-ized traditional interpretations of beauty.

A decisive moment in the history of cosmetics, the post-World War I period witnessed the emergence of an international beauty culture—an aesthetic awareness that established cosmetics as an indispensable element of modern life. Fashion was every-where, indissociable from theater, cinema, literature, and painting. Makeup, as fashion, stood for self-expression and innocent coquetry, while providing the mask that protected the wearer from the growing aggressions of urbanism. Moreover, as clothing became more revealing, it was makeup that provided women with a necessary, if gossamer, social shield, in a society where rules were being remade daily. As Colette wrote in *Les Héroes Longues* (1917), "Women stopped as though struck, with an air of having passed an invisible limit and been thrown to the other side of life."

Right: **SAVON OLIVERT-LEGRAIN, FRENCH SOAP ADVERTISEMENT, 1920.**

Below: **MOVIE STAR AND "JAZZ BABY" LOUISE BROOKS,** *MOTION PICTURE* **MAGAZINE COVER, CIRCA 1928.**

The newly established beauty culture coincided with formidable economic, scientific, and social advances which resulted from the First World War. Dissolution of the traditional structure of government and political systems caused an evolution of mores and allowed the emergence of an ideology obsessed with novelty and change. Having successfully assumed men's work during the war, women gained new confidence as they realized they could function in a professional world. Choices in work improved as well, and the number of traditionally female jobs, such as farm worker and domestic servant, decreased as a result of urbanization and the availability of electrical appliances. The increased earnings of those who did work stimulated the consumption of nonessential products, including cosmetics. The French publication *The Beauty Industry* affirmed in 1923 that the success of feminism supported, rather than discouraged, cosmetics use for women wishing to look their best as they competed with men for jobs, and concluded that such competition significantly heightened demand for toiletries.

The need for women to present an attractive public persona was intensified by the scarcity of men, yet another legacy of the war. The ratio of one man for every three to four females created an emphasis on beauty that was sexually, rather than socially, codified. Evening makeup seen in the tango palaces and the tea dances consisted of powder, bright rouge, and red, distinctly outlined lips which attracted the eye to the mouth, traditionally the most sexually charged part of the face. The eyes were shaded with bright colors (often blues and greens) or outlined in black kohl for a decorative and mysterious look.

The psychological aspects of makeup were explored, and the therapeutic aspects of powder and paint documented, when a beauty parlor for the patients of an Essex County, New Jersey, insane asylum was established in 1928, a first of its kind. Its immediate success proved to the psychiatric profession that the benefits of an artificial barrier between the outside world and the inner self should not be ignored. A 1928 issue of *Toilet Requisites* heralded the salon as a revolutionary new cure for depression and urged the formation of other such facilities in major clinics throughout the United States.

The "look" of the female face, for the first time in history, became a subject of international concern. A consequent proliferation of images helped foster an "international" style that remained consistent throughout the Occident. Photographers

THE POSTWAR RATIO OF ONE MAN FOR EVERY THREE TO FOUR FEMALES CREATED AN EMPHASIS ON BEAUTY THAT WAS SEXUALLY, RATHER THAN SOCIALLY, CODIFIED

like Alfred Stieglitz and Baron de Meyer worked in New York, London, Paris, and Hollywood, colonizing this ideal of beauty. Movie stars from Burbank to Pinewood shared the same makeup men, and cosmetics companies increasingly formulated one image for worldwide distribution. In the quest for a universal standard of beauty, contests such as the Miss Universe pageant (begun in 1928, and shut down soon after for immodesty) became popular.

Demand for cosmetics in every country rapidly increased, and the fledgling industry grew to meet this new market. Across the board, massive changes brought about by the postwar period, including scientific and socioeconomic advances, allowed a rapid expansion of production, leading to the creation of safe, mass-market products. Cosmetics that heretofore could only be bought by the wealthy, educated, "free-thinking" woman were now available to the average housewife through drugstores and mail order catalogs. By the end of the 1920s, the sales volume of American cosmetics companies alone was close to $180 million, reported *The Wall Street Journal*.

The developing world beauty culture looked to Europe for its inspiration. Paris, the postwar cultural capital, played host to an elite group of artists, actresses, and émigrés who rapidly gained prominence over an older, more traditional aristocracy. Rigid social hierarchies were supplanted by an eclectic assembly of young, talented individuals who shared artistic affinities as well as a taste for provocation and adventure. Music hall singers inspired couture designers, while diehard aristocrats befriended scandalous Dadaists.

In Paris, traditional ballet dancers socialized with bohemian painters at the café of the moment, the Boeuf sur le Toit. Led by Count Étienne de Beaumont at his sumptuous townhouse *Le Monde* (meaning "the world that counted"), exponents of nonofficial, nonacademic art mingled with classical artists. Beaumont, with his *bals transvesti*, evening entertainment with daring costumes, became the inventor of a new snobbism, one requiring "that value take precedence over title, talent over wealth, artists over establishment," wrote Edmonde-Charles Roux.

Cross-cultural exchange of new and diverse ideas brought to the upheaval of postwar Europe by the influx of émigrés from Russia, Hungary, Spain, and beyond, further altered the aesthetic surface of the decade. It resulted in the continued breakdown of traditional cultural mores and became an important catalyst in the creation of beauty trends. A vogue for African and Oceanic images invaded France and sparked a series of reactions: the desire for tanned skin, the symbolic face painting of the Dadaists, and the fashion of heavily made-up "almond eyes."

Paris was crowned the center of artistic creation at the 1925 Exposition Universelle des Arts Décoratifs. The exposition confirmed the immense influence that the decorative arts exercised over the aesthetic sensibility of the twenties, as witnessed by the Deco-inspired objects on display. Cosmetics companies such as Lancôme and Coty sponsored lavish pavilions and filled them with crystal perfume bottles and lacquer powder jars in sensuous shapes. Art Deco design, packaging, and advertising became central in the sales of beauty products and drew a logical connection between design and cosmetics. As a 1926 article in *Toilet Requisites* suggested, beauty products were considered more effective when packaged in extraordinary containers—a harbinger of the concept of luxury that would surface in the next decade.

Magazines throughout the world celebrated the exquisite, albeit artificial, elegance of the French woman. A 1925 article in American *Vogue* promised that "the French captured the secrets of attraction, and we should look to our Parisian sisters as role models of charm." Marketing therefore reinvented products under French names to assure an elite image elsewhere in the world and to link postwar beauty with international elegance and chic. American servicemen returning from Europe brought perfume and powder to their wives and sweethearts, who increasingly clamored for imported makeup, despite its high ticket price. Paris and London were still the two principal producers of creams, powders, rouge, and perfume extracts. In 1920, France furnished North America with four million pounds of rice powder, the primary ingredient in face makeup. But the United States, newly muscular in international trade, soon levied substantial import taxes on foreign beauty products.

The rise of makeup coincided with the hiking of the hemline, as French couture created a veritable revolution in the female aesthetic by introducing a shorter skirt, along with a destructured, simple, straight silhouette. This new minimalism was balanced by a more decorative treatment of the face and hair, and flagrantly made-up models appeared on the runways as early as 1917. The bobbed coiffure, which emerged as a true fashion trend in 1917 (a decade after it was introduced by Colette and other visionaries), complemented the vision of provocative artificiality. Hats—cloches and turbans—drew attention to the face and demanded a new emphasis on eyes and lips.

Although they were still considered avant-garde, fashion models were invested with improved social status, to the degree that they became role models for women in Europe and elsewhere during the 1920s. "The acceptance of mannequins in society came very suddenly. The Paris dressmakers used to show their clothes

on any willing girl of no particular looks who would wear black
maillots with high necks and long sleeves over which the model
gowns were shown. It was not until the 1920s that girls of proper
upbringing even considered modeling as a career, let alone per-
suaded their families to allow them to do so," claimed a contemporary article in the English magazine *Punch*.

In 1923, John Robert Powers founded the first prototype
of the modeling agency as we know it in New York City, and in
doing so "completed the transformation of the model from an
object of opprobrium to one of envy," reported Eileen Ford in a
1991 interview. Powers succeeded in giving the profession of modeling an image of glamour and social preferment that attracted
even haughty debutantes, who generally scorned paying work.
Models began to assume an active role in instigating fashion
trends, as creating a "look" or inspiring a couturier became part of
their professional responsibility. They applied their own makeup
and often styled their own hair. Cosmeticians who applied light
makeup at the end of a facial treatment in a beauty salon existed
for the more elite social set, but not for the professional runway
mannequin. Many of the 1920s couture models were aristocratic
immigrants from Tsarist Russia who had left their homeland after
the revolution. Chanel employed many of these impoverished and
uprooted countesses as salesgirls as well as mannequins, and
Russian, along with French, echoed in the hallways of her salons.
Even the receptionist of Chanel's Paris headquarters, Count
Koutousov (remembered in Chanel's memoirs as "a man of great
distinction"), had been governor of the Crimea in his former life.

The immigrant Russians were accustomed to a more decorative, painted look and brought with them an understanding of
products and methods of application rarely seen in the Occident.
"We were taught by older models or our families how to apply
makeup, how to wear lipstick. We would buy our products at the
department stores, or in the corner *parfumerie*, where one could
find a limited, but adequate, quantity of colors and products,"
recalled one Russian model who worked for both Hermès and
Chanel. It was the Slavic influence that was said to be responsible
for the enthusiasm for beading, a technique of putting a waxlike
substance on the end of each separate eyelash in the form of a
bead; models would have contests to see who could finish their
lashes first. False eyelashes were also used, and various powder
color combinations were tried—from diaphanous white to violet,
ochre to tan—as the decade progressed.

As makeup for the face gained widespread acceptance, a
greater range of beauty products became available. The first of the
couturiers to create a perfume was Paul Poiret, with his Parfums

Above: **JOSEPHINE BAKER IN
HER DRESSING ROOM, 1925.**
*Photograph © UPI/Bettmann
Archive.*

Right: **AMERICAN DANCER
JOSEPHINE BAKER AND HER
REVUE NÈGRE QUICKLY
BECAME THE TOAST OF PARIS
UPON THEIR ARRIVAL IN
EUROPE IN 1925.**
Photograph © Archive Photos.

Rosine (1910), named after his daughter, but it was not until the 1920s that couture perfumes became a vogue. This inclination confirmed the compatibility of fashion and beauty, and created yet another context in which cosmetics could be developed. "Every major couturier had to have a fragrance as well. This meant growth by leaps and bounds for the industry of Grasse [the city in France renowned for the manufacture of perfume essences and oils], as an entirely new approach to style emerged after the war," claimed the contemporary journal *La Formulaire de la Parfumerie*. Marylene Delbourg-Delphis, in her milestone book on fragrances, *Les Sillages des Elégantes*, emphasized that women at the outset of the decade viewed new perfumes and powders as they did new fashions in clothing—as seasonal items to be changed frequently. With the rise of couturier fragrances, scent became a prestigious symbol of chic, and long-lasting "signature perfumes" quickly came to dominate the market.

La Garçonne was the sobriquet given to a significant fashion trend in the postwar years that came into vogue with the publication of Victor Margueritte's book of the same name. Although immediately banned as pornographic, the novel became a national bestseller that would irrevocably mark the 1920s. *La Garçonne* described the short-haired, cigarette-smoking, sexually liberated young women who often dressed in men's attire, had careers, and spent late nights dancing or indulging in a favorite pastime of the artistic milieu, smoking opium. Though the euphoric atmosphere of Paris in the twenties gave rise to the Garçonne style, it was Chanel who was credited with much of its look and charm. She certified androgynous chic by adding masculine elements to the feminine wardrobe—borrowing such staples as the white shirt, the cardigan, and pleated pants from her lovers' closets and including them in her designs for couture collections.

La Garçonne may have assumed a masculine attitude, but she remained subtly feminine through the use of makeup. She used the contrast between the decorative frivolity of the heavily mascaraed eyes, red lips, and bright cheeks and the stark rigidity of the formal suit and tie to create an extraordinary sexual nuance and unconventional attractiveness. Literary and artistic figures such as Eileen Gray, Djuna Barnes, Vita Sackville-West, Romaine Brooks, and Colette immediately adopted the look. Women throughout France soon followed the trend, and even advertising pages featured the iconoclastic Garçonne as their female heroine.

Makeup also turned its face toward Africa for inspiration when American-born Josephine Baker, and her notorious *Revue nègre*, arrived in Paris in 1925. Her arrival signaled the end of orientalism and began a vogue for African art that became a major influence during the twenties. African art had been influential since 1905, but only for a small number of artists and collectors. (Interestingly, Helena Rubinstein was one of the first to amass a magnificent collection of African sculptures and masks.) By 1925, media coverage had generated interest in the various art forms associated with primitivism, and jazz was becoming increasingly popular. Socialites went to nightclubs like the Boule Noir or the Bal Nègre where they danced the "black bottom" with black musicians and American soldiers who had stayed in Paris after the war.

The eighteen-year-old Baker's first performance caused a sensation. The "banana dance" featured a costume made only of a skirt of real bananas, black lipstick, and sleek hair grease that flattened her unruly mane. Said to resemble "kinetic movement," Baker's interpretive dancing endeared her to both press and public and made her an overnight international star. Considered one of the most exquisite women in the world, Baker was a preferred model for artists, photographers, and designers. Her golden-brown body, agility, animal charm, and husky voice shattered the feminine ideal of the showgirl and created a new fashion for ethnicity.

Baker's style was quintessential 1920s: animalistic, elegant, and through makeup, ambiguously sexual. She carefully controlled her image, not only through the use of outrageous costumes but also with unusual, well-applied makeup. She developed her own look rather than adopting the traditional vaudeville "blackface" (wherein all performers, white or black, were obliged to wear burned-cork ashes and pale chalk lips). Instead, Baker used a light, powdered beige tone on her face, kohl to outline her eyes, and dark lipstick to give her lips drama. When traveling, she always brought her own specially formulated powder, as the author of her biography assiduously reports: "Josephine received her first guests [in Berlin], with her two dogs, Fifi and Bebe, surrounded by 15 trunks, 196 pairs of shoes, 1,367 costumes, assorted furs, innumerable dresses—and 64 kilos of powder."

The culmination of this artifice was an impression of feline sensuality, as theater critic Pierre de Regnier rhapsodized in a contemporary review of her performance: "Josephine Baker. Is it a man? Is it a woman? Her hair, already short, is coiffed as caviar, her voice is sharply shrill, she is agitated with a perpetual trembling, her body slinks like that of a serpent, or, more exactly, resembles a saxophone in movement and the sounds of the orchestra seem to come from within."

Mistinguett, the famous French cabaret singer, was also celebrated for her ostentatious personal style. She used makeup lavishly, with colors and shading that were often bright and strong—turquoise, green, and blue for the eyes. Brown and black were also used, "but with less success," a fellow chanteuse uncharitably observed.

The twenties also marked the transition of makeup from the nighttime to the harsh light of day. Dancing was an ever-popular pastime for ladies of society, and the "flapper," named after the dance she so energetically performed, spent afternoons in *thé dansants* doing the Charleston to newly popular phonograph records. Makeup, as employed by the flapper, was expressly meant to attract men, and the well-designed crimson mouth and shaded, shadowed eye resuscitated a method of flirting not seen since the court of Marie Antoinette. Makeup allowed the 1920s *élégante* to exhibit her legs, her arms, her cleavage—yet preserve her adolescent charm.

The gesture of applying makeup in public, heretofore considered vulgar, now became stylish and sensual, with the use of artfully made powder compacts and metal lipstick containers. Accessories such as the bracelet rouge pot, the rouge ring, and the powder compact were designed for evening use and to accompany even the most active dancer. Bejeweled powder pots by Cartier, Van Cleef & Arpels, or Boucheron became so precious (and ubiquitous) that in 1925 the U.S. government began a study to determine whether a jewel tax on the proliferating novelties called "makeup purses" would be appropriate.

As the use of makeup became more widespread, artists increasingly understood its symbolic potential and often experimented with its mask-like qualities. Man Ray painted eyes on the eyelids of the most famous studio model of the twenties, Kiki de Montparnasse (they disappeared as she slowly opened her eyes), for a film entitled *Kiki's Double*. He exploited the graphic aspect of beaded lashes, using them as a visual counterpoint to artificial tears on Kiki's cheeks. Using lipstick and eyeliner, he further accentuated the primitive suggestivity of the female face and posed his now familiar model's head adjacent to an African tribal mask. This photographic work was destined to become one of his most memorable images.

Even without Man Ray's improvisations, Kiki was renowned for her own use of cosmetics, as Thora Dardel, the wife of another artist, recalled: "My most vivid memory of Kiki was on the *terrasse* of the Dôme, emptying the contents of the case she always carried, and applying her makeup using three or four colors of green to make her eyes match her dress." Kiki was also celebrated in her circle for finding daring new uses for eyeliner, which included drawing lines to imitate hair on her sparsely covered pubic region.

Such sexual references, suggested by the use of skin

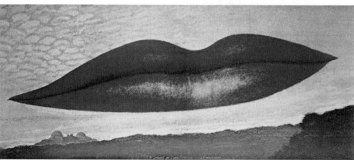

Top: **STILLS FROM THE SHORT FILM** *EMAK BAKIA,* **1926.** *Directed by Man Ray.*

Center: A L'HEURE DE L'OBSERVATOIRE, LES AMOUREUX, 1934, **MAN RAY.** *Oil on canvas. Private Collection.*

Bottom: NOIRE ET BLANCHE, **1926, MAN RAY.**

color, eye color, and lip painting, were apparent in the works of numerous 1920s artists. Foujita, in his painting *Youki, Déesse de la Neige,* accentuated the sensual femininity of his nude model by contrasting her vermilion mouth with both the pale color of her skin and the white of the painting's snowy background. Tamara de Lempicka painted scandalous scenes of sexual abandon, where exotic blue and violet eye makeup was the only body covering. Kees van Dongen (heretofore a staid society portraitist) began to introduce bright, frank colors into his works, in which debutantes and women of distinction first appeared highly made up. Makeup had climbed up and down the entire social spectrum in the most democratic tradition of fashion.

Europe's seductive image of beauty was not the sole source of aesthetic inspiration available to the 1920s public. Hollywood and the burgeoning film industry also provided potent visions of glamour. The "star system," which had existed since 1911, was now firmly ensconced in the cinematic tradition and began to radically alter the modern conception of beauty. Film audiences began to regard the hero/heroine more carefully as new cinematic devices permitted the close-up and the fade-in/fade-out techniques, which conveyed emotion as well as a sense of action. Directors such as D. W. Griffith, and later, Cecil B. De Mille, were able to exploit the expressive potential of the subtleties of the human face to involve the viewer on a visceral, not simply intellectual, level. The public identified with the idealized vision of elegance presented on the screen, and actresses were transformed into stars who, by their appearance and personal charisma, attracted thousands of moviegoers each week.

Films after the First World War continued the silent movie tradition of portraying women as conservative, Victorian icons with long flowing hair and childlike, innocent faces or, conversely, satanic vamps who embodied the essence of sexuality. Mary Pickford and Lillian Gish incarnated the vestal virgin whose appearance varied little from film to film, and whose coiffure, makeup, and wardrobe were carefully studied to conform to the public ideal of pre-Raphaelite beauty. Their faces were made up as masks, with white, powdered skin, small lips (reduced through the application of lipstick inside the lipline), and lightly shadowed eyes with an abundance of elaborate false lashes.

The vamp was a character invented in 1914 by Fox productions in Hollywood to introduce the actress Theda Bara. In stark contrast to the "sweetheart" image of Pickford, Bara was to project unmitigated evil, and in the movie *A Fool There Was,* she fulfilled the audience's penchant for a lust-driven provocateur. Her image was defined by a heavily made-up face with lips that were

Left: **SOLANGE DAVID, PARIS, 1929.** *Photograph by Jacques-Henri Lartigue.*

Above: **ALLA NAZIMOVA IN THE SILENT FILM** *SALOME,* **1922.** *Photograph by Rice.*

large and violently painted, and a hairstyle that was full and unkempt.

As the decade advanced and cinema attracted a new, sophisticated audience, the portrayal of women became more realistic. Gloria Swanson, in the comedies and melodramas of De Mille, played women who were pragmatic and hedonistic—truer to the independent 1920s personality. Aware of the evolution, Swanson, who had begun her career in Hollywood as a replacement for the waning Theda Bara, quickly changed her makeup and gave it a polished, almost urbane feel with clearly arched eyebrows, defined, delicate lips, perfectly outlined eyes, and feathered eyelashes. Her famous beauty mark, so long hidden, was now unveiled, and became her trademark. Soigné and modern, Swanson's was the first movie makeup to correspond to the trends emerging from the newly established international cosmetics empires.

Catering to a more popular audience, "jazz babies," the flappers of the twenties, were portrayed by Colleen Moore, Clara Bow, Mae Murray, and Louise Brooks. They were often cast as young salesgirls who, by sheer wits or fool's luck, landed rich suitors. Films such as *Jazz Mania*, *Our Dancing Daughters*, and the famous *It* (with Clara Bow) glorified women who were young, beautiful, and independent, but ardently dreamed of a prosperous husband. Their shining faces, round, pouting lips, and lined, heavily lashed eyes made a less sophisticated look than that of Gloria Swanson. They served as more touchable, and ultimately more influential, role models to the thousands of women in theaters around the world; women who identified their romantic hopes with the celluloid Cinderella tales in which these actresses starred.

Throughout the decade, an integral part of the creation of the Hollywood star was the recognition of the need for professional hair styling and makeup application. Movies were nearly always shot out of sequence and therefore required the services of a qualified technician to retain visual continuity. The first makeup artists began as wigmakers, since, as early as 1920, wigs were worn to guarantee a consistent image and assure the same hairstyle throughout months of shooting. "Many of the silent movie actors came directly from the stage to screen and were accustomed to applying their own makeup, but as the reaction between the film and the colors became more complex, professional cosmeticians were the only ones with sufficient knowledge and skill to blend the

new makeup, new lighting, new film, and skin colors," Hollywood historian Christopher Finch explains.

Mary Astor, in her biography, *A Life on Film*, recalls that her face was coated with greasepaint (Stein's #2) until every pore was filled, then dusted with powder until it became a mask. The lipstick used then was dark red, but it had to be carefully applied because red tended to bleed on the crude black-and-white film stock used in the early cinema. If lipstick was applied too lightly, however, it would appear white on the screen. Astor also recalled brown eye shadow and black mascara, used along with "cosmetique," a black cake of what she called "guck" that was melted over an oil lamp. This was applied to the eyelashes with a match or a toothpick to create a beading effect similar to that seen in Parisian couture salons and London music hall dressing rooms.

Most early silent movies used arc lighting and octochromatic film, a black-and-white film on which all hues of red appeared black. Since red was the base tone of most Caucasian skins (and most film actors and actresses of the time were Caucasian), performers found it necessary to apply makeup very heavily to avoid appearing dirty in the films. Arc lighting techniques also distorted the natural highlights and shadows of the face, intensifying wrinkles, posing serious aesthetic problems for the early technicians.

Max Factor, a Russian immigrant who had been trained as a theatrical wigmaker and had worked for the imperial Russian Court Opera of Czar Nicholas II, was one of the first and most influential of the Hollywood makeup artists. As studios did not install makeup departments until 1911, Factor operated out of a small theatrical and hair goods store in Los Angeles, where he would begin work before dawn to paint and coif the actresses who had waited at his doorstep for hours. Factor was the sole importer of the Berlin-made Leichner theatrical makeup, and later of Hines theatrical makeup. As he often worked directly with cameramen and directors (one of his early achievements was to devise a special foundation, with the help of cameraman Charles Roshneer, for Mary Pickford, coded 7-R) he realized the limitations of the flat, two-dimensional "grime." He developed, in 1914, a more realistic "flexible greasepaint" which was the first makeup made specifically for motion pictures and the first natural-looking cosmetic to be used in film. This thin, colored cream in a jar, was made from a

> MAKEUP HAD A POLISHED, ALMOST URBANE FEEL WITH CLEARLY ARCHED EYEBROWS, DEFINED, DELICATE LIPS, PERFECTLY OUTLINED EYES, AND FEATHERED EYELASHES

combination of existing theatrical products. It appeared natural to the camera, yet was thick enough to cover the skin's natural red tones. The makeup also permitted facial flexibility on the silent film screen—an essential and important innovation.

George Westmore, another pioneer in the Hollywood makeup field, was also well known as a wig specialist before gaining notoriety as a makeup artist. Unlike Factor, he did not chemically alter the products he used, but he developed a particularly artistic hand and convincing manner in their application. Westmore was the first to develop a permanent makeup presence on a Hollywood lot for producer William Selig in 1917, by convincing actors (including Douglas Fairbanks, Theda Bara, and Anita Stewart) that carefully controlled makeup could be critical to a successful career.

Westmore fathered five sons who all soon became accomplished makeup artists in their own right and who together would irrevocably alter the cultural aspects of female beauty. The oldest son, Mont Westmore, began his career as the personal makeup adviser to Rudolph Valentino from 1921 until the screen heartthrob's death in 1926. Around the same time, Westmore revolutionized—some say defined—the flat-chested flapper look, by using gauze on Clara Bow's nipples and adhesive plaster across Bow's breasts (instead of a brassiere) to project the effect of nudity beneath a flimsy garment. The Westmores' dynasty spanned several decades of pervasive influence on the "look" of Hollywood, long after their auspicious beginnings in the twenties. House of Westmore cosmetics still have a presence in Hollywood today.

The 1920s witnessed the development of a middle class for whom leisure time became an indication of affluence and sophistication. Women, as well as men, actively participated in sports; driving cars and swimming at the beach became worldwide pastimes. The look of tanned skin was also popular as a result of the enthusiasm for outdoor activities, and first appeared in the late teens in Deauville, France, as the *demi-mondaines* were seen taking "sun baths" in their new, revealing bathing costumes. Tanning became widely accepted as Chanel herself was caught exposing her unprotected face to the sun. "Suddenly it was extremely fashionable to be dark-skinned. It indicated that you had the money and the time to spend long hours on the Riviera, or in Normandy. We would even have contests to see who was the darkest, and would compare legs while sitting at the terrace of Fouquet's [the famous restaurant on the Champs Elysées]," remembered a Russian runway model in Paris.

So many people wanted to look tanned that different colors of powder and new methods of application had to be devel-

oped to address the trend. Jean Patou created the first sun lotion in 1924, called Huile de Caldée, and Chanel followed with her own sun lotion in 1928. That same year, "American women spent $1,835,000,000 for cosmetics, and in 1929 the figures were climbing upwards because of the sudden rage for the suntanned look, leaving women with dressing tables crammed with makeup colors that were no longer fashionable. An American manufacturer sold two million bottles of Instant Tan in the first ten days his product was on the market," reported Richard Corson in his 1955 summary of the industry, *Fashions in Makeup*. Other, often dangerous methods of tanning became the rage. "Some women even dyed their skins with a solution of permanganate or with colorants made from red ecarlate, yellow, and brown powders, or with the mixture of coconut and cade oil," Corson added. Less economically advantaged women wanted to show that they could obtain the dark skin made possible by a long stay in the country, even though they could only afford a one-week vacation. The results were predictably damaging: "They were constantly in the sun, and got spots that were rich and indelible," a contemporary document observed. To meet the popular demand, tanning booths, which used fluorescent lights called "sun ray machines" to artificially induce tans, were installed in beauty parlors and, despite warnings from beauty experts such as Helena Rubinstein and Elizabeth Arden, enjoyed great success.

The new fashion for traveling and motoring introduced a concomitant enthusiasm for traveling cases. Made of ostrich leather and sterling silver, and containing bottles and brushes along with compacts to contain makeup, these cases appeared in the lines of various companies and were often advertised in the fashion magazines. Louis Vuitton and Hermès became two innovators in this luxurious style and perfected articles designed to hold all the beauty articles of the period. In addition, accessories for the toilette proliferated in the home with the reappearance of dressing tables, which had fallen into disfavor during the Victorian age. By the end of the twenties the Art Deco preference for chrome, sculpted wood, mirrors, and glass provided an effective context in which the new makeup products, artfully packaged in crystal, cloth, or painted containers, were proudly displayed.

With the increasing popularity of photogravure in 1919, fashion magazines became an indispensable avenue of communication for news about beauty. New printing techniques made possible the improved reproduction of photographs, and thus delivered a sense of realism that immediately provoked a mimetic aspect in fashion. For the first time women could actually see the styles and makeup worn by the models, not just illustrations of

them, and they were inspired to closely imitate the latest makeup and hair styles. Most magazines and newspapers, by the mid-1920s, had beauty editors as well as beauty columns, such as American *Vogue*'s "On Her Dressing Table" and *Harper's Bazaar*'s "The Cosmetic Urge," where new products and new methods of applying makeup were discussed. Daily newspapers were also primary sources of beauty information. The traditional mother-to-daughter transfer of beauty advice was not possible when the population at large had no experience in using the new cosmetic products. It therefore became the job of the beauty columnist to give the needed information about the use of foundation, powder, and eye shadow. French *Vogue* suggested that color for the lips should be translucent for the evening, but dark for the day. "A large mouth," they admonished, "is never painted to its end, a small mouth is always lined until the corners."

American *Vogue*'s lengthy advice included introducing the first true concept of full-face makeup. "A Perfect Makeup, Is It Possible?" from a 1927 issue, presented an interview with beauty specialist Dorothy Maynard. Her advice: "Combine one's own powder with one part pink, one half white, and another part natural. Then fill a small frying pan with good dark cosmetic, and hold over lighted candle until melted. Run the tip of your finger under the pan thus obtaining enough lamp-black to darken the eyelids, powdering over, giving the eyes a soft blue effect. Then take a small camel's hair brush and carefully apply the soft cosmetic in the pan to each eyelash, making a thin ball on the end of each individual lash. Next, apply a soft cardinal red rouge to the cheeks, after which you again make the mouth look natural. The rouge must be a dark cherry red, not vermilion like one sees on the street. Then with the rounded end of the hair pin, or the broad end of a wooden toothpick dipped in your lip rouge, place a tiny speck to the corner of each eye near the nose and you will possess a pair of beautifully brilliant eyes."

The beauty editor became such a ubiquitous institution that in 1928, a local New Jersey radio station, WGBS, introduced "Miss Nell Vinick, journalist," to give lessons in beauty culture. Makeup had arrived and left its mark even in the provinces, through which its influence quickly spread. With the omnipresence of makeup came a demand for newer, cheaper, safer, and better-marketed products. In 1923, *The Nation* magazine estimated that the "factory value of cosmetics and perfumes in U.S. was seventy-five million—an increase of 400 percent in ten years." The beauty industry that before the First World War had been considered inconsequential and unimportant, was finally being taken seriously by the scientific and financial communities.

In fact, it was the scientific developments of World War I that enabled the cosmetics industry to significantly advance its production capacity as well as the quality of its products. Cheaply produced colorants, once the specialty of German chemical companies, were now available in the plants the United States and France built to process the chemicals, challenging the dominance of Germany in the field. With postwar peace came the additional need to transfer the production of wartime chemicals (including mustard gas) to new peacetime products. Cosmetics were a logical choice. Once the trend for scientific autonomy was established and a stable market developed, chemical companies were confident enough to expand their production and chemists were able to establish new laboratories.

The Dohren Company of Germany monopolized the production of oils essential to the creation of makeup until the American Lanolin Company was founded in 1918. The American Cholesterol Company appeared soon after and continued research in this field, developing the first lanolin derivative, Amerchol L101, which refined oil so that it could be used as an essential emollient in makeup. This improved the texture of creams, rouges, and lip salves greatly, and confirmed the growing reputation of the developing American chemical industry.

The demand for a greater variety of beauty products also resulted in numerous chemical innovations. In 1916, pearl essence was first extracted from the scales of herring to manufacture simulated pearls, only to be later employed in the formation of the first frosted nail enamels. An effective preservative, paraben, was introduced by Julius Penner, AG in the United States in 1927, and enabled a longer shelf life, increasing commercial viability for cosmetics. The first cosmetic sunscreen (not suntanning lotion) was developed by Klarmann for Lehn and Fink in the United States in 1928. It contained a salicylate and a cinnamate as its active sunscreen ingredients.

Another revolution occurred in 1923, when W. A. Poucher's *Encyclopedia of Cosmetics and Perfumery* was published. It made public for the first time various recipes for different cosmetic products, which aided both the development and the pirating of cosmetic articles. Any competent laboratory could produce the products Poucher described, and his encyclopedia inspired independent chemical companies to develop and commercialize makeup under names similar to those of important and established cosmetics figures, heightening competition.

Effective laws controlling the definition and safety of cosmetic products became a subject of vital concern as makeup became more accepted. Belladonna, a poisonous plant extract available in drop form and used inside the eye to brighten it, was still obtainable but widely criticized. Cases of lipstick poisoning were cited in the United States in the 1920s, while lead was still found as an ingredient in face powders. Chemical dyes were not strictly regulated, and using homemade products, such as walnut oil for lash and brow darkening, was still an accepted practice, as seen in the beauty columns of the period: "Who is the Parisienne who hasn't bought, in our day, a cream or a rouge, a milk for the face, in a place where a housekeeper or a charlatan pretends to hold the secret of great medicine, or a guru or even a Hindu? But many of these creams and powders or these rouges contain, as before, derivatives that are noxious, or poisonous: protochlorure of mercury, bichlorure of mercury, hydrate of lead, ceruse, formol, acid salicylique, antipyrine, fluorures at large doses, and silice pulverized," warned *Art, goût, beauté* in 1928.

Some cosmetics were so dangerous that it was necessary to limit their use. A law passed in the United States in 1916 restricted the use and preparation of certain products to doctors and pharmacists who could employ them only for medical purposes. France also passed a quality control bill in 1919 for cosmetics ingredients, but putting the law into practice proved difficult. *Toilet Requisites* demanded legislation in the United States to assure that deadly chemicals were not used in cosmetics, but controversy about whether a cosmetic was a medicine or a beauty product defeated any responsible efforts to effectively control the problem.

"Trademarks," or brand names, became necessary to assure the quality that the government was incapable of legislating. The individual who created or endorsed the item was assumed to guaranteed its purity. In 1924, commenting on an episode of lipstick poisoning, *Toilet Requisites* remarked: "No one can deny that there are on the market preparations that would be apt to bring disaster on most any user. It is safe to say that preparations, whether they be lipsticks or other toilet articles, when manufactured and backed by responsible and reputable concerns, are of the quality that can do no harm. The best guarantee is to carry only well-known lines."

The increase in the volume of postwar makeup sales made control of quality even more difficult. Dr. Charles W. Pabst, a noted New York dermatologist, stated that "Some women apply mixtures to their faces that would take the paint off an automobile." He registered a 50 percent increase over three years in cases of skin diseases resulting from cosmetics. Noxious ingredients such as mercury and arsenic could still be found in basic makeup, and the doctor cited one particularly dangerous example of a face powder advertised not to rub off. The makeup remover provided

Above: **ART DECO ENAMELED COSMETIC CASES BY VAN CLEEF & ARPELS, CIRCA 1925.**

Preceding page: **CLARA BOW, THE ULTIMATE FLAPPER, IN THE MOVIE** *IT.* **"IF I EVER SAW IT, THAT'S IT," SAID ONE ENRAPTURED MALE ADMIRER UPON SIGHTING CLARA, 1928.** *Photograph © Culver Pictures.*

IF THE "LOOK" OF THE 1920s WAS OBVIOUSLY ARTIFICIAL, IT WAS DEFINITELY CREATED TO BE NOTICED, TO SUGGEST INDEPENDENCE AND MODERNITY, AND TO SHOCK BY ITS AUDACIOUS USE OF COLOR AND TEXTURE

by the manufacturer, warned Dr. Pabst, "was even more dangerous than the powder." In Japan in the 1920s, one of the foremost
causes of infant mortality was a disease resulting from the mother's
use of a white face powder containing lead. "The disease usually
appeared at about eight months and was more frequent in the
summer when face powder was used in greater quantities. In cases
of fatality, the body always showed traces of lead and could
always be traced to face powder used by the mother," reported an
article in *Toilet Requisites* in 1926.

As early as 1918, the issue of trademark control became
an important factor in the development of the cosmetics industry.
The U.S. Department of National Commerce called for a "place of
origin" law to protect, at first, against the inundation of illegal
German chemical products that had become a political issue in
postwar America, and then against fraudulent claims.

The rapid expansion of the number of trademarks also
became problematic. Prestigious (often French) product names
were illegally usurped, as when the logo of the world-renowned
French perfume Origan, created by François Coty, was used by
Ernest Coty (no relation) to label various products that had nothing to do with the original. Finally, the Coty company alerted the
French High Court of Appeals, which called on a law passed in 1857
stipulating that "the fraudulent use of a trademark bearing such
indications as were likely to deceive the purchaser with respect to
the nature of the products was actionable." François Coty won his
case, and the falsely named "Origan" products were confiscated,
but industry watchers agreed that a new, more precisely defined
law was needed to control
the industry.

Problems con-
cerning the use and regis-
tration of names and
logos were further complicated by the fact that
many cosmetics were pro-
duced by modest, local businesses, and some specialty items that
ultimately attained wide distribution originated as private formulas
in beauty or barber shops. The original basis on which a product
was trademarked was defined by the previous or habitual use of
the name. This distinction was soon proven inadequate, however,
and the United States patent office was inundated by questions
concerning the lawful definition of use, i.e., was it enough simply
to use a name for a product, or was it necessary to export the
product across the state lines or to exploit the name publicly
through advertisements in order to establish a viable claim? Legal

questions became even more complicated because trademarks were traditionally granted to the individual who used a name first, and the courts were prevailed upon to attempt to protect the original owners whenever possible, although actual authorship was difficult and time-consuming to prove.

The worldwide increase in the demand for cosmetics created new methods of distribution that profoundly altered future product development, as well as advertising policies. Salons, first promoted as treatment centers for beauty ailments, became beauty shops. The principal personalities of the cosmetics world (Elizabeth Arden, Helena Rubinstein, Dorothy Gray, and Madame Leclaire) founded their images on the quality of their salons. No expense was spared in interior decoration, or in the conception of the treatments offered. "Thousands of women who have never been in an Arden salon buy Arden products in the more respectable drug and department stores all over the country," noticed *Fortune* magazine in 1929.

The market at the end of the war was dominated in the United States by Elizabeth Arden and in Europe by Helena Rubinstein. Elizabeth Arden began to experiment with makeup just after the war, when she discovered the secrets of the young, heavily mascaraed flappers in the nightclubs of Paris. A famous anecdote alleges that, with a chambermaid in the Ritz Hotel as a guinea pig, Arden experimented for hours, finally arriving at the perfect formula for eye makeup. The chambermaid apparently burst into tears after the ordeal and Arden, watching the tracks of makeup stream down her face, came upon the idea of waterproof mascara. Arden's only serious competitors in the cosmetics field were her former employer, Eleanor Adair, and the actress Lillian Russell. By 1919, Arden already had two salons and was considering locations in several other cities and resorts. She had found a chemist, A. Fabian Swanson, who was then working in the Stillwell and Gladding laboratory, and who shared her enthusiasm, creativity, and work ethic. The Arden-Swanson alliance produced a steady flow of new products that were eagerly purchased by both clients and customers in leading stores across the country. "In addition to Cream Amoretta and Ardena Skin Tonic, the first year offered Venetian Cleansing Cream, Venetian Pore Cream (for blackheads), Venetian Lille Lotion (to prevent freckling and to keep the skin from darkening), Venetian Muscle Oil (for wrinkles and hollows), Venetian Adona Cream (for the neck and bust that might be losing firmness), and a full line of rouges and tinted face powders," Arden commented in her biography by Alfred Lewis and Constance Woodworth. She considered packaging and names essential, and the metal cases in which Arden sold the Venetian

powders were attractive advertisements for her products. Years later, Helena Rubinstein was to remark that "with her packaging and my products, we could have ruled the world."

Rubinstein, who owned salons in London and Paris, arrived in the United States in 1915. She opened her first American salon in New York in 1916, at 15 East 49th Street. By 1917 there were locations in San Francisco, Boston, Philadelphia, Washington, Chicago, and Toronto. Rubinstein (in her biography *My Life for Beauty*, 1964) recalls: "The walls of the salon were covered in dark-blue velvet, with rose-colored baseboards; the period furnishings were upholstered in pale-blue silk, and the rooms were decorated with the works of the Polish sculptor, Elie Nadelman. The opulence of the surroundings pleased my customers, and journalists wrote exciting articles about the new salon with its amazing decor. There is no denying that the beauty business is made up of part theater, part glamour, on the surface at least; and I admit that I was the first to insist upon these trappings." Like Arden, she began to market her creams and makeup products in exquisite packages to create the illusion of luxury and ostentation, naming her first product line Valaze.

Professional competition between Helena Rubinstein and Elizabeth Arden was legendary and contributed greatly to the development and quality of their respective cosmetic products. When Rubinstein opened her "Maison de Beauté Valaze," she ran a full-page advertisement in *Vogue*. Arden, upon seeing the ad, took five more rooms on upper Fifth Avenue and created a new, more luxurious salon (and a new laboratory for Mr. Swanson). The decorative differences in the salons provided an interesting insight into the differences in their social aspirations. "Helena strove for the 'artistic', with dramatic dark-blue velvet walls and red baseboards. Elizabeth wanted to capture the aura of the drawing rooms of the great mansions that lined Fifth Avenue with consultations held in the white and gold Oval Room, and treatment rooms decorated in subdued pastels," Lewis and Woodworth point out. Competitors, such as Marie Earle and Dorothy Gray, were beginning to appear in the 1920s, but none became international successes or serious rivals until the appearance of Charles Revson in the early 1930s. Throughout their careers, Arden and Rubinstein represented an equal contest between two giant personalities, and between them, they created an industry.

Salons, even during the 1920s, provided a total approach to beauty, offering treatments as varied as exercise classes, makeup instruction, facials, massage, and hair shampoo and conditioning. A woman (necessarily of a certain economic stature) would spend an entire day in the salon, and meet her friends to gossip or

Above: **AT MRS. MARION'S
BEAUTY SCHOOL, A CLIENT
RECEIVES A PERMANENT
WAVE TREATMENT, AS DOES
HER PEDIGREED PUP
"BUBBLES," NEW YORK CITY,
1926.**
*Photograph © UPI/Bettmann
Archive.*

Below: **TUMMY SHIMMY
MACHINE, CIRCA 1928.**
*Photograph © The Underwood
Collection/Bettmann Archive.*

socialize. General health and physical well-being began to be considered as important as cosmetic beauty, and Helena Rubinstein employed a doctor to make a physical analysis of each "patient." Diet and weight control were a large part of the salon treatment, and the desire to be slim obviously obsessed many women even at that time. The society makeup artist, who had disappeared during the Victorian era, was reintroduced by both Arden and Rubinstein to give consultations at the end of the day as the final beauty treatment, or, at Guerlain in Paris, to prepare the woman for her evening party.

The hallowed environment of the beauty salon could not morally permit a male presence (other than the doctors), so the consultants, and later the salespeople and personnel demonstrators, were women. Both Arden and Rubinstein, early feminists, prided themselves on providing employment for women, and in their worldwide salons some seven thousand women carried their message of beauty to the masses.

The common hair salon created an excellent commercial opportunity to sell cosmetics. The new bob style was first realized in a barber shop, but quickly spurred the development of feminine coiffure parlors. The permanent wave, another recent invention, also brought a large clientele for this service. A manufacturer of hair goods rejoiced that because of the bob, "a tremendously profitable year is in store for the manufacturer and purveyor of toilet articles." Manicuring salons also continued to attract customers, and the manicure industry was considered the fastest-growing sector of the cosmetics business in 1922.

On a more upscale front, the company later called Charles of the Ritz had its beginnings in 1919 when hair stylist Charles Jundt came to America from Alsace-Lorraine, France, and opened his first beauty salon in New York at the Ritz-Carlton hotel. Best known for his finely textured powders available in an array of shades (green, violet, orange), Jundt personally blended his signature colors to match skin color at innovative "powder bars," boutiques he opened at a select group of stores across America. The idea was subsequently embraced by many manufacturers in the U.S.. He later launched a group of exclusive beauty salons throughout the country and a line of cosmetic and skin treatment products. In 1926, a company was established to distribute these products in his name.

In America, drugstores continued to attract a wider clientele. Lower prices, a warm, personal approach, the close proximity of medicine and cosmetics, and a more accessible fashion image served as catalysts to increase sales. Small-town pharmacies, such as the Owl drugstore in Hollywood, initiated beauty contests, sometimes sponsored by famous actresses, to search for "the new starlet." Specialty stores (*parfumeries* in Europe) had a large following, and the department stores, a worldwide phenomenon that increasingly cultivated a "middle of the road" public, further developed their market through the use of adventuresome window dressing and changing seasonal displays. Live demonstrations were introduced and even included "putting on a show" in the window to promote novelty treatments such as mud packs. Women pressed against the glass to take in the free demonstrations and, trusting in the miraculous powers the new fad promised, rushed inside to purchase.

Marketing took on new meaning. When Helena Rubinstein first began to sell products in department stores, she went with her sister, Manka, to launch her Valaze creams. She trained technicians to give treatments, and gave personal customer consultations. "Manka and I made it a point to wear the clothes we had brought over with us from Paris. We were well aware that many women came to see what we were wearing—and we really gave them something to look at." After one appearance at Jordan Marsh, in conservative Boston, the following mention appeared in the morning newspaper: "Madame Rubinstein wore a tomato-colored dress and eight strands of black pearls. Eight hundred women were enraptured by her lecture on treating the skin and on makeup for formal occasions."

Marketing even spread to the hinterlands. The American rural population became a significant share of the cosmetic business during the 1920s, as mail-order businesses such as Sears and Roebuck were firmly established. The passage of a bill granting free postage to farm families added incentive to buy, and the attractive pictures and illustrations in the catalogs increased the desire for makeup. Improvement in the rapidity and efficiency of delivery also provided the assurance that the cosmetics would arrive fresh and in good condition. In 1929, *Fortune* magazine announced that Sears and Roebuck sold more powder in that year than it sold soap, toothpaste, and shampoo combined.

"The soul of the business is advertising," said another *Fortune* article on cosmetics in 1930, commenting that women's magazines provided an excellent opportunity to sell these newly developed products. Cosmetics companies had quickly recognized the power and benefit of such exposure. In 1929, the article went on to report, the beauty business spent more than thirty-five million dollars on magazine advertising space. It was already a big business, and through a process of consolidation, makeup was becoming a bigger business. "The man in Cosmetics might well be envied by the man in Copper, or by the man in Coal," said *Fortune* optimistically one year after the Great Depression had begun.

Great care was taken to attract the potential client with catchy slogans, informative text, or exquisite artwork in ads. For the first time, full pages in fashion magazines were devoted to selling Bourjois powders, or Winx eye mascara. Expensive black-and-white pictures, portraits of actresses, and suggestive designs revolutionized the look of advertising. The idea of wearing makeup, so often shrouded in mystery, was touted with great fanfare. Catch phrases such as Elizabeth Arden's "The Eyes of Youth" or "Kissproof: lipstick, rouge, face powder, products which will give you new beauty instantly, a different kind of beauty," reflected commercial sensitivity to the allure of youth and novelty. Dorin of Paris introduced a new line of powders with the heretofore scandalous salespitch, "What attracts men most? Blond beauty or the charms of dusky hair and skin?" The French firm Vivaudou suggested that their powders and rouges would "Envelop you with mysterious charm," as they "guard the most famous secret in the world!" (presumably the key to sexual attraction).

Endorsement advertisements originated during this period, and socialites, actresses, and music hall performers lent their names to various products. Lucretia Vanderbilt, a prominent member of New York's Social Register, launched her new line of products with the slogan "What is fashionable without fashionable toiletries?" Tangee took a more liberated approach, with the statement "The smartest women achieve lovely lips," while Elizabeth Arden also traded on women's intelligence, asking them to buy the "Smartest Tan—the Rosetta Bronze." Cosmetic companies were still empowered to make outlandish claims for their products, since no effective laws existed to control the validity of the advertisements. Suggestions that cosmetics restored lost youth, guaranteed happiness, and attracted men were common. "Permanent" rouge, or miraculous "lash-lengthening" mascara, was supposed to provide instant beauty, and no superlative was adequate to sell the ever-expanding number of new products.

If the "look" of the 1920s was obviously artificial, it was definitely created to be noticed, to suggest independence and modernity, and to shock by its audacious use of color and texture. Eyebrows were plucked to a thin, arching line and then redesigned with an eyebrow pencil. Eyes, especially with the newly significant evening dress, were brightly colored with turquoise or green cream shadow (for blue-eyed women) or brownish-black tones (for brown-eyed women). Mascara was employed sparingly, as were false eyelashes and kohl eyeliner, although all of these products were readily available in specialty and department stores. Rouge was applied to the cheeks in a round circle without any attempt to shade or sculpt the face.

Above: **PARISIAN CABARET SINGER MISTINGUETT, CIRCA** 1927. *Poster by J. D. Van Caulaert.*

Right: **SHEET MUSIC FOR THE SONG** *YOU DROVE ME MAD (DU HAST MICH TOLL GEMACHT),* **BERLIN, 1922.** *Illustration by Herzig.*

YVONNE PRINTEMPS
SUNBATHING IN ROYAN,
FRANCE, 1926. *Photograph by
Jacques-Henri Lartigue.*

Lipstick, the favorite product of the 1920s, was first applied with the fingers, using two fingers for the upper lip and one for the lower, creating a pursed, full effect. Gradually, the application of what in France was known as *raisin* was perfected and the style called for the outer corners of the lips to be covered, using brushes or pencils.

Powder was applied over a cold-cream base with a hoop of feathers or lamb's wool, or it was used with a puff, moistened and applied wet to form a paste that was thicker than powder. As early as 1921, matching the correct shade of makeup to hair and facial coloring was popular.

While it was a new plaything for most women in the 1920s, makeup was not always well chosen, well applied, or of good quality. Numerous commentaries criticized the outlandish aspects of makeup, and American *Vogue* ran one such article in 1926 entitled "What Men Really Think of Women's Vanities," in which John McMullin railed, "The ladies now have a corner on boldness, and the sensitive male turns in grieved dismay from too-low frocks and stockings rolled beneath the knee, while lips shaped with cupid bows are viewed with sentiments far removed from love. We hate women who wear makeup on the golf course. Mascara is applied like the tar paving on Fifth Avenue, and the eyelashes stick out as if applied by the yard."

The average consumer grappled with exactly these problems. Not only were colors more intense after application than initially thought (common with the indelible rouges and lipsticks), but they were thick and cakelike (a fault of the powders).

Electric lighting also made the makeup seem faded and white, a dilemma compounded by the fact that women often tried to wear products for all circumstances, as an article in a 1925 *Ladies' Home Journal* mentions: "Everybody wears rouge too light for them....One firm alone makes eight shades, and I tried every one at home by daylight and electricity too. There wasn't any of them that seemed exactly to hit it. So when I go to dinner, I poke around to find from my hostess in advance whether there will be candles or dim lamps or electricity. And then I get all set for the lighting." Although it had jumped the hurdle of popular acceptance, the science of makeup and its practical application still had a long way to go.

PRODUCTS

LIPSTICK

LIPSTICK IN THE TWENTIES EXISTED IN THREE PRIMARY FORMS—SALVE, LIQUID, OR STICK. THE CREATION OF THE METAL LIPSTICK CONTAINER IN THE UNITED STATES BY MAURICE LEVY IN 1915 TOUCHED OFF A GREAT INTERNATIONAL PASSION FOR LIPSTICK. IT WAS OFFERED IN THREE SHADES, FROM ORANGE TO RED TO DEEP ROSE. INDELIBLE STAINING PRODUCTS WERE IN GREATEST DEMAND, AND BOTH TANGEE AND MAYBELLINE MADE A "KISSPROOF" VERSION. "ROUGE BAISER," INTRODUCED IN FRANCE BY THE CHEMIST PAUL BAUDECROUX, WAS SOLD AS THE "LIPSTICK THAT PERMITS A KISS," (BUT THE PRODUCT WASN'T A HIT UNTIL THE 1940s "MASKED WOMAN" ADS BY ILLUSTRATOR RENÉ GRUAU MADE IT A STAPLE OF FRENCH BEAUTY REGIMES).

AS THE LIPSTICK TREND TOOK HOLD, "NATURAL" LIPGLOSS WAS INVENTED, CONTAINING ONLY BROMO ACID AS COLORING, AND PRODUCING A RED SATIN EFFECT AS THE SALVE REACTED TO THE WEARER'S SKIN. THE PRODUCT WAS SAID TO BLEND WITH ANY SKIN, LOOK DIFFERENT ON EACH WOMAN, AND "WEATHER ANY STORM." IT WAS THE CULMINATION OF A PRODUCT EVOLUTION SPURRED BY THE DEMAND FOR AN ACCEPTABLE LIP COVERING THAT WASN'T A SHOCKING, UNNATURAL SATURATION OF RED. ANOTHER ENDEMIC LIPSTICK ISSUE WAS CONFRONTED WHEN HELENA RUBINSTEIN CREATED CUPID'S BOW, A "SELF-SHAPING LIPSTICK THAT FORMS A PERFECT CUPID'S BOW AS YOU APPLY IT." THE PREOCCUPATION WITH DESIGNING THE MOUTH WAS ALSO NOTED WITH THE FIRST METAL LIP TRACER, MADE IN SIZES TO CORRESPOND TO THE WEARER'S MOUTH TO ASSURE PERFECT APPLICATION OF COLOR. IN ORDER TO BETTER CONTROL THE DESIGN PROCESS, THE MIRRORED LIPSTICK CONTAINER, ANOTHER TWENTIES INNOVATION, WAS ISSUED BY LA BLOOM IN PARIS, AND BECAME EXTREMELY POPULAR ON BOTH SIDES OF THE ATLANTIC. FINALLY, IT IS WORTH NOTING THAT IN THE TWENTIES FLAVORED LIPSTICK ALSO BECAME THE RAGE, AND THE FLAVOR MOST IN DEMAND (ANNOUNCED *AMERICAN COSMETICIAN* MAGAZINE) WAS CHERRY.

ROUGE

ROUGE IN THE TWENTIES REDEFINED AN ALREADY VENERABLE BEAUTY PRODUCT IN A NEW, MODERN CONTEXT. A DESIRE FOR SIMPLICITY, PORTABILITY, AND PRACTICALITY TRANSFORMED THE MESSY ELIXIRS OF THE PREVIOUS GENERATION AS ROUGE BECAME AVAILABLE IN VARIOUS FORMS: CREAM, POWDER, LIQUID, AND ROUGE PAPERS. THE CREAM WAS SOLD IN A SMALL, ROUND CONTAINER, OFTEN METAL OR PORCELAIN, AND APPLIED WITH THE FINGERS OR A PIECE OF COTTON; A TYPICAL RECIPE USED A MIXTURE OF CARMINE, TALCUM, AND GUM ACACIA. THE LIQUID WAS SOLD IN A BOTTLE, AND OFTEN CONTAINED AMMONIA, CARMINE, ESSENCE OF ROSE, AND ROSE WATER. THE MIXTURE REQUIRED TEN DAYS OF MACERATION, AND TWO OR THREE MORE TO SETTLE, AND THEN COULD BE OPENED. BEGINNERS WERE ADVISED TO USE THE LIQUID, AS THE OTHER TYPES WERE DIFFICULT TO APPLY. POWDER ROUGE GAINED POPULARITY AS SPILLPROOF CONTAINERS AND THE COMPACT (USUALLY A METAL CONTAINER SMALL ENOUGH TO PUT IN A PURSE) WERE DEVELOPED. ROUGE AND POWDER, AND EVENTUALLY LIPSTICK, NOW CAME IN THE SAME PACKAGE.

AS WITH LIPSTICKS, INDELIBLE ROUGE PRODUCTS WERE POPULAR; MOST EXISTED IN ONE COLOR THAT LOOKED DIFFERENT ON EVERY SKIN, BUT SOME MANUFACTURERS, LIKE TREJUR AND BOURJOIS, OFFERED SEVERAL SHADES, RANGING FROM DEEP REDS TO ORANGES AND PINKS. A PRODUCT CALLED HEALTHGLOW, WHICH WAS ADVERTISED AS THE "COLOR OF RICH GLOWING BLOOD," AND GUARANTEED TO LAST THROUGHOUT THE

DAY, WAS AVAILABLE IN TUBE FORM OR IN A SILK CASE WITH APPLICATION PAD. PERT MADE A WATERPROOF ROUGE, WHICH WAS PERHAPS THE MOST-ADVERTISED PRODUCT ON THE AMERICAN MARKET (ALONG WITH WINX MASCARA). A CHARACTERISTIC AD FROM 1923 RAN: "HERE'S MISS MELISSA MARY SUE, WHO PERTS HER CHEEKS WITH ROUGE SO NEW. SHE POUTS HER LIPS AND PERTS THEM TOO, AND WINX HER EYES TO FLIRT WITH YOU." THE FASHION FOR CUSTOM-BLENDED ROUGE WAS RECORDED IN THE BRITISH MAGAZINE *QUEEN*, BUT SUCH A PRACTICE CAUSED COMMERCIAL PROBLEMS BECAUSE OTHER WOMEN COULD DEMAND THE SAME SHADES, WHETHER THEY WERE BECOMING OR NOT. "THE TANGERINE ROUGE, WITH ITS APRICOT SISTER, THE SUNTAN POWDER, THAT QUEER PURPLISH POWDER ONLY TO BE USED AT NIGHT UNDER ELECTRIC LIGHTS—THESE WERE ALL MADE FOR SOME PARTICULAR WOMAN WHOSE SKIN AND STYLE THEY SUITED," WARNED THE MAGAZINE IN 1928.

POWDER

STILL THE MOST IMPORTANT AND COMMON ELEMENT IN A WOMAN'S MAKE-UP, BY THE 1920S POWDER WAS OFFERED BY MOST COSMETICS COMPANIES, AND COMPETITION AMONG THEM WAS FIERCE. POWDER, WHOSE CHEMICAL COMPOSITION AND FORM HAD CHANGED LITTLE FROM EARLIER DECADES, EXISTED IN FREE FORM AND IN NUMEROUS SHADES: NATURAL, RACHEL (FOR OLIVE COMPLEXIONS), DARK RACHEL, ROSE, GREEN, LAVENDER, ORANGE, WHITE, PEACH, AND CINNAMON. IT WAS FREQUENTLY PLACED OVER A HEAVY BASE OF CREAM, CREATING A COVERING SIMILAR TO TODAY'S FOUNDATION. THE LIQUID FORM, ALTHOUGH DIFFICULT TO APPLY, WAS CONSIDERED THE MOST EFFECTIVE AND LONG-LASTING APPROACH; IT WAS USED TO COVER BLEMISHES AS WELL AS TO PROTECT SKIN.

COLOR IN POWDER WAS CONSERVATIVE, AS A CONTEMPORARY INDUSTRY WATCHER, HENRY TETLOW, POINTED OUT, NOTING THAT WHITE POWDER WAS STILL THE MOST POPULAR SHADE AND THAT "LATINS WOULD USE NOTHING ELSE." WOMEN OF BRITAIN AND NORTHERN EUROPE, ON THE OTHER HAND, PREFERRED A YELLOW TINT USUALLY CALLED "CREAM." AMERICANS PREFERRED PINK, WHICH THEY CALLED "FLESH," THOUGH "BRUNETTE" (A PINKISH-BROWN POWDER, "SOMEWHAT LIGHTER THAN THE FRESHLY CLIPPED COAT OF A CHINCOTEGUE PONY") WAS COMING INTO FASHION AND WAS OFTEN USED FOR TOUCHING UP THE NOSE, EVEN WHEN THE REST OF THE FACE HAD BEEN POWDERED WITH PINK OR WHITE.

IN PARIS, CARON INTRODUCED THE CONCEPT OF PERFUMED POWDER IN 1920, WITH PEAU FINES AND TABAC BLOND, AND INSTANTLY REVOLUTIONIZED THE PERFUME MARKET, CREATING AN ENTIRELY NEW USE FOR THE PUNGENT ODORS THAT ISSUED FROM THE COUTURIERS. BEAUTIFULLY DECORATED CONTAINERS FOR POWDER WERE AN IMPORTANT BUYING INCENTIVE. IN SILK OR BROCADE, AND DESIGNED TO HOLD THE LOOSE POWDER AND POWDER PUFFS, THEY WERE PLACED ALONGSIDE OTHER ACCESSORIES ON THE TWENTIES VANITY TABLE. THE MID-1920S WITNESSED THE RETURN TO SPECIALIZED COSMETICS SERVICES, AS STORES BEGAN FURNISHING PERSONALLY BLENDED POWDERS AND THE RAGE FOR INDIVIDUAL FORMULAS TOOK HOLD. SOON MOST DEPARTMENT STORES WERE PROVIDING THIS SERVICE FOR THOSE WILLING TO PAY HIGHER PRICES AT THE "POWDER BARS."

Above: **WORKERS IN POWDER FACTORY, GREAT BRITAIN, CIRCA 1920.**
Photograph © Hulton Deutsch.

Left: **CROPPED HEADS DISAPPEARED UNDER CLOCHE HATS AS THE YOUNG AND GAY TOOK THEIR NEWLY PORTABLE MAKEUP EVEN TO FOOTBALL GAMES.**
JUDGE MAGAZINE COVER, 1927.
Illustration by Ruth Eastman.

As the decade continued, powders that catered to the fashion for suntans and sunburns were offered from every major manufacturer. Important brands included Lablache and Hygenol, which, while extremely heavy in texture, suggested the soon-to-be-developed liquid foundation rather than traditional powder.

EYE MAKEUP

Eye makeup was the most experimental aspect of beauty in the 1920s, and development of eye products was the most difficult. Not until the end of the 1920s was the use of eye makeup understood and effectively employed by the consumer. Nevertheless, cake, tube, or liquid mascara used to darken lashes was widely advertised in magazines of the time. Eyebrow pencils existed in black and brown, and were often suggested as a charming accent to define the face. Several beauty authorities suggested using a spot of black pencil at the outer and inner extremities of the eyes to give them an oriental look and to elongate the eyes.

In 1915, nineteen-year-old T. L. Williams saw his sister Mabel applying petroleum jelly to her lashes, to moisten them and "to make them healthy and more noticeable." Taking this cue, he developed Lash-Brow-Line, which sold for twenty-five cents. He named the company Maybelline after his sister, and sold its goods through the mail, dominating this arena in the twenties. Rimmel, a perfume company, expanded into cosmetics in 1920, taking its name from a French chemist and perfumer who had established his business in London in 1834. Mascara 612 by Edouard Pinaud was launched in France in 1926, inspired by the Hungarian pomade Napoleon III used to groom his mustache. Containing Arabic gum, it was sold in a tube form and applied with a brush. Winx and Lashlux were other popular brands available in the U.S., and Kurlash, a tool for curling eyelashes, was introduced to the market in 1923. Meanwhile, shadows and kohl, offered in paste and pencil forms, continued to exist, and false eyelashes were available as well. An article in *Toilet Requisites* of 1921 documents their presence: "The modern tendency to facial decoration knows no limits....Borrowed from stage, and available in department stores, artificial lashes offered in shades to match the individual coloring are practically indiscernible. They are adjusted by spreading a film of liquid adhesive over the lash foundation. Indispensable for Vamping!"

BODY MAKEUP

Makeup was not confined to the face alone in the twenties. Leg makeup was used to color skin exposed by the fashion for short skirts. Called Bas de Soie, this cream makeup, sold in a tube, was made in France by Dorin. It was indelible unless washed off with soap and water, and came in three shades: rose, mode (sunburn), and ochre (dark sunburn); it sold for $1.50. In 1925, Max Factor completed the largest makeup order of all time—more than 600 gallons of body makeup for the motion picture *Ben Hur*.

Attempts to create permanent body makeup persisted on a limited scale, and such fashions as tattooing and skin staining were documented in England, where one tattoo artist had found a method to permanently fix the bright glow of youth on the cheeks: "It could no longer be said that the rose and lilac tints were painted on the faces, but that they were tattooed. Until today, elegant women of London were contented with a tattooed butterfly on their shoulders, and a flower on the calf of their legs," a contemporary English newspaper reports.

PLASTIC SURGERY AND BEAUTY TREATMENTS

The carnage and disfiguration that resulted from chemical warfare and mining in the First World War created an unprecedented interest in plastic surgery. Clinics were established in battlefields, and during the Battle of the Somme the eminent English plastic surgeon Sir Harold Gillies operated on two thousand "ruined faces" in ten days.

The 1920s witnessed the refinement of three essential aesthetic operations, reported *Toilet Requisites* in 1921. The correction of the nose was immensely improved by a Berlin practitioner named Joseph who employed the technique of reconstruction through the interior of the nasal passages, thus avoiding obvious scars. The second operation, the effacement of wrinkles, was performed in 1918 by cutting the skin and stretching it, and was developed by Raymond Passot in France. The third was the breast lift, by a Marseilles doctor named Aubert. For the first time, the medical community began to consider these interventions both safe and effective, and repairing a face for aesthetic reasons was even recommended by certain beauty specialists. In 1928 Jeanne Piabert opened the first institute of electrotherapy in Paris, specializing in the reabsorption of fat deposits.

NAILS

Polish was first commercialized by Cutex in 1917, but it wasn't until 1925 that the first true liquid nail lacquer appeared. The polish was a strong pink that was applied only to the middle of the nail, leaving the tip and the half moon bare. Manicures took on a special importance in the twenties, and there were many accoutrements available. Pink paste polish, white cake, and a buffer were the basic items in 1920. Nail white gave the nail tips a pleasing white effect. Style dictated against cutting the cuticle—instead of scissors, a bottle of cuticle remover was used with an orange stick. There was a nonbleach cream for removing stains under the nails. There was also a white bleaching powder that took care of all discoloration, including that of cigarettes, a habit that women were taking up increasingly as a defiant sign of their freedom of expression as the twenties roar sank to a whisper and the shadow of the 1930s loomed.

Sculpted Beauty *1930s*

LANCÔME soins de beauté

entre tous le plus sûr
pour se garder belle

IT WAS A DECADE OF UTTER PERFECTION, OF CLASSICAL BEAUTY, OF PERFECT PROPORTION. THE 1930s FACE REPRESENTED A PLATONIC IDEAL OF BEAUTY—SCULPTED, SENSUOUS, AND SEXUALLY UNDETERMINED—MARKED BY SYMMETRY OF FORM AND FEATURE.

THE 1930s FORMED A PERIOD OF CONSOLIDATION RATHER THAN INNOVATION FOR THE COSMETIC INDUSTRY, AS THE PRESENCE AND INFLUENCE OF AN INTERNATIONAL BEAUTY CULTURE, ESTABLISHED IN THE 1920s, WAS CONFIRMED BY AN INCREASING SOPHISTICATION.

Preceding pages: **MONTAGE, CIRCA 1930.**
Photograph by Gordon Coster.
Courtesy Keith de Lellis Collection.

Opposite: **LANCÔME ADVERTISEMENT, CIRCA 1939.**
Illustration by Pérot. Courtesy Musée Lancôme, Paris.

Right: **LANCÔME LIPSTICK CASE, DUBBED** *CLEF DE COQUETTE* **(COQUETTE'S KEY), CIRCA 1930.**
Courtesy Lancôme.

The painted, decorative face was now obsolete—even vulgar—and was replaced by a new cinema-perfect glamour that reassured the fragile sensibilities of a Western culture shocked and disillusioned by worldwide economic collapse.

Makeup in the thirties provided an escape from the unfathomable depths of the Depression. Image, not reality, was required, and the desire to create an individual look rather than follow a fashion transformed the aesthetic of the period. Makeup was no longer used to disguise the self, as in the twenties; now it was intended to reveal it. The 1929 stock market crash caused the widespread abandonment of the liberal attitudes identified with postwar prosperity. Gone was the adventurous spirit of a newly liberated civilization. It was replaced by a cynical and despairing realism which, as the decade progressed, evolved into a desire for structure, regulations, and legislated culture. Suddenly beauty and cosmetics needed to be capable of converting even the simplest country girl into a ravishing glamour queen. Popular magazines of the time spoke of every woman's "responsibility" to be "as attractive as possible" and to conform to the "standards" of beauty as dictated by various cultural and political powers. After the excesses of the 1920s, puritanism returned with a vengeance, symbolized by fashion's longer skirts and hair.

Everything had its place, and woman's place was again in the home. "The work of women increases unemployment and harms the family," the French newspaper *Le Matin* inveighed in 1931. With one in five men without a job, most countries affected by the economic crisis agreed that a woman who worked took the rightful place of a man. In 1930, the systematic layoff of women became accepted policy and even unions in Europe and the United States posed no objections. In 1932, Germany passed a law authorizing the firing of married women whose husbands earned a salary adequate for supporting a family. In the United States, a similar decree forced all female married civil service workers to leave their jobs. Teachers were similarly forced to surrender posts when they married. (The laws were repealed later in the decade when it became apparent that sending women home did not create jobs for men but instead deprived some households of their only means of support.)

The Depression reversed 1920s attitudes toward relations between the sexes almost overnight. Women searched for a way to render femininity more sensual, albeit less sexually demanding. The type of beauty had changed; no longer was the ideal a sexually approachable dilettante, as in the twenties, but rather an untouchable image of perfect womanhood. In 1929, in the United States alone, there were three million people out of work; by the next winter, four to five million. In the fall of 1932, *Fortune* magazine estimated that 34 million men, women, and children—better than a fourth of the nation—were members of families that had no regular full-time breadwinner.

Hard times isolated women in the city as traumatically as the farms had tethered an earlier generation of mothers, who taught their daughters to look for jobs in town. This rapid reversal resulted in confusion and uncertainty, as Mrs. Frances Woodward Prentice wrote in *Scribner's* as early as 1932: "I who am 37 in this year of 1932, have fallen into a chronic air pocket, an air pocket inhabited by most of my female contemporaries. In these days when it is smart to claim significance, we feel peculiarly without point. We are trying breathlessly to straddle the tremendous gulf the war really did create; awkward Colossi, prevented from getting our feet planted either THEN or NOW....We were reared, educated, and married for one sort of life, and precipitated, before we had a chance to get our bearings, into another."

This emotional need could be approached only by an idealized femininity, which planted the seeds of an obsession that

would affect the appearance of women for the rest of the century. The ideas of "looking good" and "feeling good" became inextricably connected for the first time, and the identification of goodness with beauty is crucial to the understanding of the thirties woman.

By the 1930s, the most popular medium for the creation and dissemination of mass values was the cinema. Unemployed men and women throughout the occidental world flocked to see films, and Hollywood, in contrast to Paris in the twenties, dictated aesthetic standards. The ideal of Hollywood beauty was the perfectly proportioned, photogenic face, not the decorative mask of the past decade. And it was makeup that created this flawless beauty—used to sculpt, shade, and give surface texture to the face. In 1933, the passage in the United States of the Hayes Production Code barred open sexuality in film, and the overtly sexual look of the twenties was superseded by an emphasis on "natural" effects.

Makeup as mask was replaced by makeup as sculpture, and the face—measured, analyzed, polished, and shined—became a work of art in the hands of makeup "artists." Transformation from plain country girl to glamorous starlet became the leitmotif of the decade, as makeup offered the hope of bettering a dismal existence, promising women a kind of equality. American *Vogue* proclaimed in 1933: "From dolls, women of fashion have become individual works of art. The creed of modern beauty is personality. And now, from the greenish or umber sheen of her eyelids to the flame or saffron of her lips and nails, the lady of today is a subtle and marvelous creation based on the entity that is—herself."

The movement toward naturalism reflected this quest for perfection. As American *Vogue* also remarked, "You have to use more cosmetics than before, but they have to look like less. Your exposed face has a startled, undressed look unless it is properly made up; but even a trace of heaviness looks blatant, especially in daytime." The trend can be traced to growing Germanic influences in the early thirties. Nudism, sunbathing, and hiking had all boomed in Germany at the time of the Weimar Republic, and throughout the decade, Austria and Germany were the fashionable places to spend holidays. The internationally acclaimed Leni Riefenstahl film, *Das blaue Licht* (The Blue Light), chronicled the spartan beauty and simplicity of mountain naturalism, and further confirmed a neoclassical aesthetic. Translations of Freud from the German became available in most countries and greatly changed the understanding of human behavior. In this view, the importance of the subconscious, dreams, and the inner self caused one to question the relationship between the appearance of the outer self and the essence of inner being, to consider its inherent dissonance

and search for reconciliation. This had practical applications, such as those of German nutrition guru Gaylord Hauser, who espoused the idea that beauty came from "the inside out" and introduced a low-fat, high-fiber diet that became the basis for spa menus at Elizabeth Arden's luxurious salons.

Naturalism quickly spread throughout Europe and to the United States. Open-air living became increasingly fashionable and, ironically, a symbol of monied sophistication. (One staunch practitioner, Helena Rubinstein, took solace at a health farm in Vienna after she divorced her first husband.) Camping, fishing, and hiking were popular activities, and country resorts sprung up throughout Europe and the United States. Sunbathing was confirmed as a popular obsession in the thirties. Newly built public swimming pools like the Piscine Deligny in Paris attracted hoards of unemployed men and women, and as the paid vacation became law in the late 1930s, the sport of swimming gained even more adherents. Doctors and health advocates extolled the benefits of the sun, suggesting it could heal such varied afflictions as tuberculosis and asthma. In 1936, the same year that paid vacations became law in France, Éugene Schueller of L'Oréal introduced L'Ambre Solaire, a tanning oil promising the golden glow of health, which had immediate success.

Nudism, another legacy of Germanic influence, was widely embraced, with nudist camps appearing in most occidental countries. The German psychologist John-Carl Flügel published an influential study called *The Psychology of Clothes* in which he voiced a sentiment that was to become characteristic of the entire naturalist movement: "Dress is, after all, destined to be but an episode in the history of humanity, and man will one day go about his business secure in the control of his body and of his wider physical environment, disdaining the sartorial crutches on which he previously supported himself during the earlier tottering stages of his march towards a higher culture." In spite of the currency of these sentiments, makeup was far from being abolished. Instead it was common to see "nudists" wearing lipstick, eye shadow, and mascara—and nothing else.

Naturalism made the 1930s woman uniquely conscious of her body and health. Slimming crazes were more popular than ever, with a new emphasis on physical fitness. American *Vogue* stated: "It takes more than a new color lipstick to make you look like a new woman this year—you must begin at the beginning, with your figure." The new naturalism required makeup that suggested a healthy glow, imitating unadorned skin yet improving its color and texture. Artificial, unbecoming shades of eye shadow, powder, rouge, or lipstick were considered in bad taste. "The fash-

ion of the red-and-white face has gone," affirmed *Harper's Bazaar*. "Nature's colors are in order and we seek the powders that bring out the natural luster of the skin, the rouge that blends with our own color or provides it naturally, when we have none."

Cosmetics companies therefore offered a much greater variety of colors, sometimes up to eight shades of powder rouge, from bright red to delicate pink, along with similar ranges in cream rouge and lipstick. Women were told to base their cosmetic choices on both hair color and eye tint. *Collier's* magazine noted the shift away from slavish adherence to fashion, claiming women in the past "looked more like a billboard than a work of art. All girls were abjured to do the same thing, so that we can remember whole eras like the nose-in-the-flower-barrel...or the recent all-over mahogany finish." The writer added, "This thing is different. The keynote is individuality, the watchword, subtlety. The colors and shadings are as delicately varied as those a painter puts on a canvas." Eye makeup was less blatantly applied; the heavy cosmetic wax was replaced by a lighter mascara available in numerous colors such as blue, green, black, and brown.

"Ethical" cosmetics were introduced during the 1930s by the oldest drug manufacturing company in the United States, Schieffelin and Company. They claimed that their complete line of makeup and creams, called Almay, had been formulated by doctors specifically for women who suffered allergic reactions or from skin diseases. Advertisements for the products appeared in medical journals, an unprecedented marketing strategy, and Almay was deemed an immediate success. Other health concerns were reflected in the use of vitamin supplements in makeup. The newly invented estrogen creams were all the rage, although the efficacy of such products was greatly disputed.

Athletic stars became increasingly influential. Almost every sport had its women champions, and the public celebrated their victories. The Olympics of 1932 and 1936 also increased popular interest in sports, and stimulated the growth of several sportswear companies and the proliferation of waterproof eye makeup, lipstick, and rouge. American tennis star Helen Wills's match with the French star Suzanne Lenglen created an international stir. Gertrude Ederle swam the English Channel and the Norwegian Sonja Henie electrified the world with her brilliant skating. Amelia Earhart captured the emotions of millions as she became the first woman to fly across the Atlantic Ocean alone. When interviewed concerning this adventure, Earhart commented that while it was exhilarating, she regretted the absence of a "powder room" and suggested that future plane designs place greater emphasis on feminine comfort.

By 1930, 23,000 movie theaters were showing films for 90 million people in the United States alone. In the same year, over 500 movies were made in Hollywood (a statistic never equaled before or since). Cinema provided an inexpensive escape from the stark reality of the decade, and the business of Hollywood rapidly became the major source for style and fashion worldwide.

A nexus of talents of many countries and backgrounds, Hollywood attracted Europeans who sought to escape the growing totalitarianism in Germany and Italy, and it provided hope for poor immigrants seeking fame, fortune, and influence in a new and unexploited industry. The chance to make a career overnight fortified the rhetoric of the American dream, and was idealized as a shortcut to the decade's longed-for perfection.

The movies' perpetual flow of images introduced the idea of beauty-by-imitation to many women of middle or lower class background. This pedagogic aspect of makeup was enthusiastically embraced by Hollywood cinema, whose 85 percent domination of world film production infused a peculiarly American aesthetic into a universal definition of beauty. The idea of the outlandish, Europeanized sophisticate quickly became outdated, and was replaced by a home-grown silver screen glamour queen.

As opposed to the 1920s' ingenue-vamp stereotypes, 1930s movie scripts introduced a complex older female character of passion and depth. "The glamour and maturity Garbo personified indicated a new standard of beauty and behavior for American women—a standard that became predominant in a time of economic distress," sociologist Lois Banner observed in *American Beauty* (1983). Garbo's look of assertive, self-confident, yet ambiguous sexuality, as well as her almost perfectly symmetrical face, afforded a strong and naturally defined image. Her influence was so great that it could well be said that Garbo alone changed the idea of femininity in the twentieth century.

The first true "glamour" makeover, Garbo was also the first example of the success and potential of makeup's role in the Hollywood system. "They smartened her up. They fixed her blonde hair, gave her a shape, and realizing that those eyes were her finest feature, they made them up magnificently, and then affixed spurious eyelashes so long that they dipped in her consommé in the commissary," quipped Hollywood columnist Frederick Hall in a 1934 issue of *Stage* magazine. He went on to argue that "the past decade has seen the full flowering of the glamour business. I date it exactly from the arrival of Greta Garbo on the unfriendly shores....In my belief [she] was the first to be glamorized in the modern Hollywood sense, and she remains to this day the outstanding product of the art."

Preceding page: **LORETTA YOUNG EXEMPLIFIES 30s BODY-CONSCIOUS NATU-RALISM IN THE FILM** *TOO YOUNG TO MARRY*, **1939.** *Photograph by Irving Lippman.*

Above: **MELLO-GLO, "NEW" FRENCH PROCESS POWDER IN COMPACT-SIZED PAPER BOXES.** *Photograph by Underwood. Courtesy Keith de Lellis Collection.*

Right: **WEIGHT REDUCING BUBBLE BATH, FEATURED ON** *VOTRE BEAUTÉ* **MAGAZINE COVER, 1939.**

Opposite: **GUERLAIN ADVER-**
TISEMENT, CIRCA 1935.
Illustration by Darcy.
Courtesy House of Guerlain.

Right: **JOAN CRAWFORD CAR-**
RIES A BROWN LEATHER
BAG WHOSE WOODEN HAN-
DLE CONCEALS A LIPSTICK
IN ONE END AND A PERFUME
BOTTLE IN THE OTHER,
CIRCA 1930.
Photograph ©Culver Pictures.

Garbo was initially overlooked by the major studios, who considered her large size, poor teeth, unruly coiffure, heavily made up eyes, and unbecoming mouth liabilities. She had spent six months in New York with her mentor, the director Mauritz Stiller, without success, until photographer Arnold Genthe took pictures of her and sent them to Metro-Goldwyn-Mayer. Legendary studio mogul Irving Thalberg immediately saw a new talent and gave her a role in a 1926 silent movie, *Flesh and the Devil*. Hall documented the sea change: "Before long, in the close-ups with sloe-eyed Jack Gilbert we were all believing that we had seen a downright divinity who had just slid down a brass pole from the heaven of gorgeous gals. At that moment was born the astounding Garbo Cult, the like of which had never been known before or since."

As different as possible from Swanson, Bow, or Theda Bara, her screen predecessors, by 1929 Garbo was the biggest female attraction in Hollywood. Garboites filled the theaters and bought the fan magazines. Her fervent admirers were described as "Garbomaniacs," a mild term for the almost psychotic adulation she inspired. She had such a sweeping effect on women everywhere that they even adopted her style of wearing shoulder-length hair and a slouch hat.

Her screen makeup concentrated heavily on her best feature—her long-lashed eyes—in an unusual and elaborate adaptation of a style originally used on the stage. Larry Carr, in *Four Fabulous Faces* (1970), described the process: "First, while the eyelid was closed, the eyeball was outlined, then softened and blended. Next, a heavy black line was drawn across the bottom of the lid to blend into the eyelashes. At the corners, two additional lines were drawn down and out, making a triangle, to extend their size and shape. Garbo's face was left natural, except for shading which hollowed her cheeks. Her lips were red and shined with lip gloss."

Garbo's enormous success ushered in the age of glamour, imposed as an ideal on those who didn't have it, and deified even further by those who did. The transformation of truck driver's daughter into cinema star was an uplifting fiction for the Depression-shocked audience. Makeup artists who played important roles in the creation of "overnight successes" became celebrities in their own right. An article entitled "The Glamour Factories of Hollywood" in a 1936 issue of *Stage* magazine states: "At the present time, so important is the glamour business that makeup men rank just above directors and just below Adolph Zukor in the studio hierarchy. Every lot in Hollywood possesses a small herd of these makeup *maestri*."

These makeup mavens of the thirties claimed adherence to a "photogenic formula" based on classical Greek ideals of beauty and proportion. The perfect camera face, male or female, was oval, with features balanced symmetrically, and the Hollywood version of the Pythagorean "golden mean" stipulated that the face be able to be divided vertically into three equal sections, and horizontally into five eye widths. The mouth was sensuously curved, slightly wider than the width of one eye, the upper lip a little fuller than the lower. Eyes were large and open to brighten the expression, and an eye's width apart. As few would-be stars possessed such faces, makeup men used the ancient technique of chiaroscuro, applying darker shades to parts of the face supposed to recede on film and highlights on areas they wanted to appear more prominent.

Chief among the *maestri* were the sons of George Westmore, who dominated Hollywood studio makeup. Mont, the eldest, worked for Cecil B. De Mille and freelanced successfully before heading the makeup department at the powerful Selznick International studio. Twins Perc and Ern were bitter rivals. Perc headed the makeup department at First National and Warner Brothers' studio for a quarter of a century (presiding over a staff of thirty sculptors, hairdressers, wigmakers, and plastic workers), while Ern held the same position at R.K.O.. Wally, the fourth son, ran Paramount's makeup department, and Bud was in charge at Universal for twenty-three years.

The Westmores, who were known throughout the world as the reigning makeup dynasty, were responsible for many of the major makeup trends of the middle and late 1930s. Ern changed the shape of Bette Davis's mouth in 1931 for a movie called *Way Back Home* and Hollywood took notice. Until then, many actresses still wore the twenties' elaborately drawn cupid's bow. This heart-shaped mouth did not suit women whose features were not small and delicate. For Davis, Ern drew the mouth almost straight across, extended the length of her lower lip, and made it slightly heavier to correspond to the upper lip. The effect emphasized her large eyes and improved the symmetry of her face. The electric effect of the change caused Katharine Hepburn, who was to star in *Bill of Divorcement* that same year, to adopt the same mouth.

Bette Davis, in fact, was one of the first actresses to challenge the Hollywood makeup code. Once a star's image was established, it was carefully maintained. Neither studio nor star was willing to tamper with a successful screen presence. Audiences wanted to identify with the performers on screen, even if the film was set in an earlier historical period, and to have their heroes and heroines appear modern, strong, and beautiful. Thus, though costumes and staging strived for authenticity, makeup rarely did. Davis, however, fought for realism. When asked at age thirty-one

to portray Queen Elizabeth I in her last years, she demanded that Perc Westmore shave her forehead, her eyebrows, and cut her eyelashes in order to appear as much like the notoriously vain queen in her dotage as possible.

Perc was known for meeting even more radical makeup challenges. Carole Lombard called in 1934 with an unusual problem: "I'm over here at Columbia making a picture called *Lady By Choice*, and I've got this low-cut dress, and my tits just don't look big enough," the star told him. Westmore recommended highlighting the upper part of the breasts by applying a lightweight, light-colored liquid foundation. Flesh-colored powder was applied sparingly over the foundation; even more intriguing highlights were attained by using cold cream or a film of Vaseline over the foundation, instead of the powder, and toning it down with tissue. A thin line of dry rouge applied with a brush between the breasts completed the transformation and deepened the cleavage. (Lombard was thrilled with the results.)

One of the most difficult makeup problems of the decade was posed by the epic saga *Gone With the Wind*. Producer David O. Selznick, a noted perfectionist, became obsessed with the color of Scarlett O'Hara's eyes, which were green in the novel. Selznick wrote memo after memo to Mont Westmore, raging that in various scenes Vivien Leigh's eyes were not green but "violet, gray, blue, and nearly every other color in the spectrum." Mont finally solved the problem with colorful clothes highlighting the green in Leigh's multi-hued hazel eyes, intensifying the effect by extravagant use of green eye shadow. Selznick, said Hollywood wags, never could figure out how Mont wrought the "Miracle of the Green Eyes."

According to the Westmore system, all faces could be classified according to the following general types: oval, round, triangular, oblong, diamond, square-jawed, or inverted triangle. As a rule of thumb, Westmore held that curves are feminine, angles and squares masculine. The oval face was considered the ideal of feminine beauty because it had the most curves, and the square was the least desirable for the opposite reason.

Following this phrenologic frenzy, Max Factor developed a more precise way to examine the faces of the stars, with the use of his Beauty Calibrator, a machine that measured the face mechanically, establishing exact proportions. He also designed the Mechanical Oscillator, more commonly known as the "kissing machine," a hand-operated device to test the indelibility of lipstick formulas that pressed two pairs of rubberized lips together under ten-pound tension (said to be the ideal kissing pressure). In 1930, Factor, a true innovator in makeup, revolutionized the movie industry by creating the first lip gloss, which eliminated the need

AMERICAN VOGUE **COVER, 1939.**

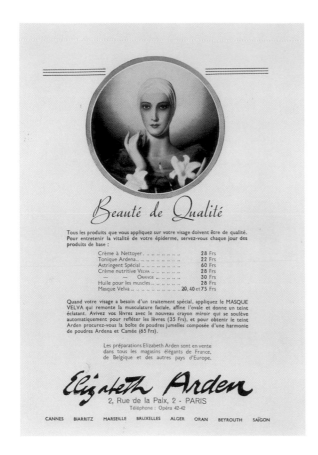

Top: **FRENCH ADVERTISEMENT FOR ELIZABETH ARDEN, 1937.**
Courtesy Elizabeth Arden.

Above: **SHISEIDO PRODUCTS, 1931.**
Courtesy Shiseido.

for actors to perpetually moisten their lips. Factor also created Pan Cake Makeup (1938) to solve a growing problem presented by the use of color film, in which traditional greasepaint on the actors' faces reflected the colors of the surrounding environment. Pan Cake Makeup, which gave a perfectly natural matte finish to skin and eliminated reflections, was such a success that studio actresses stole quantities of the product from movie sets for their own personal use. After overwhelming word-of-mouth publicity, the product was made available to the public.

The fascination with perfection and the limitations of makeup were manifested in the profusion of horror films made during this period. In *Dracula* (1930), starring Bela Lugosi, the only makeup that Lugosi would allow was a light green greasepaint, created by Universal Studio's Jack Pierce and exclusively manufactured by Max Factor. An artificial hairline and grayed temples completed the makeup process. Pierce's next film, the 1931 rebirth of the horror classic *Frankenstein*, with Boris Karloff as the monster, was to change the history of cinema. With little more than a cursory description of the monster given in Mary Shelley's classic novel, Pierce was obliged to invent the physical aspects of the character. He delved into medical and anatomy books, learning the various techniques that a nineteenth-century surgeon would employ in operating on the human skull, and conceived the now-familiar flat-topped head with scars and clamps. As the monster was to be created from the decomposing bodies of executed criminals, which would have had abnormally bloated extremities, Pierce gave the monster grotesquely proportioned hands and feet. The makeup took six hours to apply and included such revolutionary elements as wax eyecaps, lime-green foundation, and steel struts to create the monster's height and heavy walk. The picture grossed twelve million dollars in theater rentals alone. It also inspired the long and lucrative series of horror films that included *The Mummy*, *The Bride of Frankenstein*, and *The Mummy's Ghost*—all containing characters rendered unforgettable by the talents of Jack Pierce.

Aesthetic advances in cinema had their price, and makeup was part of the investment. In January 1937 Darryl Zanuck told an interviewer for *Motion Picture Insider* that "the average cost of launching a film star is about one million dollars. We select someone we think has the necessary personality, then we place him or her in strategic film roles from time to time and await the public's reaction. Some players quickly reach success, some never quite attain it. The salaries and expenses go on just the same while personalities are being groomed. And the cost of makeup, wardrobe, etc. is a considerable item in the whole."

Within the star system, Garbo's spiritual daughters were Joan Crawford and Marlene Dietrich. Crawford, who successfully made the transition from silent to sound movies, reinvented her appearance from one decade to another. During the 1920s she was a flapper with small breasts, a round face, a small mouth, and the obligatory short, waved hairdo. By the 1930s, her shoulders and face were square, her figure buxom, her eyes and lips large, her hair shoulder-length and smoothly coiffed. "I'd been a flapper in an age of flappers," she explained, "and a sophisticated lady in an era of sophistication." To achieve her new look, Crawford tried numerous styles, but it was not until she accentuated the size of her mouth and eyes through makeup that she acquired the look of assertive self-confidence attributed to the influence of Garbo (a debt Crawford herself freely acknowledged).

Nothing could compare to the machinations of the competing Hollywood studios to create their own Garbo. Dietrich, the cult star of Josef Von Sternberg's *Der blaue Engel* (The Blue Angel) (1930), was the logical candidate, and her arrival in Hollywood was heralded with articles comparing the two actresses. Dietrich's own personality and appeal were so immediately apparent, however, that she quickly became a widely copied star in her own right. Renowned for her independence in the realm of makeup Dietrich often did her own, or changed makeup she didn't like. She was credited with teaching the Westmores several techniques of makeup, as Perc Westmore admits: "She took a saucer from under the cup of coffee she was drinking, and held it about four inches above the table top. Then she lit a common wooden kitchen match and let it burn just beneath the bottom of the saucer. When she turned the saucer over, there was a black smudge of pure carbon in the indentation of the saucer's bottom. She then poured a few drops of baby oil into the indentation, and, with her finger, mixed the oil with the carbon deposit from the match. With the same finger she applied the mixture to her eyelid. She started just above her eyelashes, where she allowed the black color to be the heaviest. Gradually she blended the 'shadow' up toward the outside of her eyebrow, where it subtly faded away."

Throughout Dietrich's career, makeup artists would suggest that she refrain from plucking her eyebrows and adopt a more natural style, but she resisted, preferring instead the use of eyelashes fixed to the outer half of the lids, intensifying the wide spacing of her eyes and giving them a provocative upward slant. Her lower lids were deliberately not accented with black (which would have emphasized the boundaries of her eyes and so limited their size). Her natural eyebrows were blotted out and soaring new ones were etched far above.

Hollywood goddesses of the 1930s were made, not born, and sometimes more than makeup was required. Cosmetic surgery and dental work were common. According to the magazine *Modern Screen* in 1932, surgeon Josef Ginsberg had performed over a thousand operations on Hollywood personalities in the previous two-year period. Bebe Daniels, Carmel Myers, and Vivienne Segal all had their noses remodeled, and a spectacular transformation was achieved when a sizable lump was removed from Johnny Weissmuller's nose prior to his debut in *Tarzan*. Valentino's and George Raft's ears were surgically flattened early in their careers, though "bat ears" could also be held down with the aid of a fine fish net. The same net could be used to produce the effect of a facelift, a method that was employed to make John Barrymore appear ten years younger for his role in *Eternal Love* (1929), an early talkie. Douglas Fairbanks's double chin was eradicated by the application of heavy shadow. Extensive dental work was common as well. *Collier's* readers were told that discolored teeth could be given a coat of collodion enamel paint, which would last the day, while more serious dental problems could be rectified by "shells" that slipped over the teeth like thimbles. It was also possible to dramatically alter the shape and bone structure of the face by extracting back molars, and actresses such as Joan Crawford completely changed their appearance using this method.

The backdrop for such transformations in cosmetics was the dramatic spectacle of fashion and design, a necessary preliminary to the 1930s aesthetic. "New Objectivity," the catchword of the decade, demanded subdued colors, a harsh metallic sheen, and elegant contours in design and furniture. The doctrinaire angularity that characterized 1920s architecture was transformed; curves appeared again, and formerly strict, cubelike designs began to incorporate variations in structure and material. American *Vogue* described an ideal interior as "dead white and luminous, stripped of all useless walls and doors, with polished floors and a cocktail bar of mirrors and glass." A craze that began with the crash of 1929, the fashion for white or reflective surfaces continued until the outbreak of the second World War, and manifested itself in the new style for platinum hair and oiled, glowing skin.

The sleek, luminous surfaces of this modern style inspired a new treatment of clothing, as couturiers attempted to capture the new naturalism. Vionnet's bias cut created a fluid shape that changed as a woman walked, thus constantly redrawing the silhouette. The materials commonly used in 1930s apparel—silk and satin—melded with the lines of the body, and even though the skirts became longer, they were more revealing. Exposing the curves of the body in a flaunted femininity became the primary aesthetic concern. As American *Vogue* put it, "Flat breasts are finished."

Nevertheless, the economic crisis left an indelible mark on the haute couture industry. Suddenly necessity dictated that it was no longer fashionable to be rich. "If you haven't lost money, pretend you have," advised British *Vogue*. In the first season after the Wall Street crash, not a single American buyer came to Paris; most did not return to Europe until 1933. Fashion changed to meet the needs of the newly democratic spirit, and less expensive lines based on couture models were launched by most designers.

This popularization of haute couture was accompanied by a new need to establish perfumes and beauty products as desirable symbols of luxury. In June 1932 in America, a Cosmetic Tax Law was levied on all products of "luxury definition," increasing their cost by 15 percent. Perfume served as a base and was often added to powder and lipstick, thus expanding the product possibilities of the couture houses. Jean Patou, who continued to be an active force in cosmetics in the 1930s, created a lipstick, Sex Appeal, which was sold in the unique "Lift" container—a metal tube that had a flip-down cover instead of a removable top, that could easily be used with one hand while hiking, skiing, and even flying. Patou revolutionized fragrance marketing by opening "perfume bars" (the first one named Cocktail Dry) where women could smell his various scents as well as discuss the latest fashions. His most influential perfume, Joy, appeared in 1931, at the height of the Depression, and was immediately touted as the most expensive essence ever made. Although it was difficult to obtain (as it was sold exclusively through Paris), Joy was a runaway success.

Elsa Schiaparelli's vision of beauty and fashion stood apart from that of other couturiers of her epoch. She believed that fashion existed as a medium to express art, not decoration, and that woman was the perfect canvas. Schiaparelli often asked artists to participate in her creations, and collaborations with Cocteau and Dali were common. Artist Leonor Fini was called upon to create an hourglass-shaped vial based on Mae West's silhouette, and Schiaparelli filled it with a new fragrance, called Shocking, following her predilection for names starting with "S." She then introduced a cologne for men entitled Snuff, which came in a tobacco-brown package and whose flacon consisted of a pipe made of glass surrounded by brown tissue. "Sleeping," her own interpretation of a night perfume, was advertised as "caressing, intoxicating, lingering," with a bottle shaped in the form of a candle, "suggesting [according to Richard Martin in *Fashion and Surrealism* (1987)] the transition between the darkly subconscious and the illuminated conscious." Schiaparelli was also known for

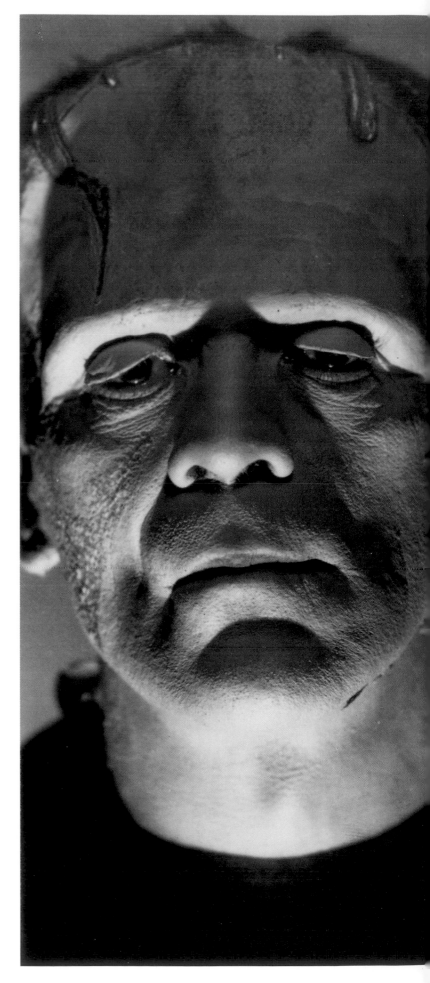

her range of lipstick shades, including the bright purple Frolic.

Art and artistry were essential to the aesthetic of makeup in the 1930s. "It takes both art and skill to acquire new beauty for your face," advised American *Vogue* in 1931. "In the daylight, you concentrate on looking your natural best. At night, you do things to your face that you have never done: You touch up your ears. You paint yourself a new mouth. You put a startling color on your lashes. You make up your neck." The human face, viewed as a canvas (rather than the mask of the previous decade), acquired added significance. It was no longer decorative but rather symbolic, sculptural—a referential art form. Makeup was not simply a matter of powder and paint, but a possibility for inspiration and artistic expression.

Surrealism fed that potential in the 1930s, as major art world figures entered the realms of fashion, fashion advertising, and window display. Artists such as René Magritte, Man Ray, Christian Bérard, and Jean-Michel Frank worked for fashion publications or with couturiers, bringing a new intellectualism to a heretofore decorative discipline. Reflecting the popular interest in psychology, the creation of beauty through makeup or fashion acquired twofold signification—as the symbolic language of dreams, and as the objective expression of the individual.

Surrealists transformed the face and body by isolating, modifying, and separating eyes, mouth, hands, and feet. Body parts became symbolic through their displacement—acquiring an exaggerated sexual or visual presence, becoming a vocabulary that had little to do with their original function. Among the most sensuous expressions of Surrealist body language were lips, liberated from the face and floating alone (as in Man Ray's *L'Observatoire*) or molded in goose down (as in Salvador Dali's shocking pink *Lip Sofa*, acquired by Schiaparelli for her Place Vendôme boutique). Painted red, Surrealist lips suggested female genitalia and therefore the sublimated sexuality of the woman herself. Then too, Surrealists viewed the eyes as the legendary windows to the soul, and Surrealist manifestos like Luis Buñuel's film *Un Chien Andalou* (1928) prophesied "Seeing with eyes closed," in an oxymoron of insight and blindness. Depicted by the Surrealists in a variety of ways, eyes could be found mascaraed, eyelashed, or waxed (as in Man Ray's *Tears*), rendered in rubies and diamonds by Salvador Dali, or winking in a glass by Marcel Duchamp. Hands and feet also played a prominent role in Surrealist vocabulary. Decorated by Picasso, or sculpted by Dali, their lacquered, brightly colored nails perfectly expressed the artist's need for artifice and surface, while the elegant, lithe forms suggested delicate, ethereal beauty.

Preceding pages:

Left: **BORIS KARLOFF IN** *FRANKENSTEIN,* **1931.**
Photograph © Bettmann Archive.

Right: **MARLENE DIETRICH, WHOSE GLOWING, POLISHED SKIN AND FLAUNTED FEMI- NINITY DEFINED THE ERA, 1933.**
Photograph © Culver Pictures.

Above: **FILM POSTER FOR CAROLE LOMBARD IN** *LOVE BEFORE BREAKFAST,* **1936.**
Photograph by Walker Evans.

Surrealism greatly altered the evolution of makeup culture. Following its mandate, "Beauty must be convulsive," it validated the idea of beauty as illusion—the power of the made-up face to symbolize other, more primitive realities. Moreover, the Surrealist vision of the dislocated, disintegrated body permanently altered the manner in which women viewed themselves. Beauty was no longer a question of a unified "whole" but rather the sum of various, often displaced parts.

This artistic and often dreamlike conception of feminine form was supported by the photographs of the day. Horst P. Horst, Hoyningen-Huene, and Cecil Beaton, among others, introduced a formal approach to fashion photography by creating photos that accentuated the spectacular aspects of the subjects, yet retained a sobriety of light, line, and form. New equipment like the German Rolleiflex, whose fixed lens, larger film, and larger negatives resulted in clear, high-definition photographs, demanded increased attention to makeup application. The resulting precision allowed an image of beauty that was glittering and polished on the surface, yet suggestive of softness and fluidity underneath. Face shading and body makeup helped construct these often elaborate fantasies.

The exhibition *Fantastic Art, Dada, Surrealism* (originating at the Museum of Modern Art, New York), which showed in London and Paris in 1936, stirred further interest in Surrealism. Man Ray, who had begun to work as a photographer for Carmel Snow at *Harper's Bazaar* in 1932, indelibly marked that publication with his Surrealist vision. *Bazaar* supported and encouraged photographers to experiment and to show fashion as it had never been shown before, and Man Ray's photography at its best created an atmosphere of ambiguity and mystery. It was through the power of such photographs found in mass publications like *Bazaar* that the Surrealist conception of makeup was disseminated to an audience far larger than the followers of the avant-garde.

The 1930s also witnessed the refinement of the classic Hollywood studio portrait. In 1938, eighty million moviegoers (65 percent of the population in the United States alone) demanded constant coverage of their favorite stars. An important factor in making this information accessible was the Hollywood portrait. Nearly two hundred photographers worked in Hollywood in the heyday of the studio, providing the publicity stills that "instantly identified" the stars, a publicity effort that was unprecedented.

THEIR QUEST WAS FOR THE FACE THAT WOULD PROVOKE IN MILLIONS THE DESIRE TO IDENTIFY

Moving away from the standardized romantic images of the twenties, the portraitists of the 1930s highlighted instead the individuality of their subjects. Their quest was for the face that would provoke in millions the desire to identify. To this end, they either collaborated with makeup artists or themselves created the made-up faces that would remain eye-catching on magazine covers even at a distance (and surviving even the crudest printing processes). The close-up of the face was soon established as the standard format of the Hollywood photographic portrait; the power of the close-up was transferred from the screen to the still.

The studio photo sessions were key in defining a star's particular look. As Bette Davis recalled: "Roman Freulich was the first portrait photographer to do a sitting with me when I got to California. When they looked at me, they called me 'the little brown wren', because with Harlow around, my hair was just mousy blonde. So they made me bleach it. They had me looking like everybody. They even made up my mouth like Garbo. Now I ask you, do you see anything like Garbo about me?"

By 1930, most important studios boasted their own photographic departments, skilled in their own makeup tricks. Makeup for the photographer was significantly different from that for the filmmaker, who required a heavier base and powder to conceal red tones highlighted by film. George Hurrell, resident photographer at MGM, was one of the exceptional talents. Loretta Young recalled: "He made you look so glamorous. Your skin looked so shiny—as if you could reach out and touch it. I know the secret with him—he was the first man who said he didn't want any makeup. You used to put a little oil on your face, and that was about all." Joan Crawford added her experience: "George Hurrell used to give me just one key light, and for him I never wore makeup...except for my eyes and lips, of course."

Director Josef von Sternberg made a lasting impression on the use of lighting and makeup during his Hollywood period through what began as experiments in the studio portraits of Marlene Dietrich. As Dietrich herself explained to Perc Westmore: "My body weight didn't bother von Sternberg at all, but my nose did. One day he got me onto a bare sound stage, pulled out a small vial of silver paint, and drew a line right down the middle of my nose. Then he climbed up onto a catwalk and adjusted a tiny spotlight to shine directly on the silver line from above my head. It was like a miracle. When he made a film test, I realized that he had reduced the width of my nose by nearly a third." Von Sternberg took charge of the publicity photographs of Dietrich, working with photographers Don English, Eugene Robert Richee, and William Walling, Jr., among others.

Robert Coburn, the photographer for Goldwyn, influenced the filming of Merle Oberon in the 1936 film *Beloved Enemy*. "She wasn't wearing much makeup when I took the picture. Actually, I didn't like it when they wore too much, and besides, I could cover any problems with lighting. She was still recuperating from makeup poisoning which had scarred her face, and she couldn't wear makeup to disguise it. I figured out that if you lit her flat, nothing would show. The cameraman on this film, faced with the problem of how to shoot her close-ups, saw what I was doing and used the same lighting setup."

Movies were just one of the communications revolution that characterized the decade. The thirties also witnessed an explosive rise in the popularity of visually oriented magazines and books, which provided rapid and wide dissemination of photographic images. *Fortune* had introduced pictures to accompany text in 1930, while *Life* appeared in 1936, featuring numerous picture stories of public life. Fashion magazines such as *Vogue* and *Harper's Bazaar* became serious arbiters of fashion, and new magazines (*Marie Claire* and *Votre Beauté* in France and *Glamour* in the United States) were founded.

Interest in the beauty industry skyrocketed as the fashion magazines supplemented their usual clothing coverage with a special beauty issue four times a year. As the influence of haute couture waned with the Depression, editors relied on less expensive (though more time-consuming) solutions to beauty problems—namely the application of cosmetics—to provide the needed direction to their pages.

Along with the fashion magazines, "fanzines" such as *Photoplay, Motion Picture, Movieland*, and *Modern Screen* doubled circulation while divulging the secrets of the Hollywood stars. Most of the writers (as well as the readers) were women, and most periodicals carried a column designed to provide beauty tips from the stars. Articles such as "What Is Camera Beauty" analyzed particular aspects of face shading and hair color, while others featured interviews with the stars about their shortcomings (for example, Joan Crawford on her square jaw). More frequently, they chronicled the transformation of the destitute country girl into a big-city avatar of beauty.

The extent of interest in the movie industry can be gauged by the fact that the Hollywood press corps, in its heyday, was the third largest in the country. There were some "three or four journalists for every star of any consequence, including has-beens and singing cowboys," said Christopher Finch and Linda Rosenkrantz in their book *Gone Hollywood* (1979). Publicity departments in the major studios would often stage outlandish stunts to attract the interest of these journalists, and one such event was described by Metro-Goldwyn-Mayer studio makeup artist Bob Shiffer: "We concocted a special makeup for Jeanette MacDonald. To get an iridescent effect, I mixed gold dust in the powder. The publicity department picked up on it and said, 'What a great gimmick!' They hired an armed guard and cooked up a story about how they needed him to bring the gold in. What happened, though, was that when Jeanette would start to sing and dance her body heat would turn all the little gold flecks green. She looked as if she had the measles." Magazines available during the thirties also included a number of well-established trade journals—*Beauty Culture, The American Hairdresser, The Beautician, Beauty Shop News*, and *The National Beauty Shop*, which existed for professionals in the cosmetics industry. Added to the proliferating five-to-fifteen-cents-a-copy fan magazines, there was ample reading material on beauty available to the unemployed millions.

The thirties concomitantly witnessed phenomenal growth in cosmetic advertising. By 1935, one magazine alone might carry as many as sixty-five different ads concerning cosmetics, and the companies were spending up to 10 percent of their profits in publicity. The cosmetic industry radically changed its commercial approach during the Depression and pre-World War II period. Advertising became the art of depicting a fictional "reality" to the public, with an emphasis on naturalism, artificially achieved. Elizabeth Arden entitled one such ad in the early thirties "The New Importance of Makeup," describing her new translucent colors and lipsticks to flatter all complexions.

Cosmetics advertisements highlighted the practical advantages of makeup, as customers could no longer afford "luxury" indulgences. According to Helena Rubinstein's new ads, makeup indisputably gave its wearer "a competitive edge when applying for a job or attracting the right man." Powder and foundation were found to be "effective against sunburn," and lipstick "protected the skin from dryness." In fact, a 1932 advertisement for Elizabeth Arden warned: "Beauty is a very tangible asset in these days of fluctuating values. If your face isn't your fortune today, who knows that it may not be tomorrow—and what kind of a fortune is it going to amount to?"

Hollywood's influence reached its apex in the mid-1930s when advertisements began to regularly include movie star endorsements in their copy. In the late 1920s, Max Factor pioneered the first such arrangement between a cosmetic company and a motion picture studio with campaigns featuring the screen's most glamorous stars in dramatic full-page ads. Showcasing Joan Crawford, Claudette Colbert, Jean Harlow, and others, the ads promoted the star's latest film release along with Max Factor's newest line of cosmetics. The practice became so well established in the late 1930s that Garbo, when she negotiated her never-to-be-realized comeback, included a clause in the contract stipulating her right to refuse the use of her image or name to sell products.

Color photography proved to be an early boon for the cosmetic industry, with bi-color advertisements soon appearing, as in the Cutex nail polish and lipstick campaign of the early thirties, in which dazzling red lips and nails were set against a black-and-white background. Full-page color ads appeared in the late 1930s. *Beauty Fashion*, the trade magazine that succeeded the defunct *Toilet Requisites*, supported taking the offensive, arguing that the advertising budgets of major cosmetics companies during the Depression should be stepped up (rather than cut back) to keep interest in beauty products high throughout the economic crisis.

Even the United States government took an interest in cosmetics advertising, although in a restrictive manner. The Federal Trade Commission passed a series of restraining laws during the 1930s, beginning with the creation of a Bureau of Standards in 1936 to legislate advertising copy and claims. The bureau was empowered to survey trade practices of the industry and to make recommendations to the board. Though the vast majority of "bad" advertising was blamed on mail-order houses, even among known brand names there were problems, such as the claim of the Lady Ester cosmetics company that certain face powders would "paralyze" the pores of the skin, making them desirably inconspicuous. When commission experts pointed out that pores have neither nerves nor muscles (and therefore could not be paralyzed), the advertisement was withdrawn. Even such renowned beauty companies as those of Elizabeth Arden and Helena Rubinstein were required to revise certain misleading ads.

The beauty salon was one sanctuary for women seeking to escape the bleak reality of the Depression and realize some of their fantasies. An estimated 40,000 salons existed throughout the United States, grouped into organizations like the National Hairdressers and Cosmetologists, whose role was to validate the quality and legitimacy of each establishment. Most department stores had beauty salons where women could have their faces massaged, cleansed, nourished, painted, and powdered. During days spent entirely in the salons, their bodies were analyzed, waxed and buffed to a glossy sheen, and "exercised" via machines

MANNEQUIN, PARIS, 1931.
Photograph by Jacques-Henri Lartigue.

that conveniently did all the work for them. In Paris, the trend for customized makeup lessons and beauty treatments became a big enough business that even the French writer Colette, tired of life as a starving artist, decided to open a salon. Colette, in her own words, wished to "play the saleswoman, try the perfumes, the pots of cream and colors...as the [transformation of] women's faces was certainly very amusing."

Renowned for her stage makeup, Colette was skilled at the use of kohl, gray antimony, and at whitening the teeth by powdering the tongue and the gums with lacquer of *garance* (madder root). She knew how to accentuate the best features in a face while hiding the mundane. She could discern "the pastel tones which favor a tan, and...which awaken a white complexion" and she had a special fondness for the recipes of "Syrian women, harems and Arab magicians." Colette concocted her own cosmetics (which she spent a year developing and selling throughout France) at a Paris laboratory. Her beauty salon, which opened in 1932, was financed by her friends the Princess de Polignac, the Pasha of Marrakech and socialite Simone Berriau. *Le Tout Paris*, the French fashion elite, attended the opening at 6 rue de Miromesnil, for which Colette's invitations read: "I will be happy, Mesdames, to receive you myself, and to offer my advice concerning the best makeup for you, for both the stage and street." Her salon initially enjoyed a huge success but as her street makeup proved to be just as flamboyant as that for the stage, her clientele diminished until she was forced to close the salon in 1933.

Salon fever spread. Max Factor opened a salon in Los Angeles in 1935, and the gala inauguration included more than eight thousand invited guests. Lancôme, the famed perfume company, followed suit in 1936 with its Paris salon, and the Guerlain brothers responded two years later with a magnificent establishment, decorated by artist Christian Bérard, on the Champs Elysées. Innovations included numerous "treatment cabins," each given the name and odor of a different Guerlain perfume.

Elizabeth Arden was also expanding, to twenty-nine salons worldwide, in France, in Los Angeles, Palm Springs, and Miami Beach, as well as in department stores. Arden was the sole proprietor of all except the two in France, which belonged to her sister Gladys. One of the world's most prominent business successes, Arden provided a role model for aspiring women everywhere. She redecorated her beauty clinics in modernist style and installed complex equipment to perform treatments like the Ardena Bath, during which the woman's body was coated with paraffin wax, resulting in a loss of moisture and, temporarily, of weight. Exercise machines were so ubiquitous in her salons that

Above: **FOUR OF THE WESTMORE BROTHERS, THE MAKEUP DYNASTY OF HOLLYWOOD, LEFT TO RIGHT: MONTY, PERC, WALLY, AND BUD, 1935.**
Photograph courtesy of the Academy Foundation/Margaret Herrick Library, Los Angeles.

Opposite, above: **THE WESTMORE SALON, HOLLYWOOD, CALIFORNIA, 1935.**
Photograph (with original retouching directions) courtesy of the Academy Foundation/ Margaret Herrick Library, Los Angeles.

Opposite, below: **THEATRICAL BOUDOIR.**
Photograph © Culver Pictures

one somewhat cynical operator observed: "We've got an instrument of torture here to suit the fancy of every fat ass in the world." Undaunted by the Depression, in 1934 after a year's preparation, Arden opened her Maine Chance retreat, a cross between a very posh women's club and a European spa. Twenty women were admitted weekly, paying between $250 and $500 to attain the average six-pound weight loss, through means including an exercise regime prescribed by certified doctors and nurses.

Four of the Westmore brothers (Ern, Perc, Mont, and Wally) opened the House of Westmore in 1935. According to the press accounts, the unveiling was a Hollywood event: "Kay Francis, reigning queen of the silver screen, turned a golden key which opened this magnificent salon of beauty. Joan Blondell threw the golden switch which flooded the interior with light, and Claudette Colbert, gowned in gold, pressed a gold button to light the exterior." The Westmores' salon was decked out with pure white silk draperies with crystal fringe, while bronze, coral, and white furniture graced every booth, each boasting its own white and gold telephone. An announcement system allowed messages to be crooned softly into the booth. The cosmetic products were created in a nearby Hollywood plant and were the most expensive of their kind on the market. Clients included the Duchess of Windsor, Madame Chiang Kai-shek, Dolores Del Rio, and Barbara Hutton, and the salon rapidly became a meeting place for movie personalities. The backstage action became legendary. "Ann Sheridan...always came in to have her hair, nails, and makeup done during lunch....She always consumed the unusual combination of mashed potatoes and gravy and a hot fudge sundae....[One] particular day, Hedda [Hopper] had written something snide about Ann in her column. The minute Sheridan heard that Hopper was there, she took her plate of mashed potatoes into Hedda's booth and dumped the whole mess right in Hedda's lap," recalled Frank Westmore.

For the cosmetics industry, the "age of belief" was past, as scientist E. G. Thomssen put it in *The Drug and Cosmetic Industry*'s July 1937 issue; it was to be succeeded by the "age of science which looks for evidence and fact." Cosmetic products throughout the occidental world were, for the first time, subject to scientific scrutiny, their contents analyzed for noxious ingredients, their colors controlled, and their textures tested for quality. New technical discoveries helped refine the products and also led to new methods to test cosmetics already in existence.

Government agencies in France, England, and Germany began to pass legislation to give governments sweeping powers to regulate different aspects of the cosmetics industry. In the United

States, the Volstead Act creating prohibition was repealed in 1933, making it easier to use alcohol in cosmetics, which in turn aided in making products with finer texture and scent durability. Also in 1933, a complete revision of the obsolete 1906 Food and Drugs Act was recommended by the FDA to President Franklin Roosevelt, and the first bill was introduced into the Senate, launching a five-year legislative battle that pitted a traditionally private cosmetics industry, whose product ingredients were carefully guarded secrets, against a powerful and public government force. Meanwhile, reports of dangerous products, such as Lash Lure (which, according to the journal *Hygeia*, could cause death or partial blindness), corrosive freckle creams, and lead-based hair dyes could still be widely found.

The United States Senate passed the milestone Federal Food, Drug, and Cosmetic (FDC) Act, or the Copeland bill, in 1938. It extended the control of the Food and Drug Administration to include cosmetics, subjecting them to the stringent control usually reserved for drugs. It authorized standards of identity and quality for products, and required pre-distribution clearance to ensure safety of new substances. The FDC act also authorized factory inspections to help enforce these provisions, and added the possibility of court injunction to previous remedies of prosecution.

Such restrictive legislation did not entirely slow scientific advances, and several new products appeared in the thirties. As early as April 1930, a "disintegrator," which had been widely used by the paint industry, was recommended for the refinement of face powder, and it resulted in perfectly mixed color and even distribution of scent. In 1931, the Atlas Powder Company discovered sorbitol, which served as a humectant in numerous cosmetic products. Accompanying the move into a more scientific age was an increased insistence on cleanliness. The Jergens Company responded by using mercury ricinoleate to produce "germ free" cosmetics, a radically new idea. Another major chemical breakthrough occurred when Dr. Lloyd Hall of Griffith Laboratories developed an oxide sterilization process for cosmetic pigments. Mearl Corporation began producing a natural pearl essence, Mearlmaid, which served as a source of iridescence and gave a new finish to various products. Monsanto labs discovered Sanolite resins, which made opaque shades of nail polish possible and so expanded the variety of colors available beyond the traditional transparent red-based hues. Several chemical publications concerning cosmetics appeared in the 1930s. Books by Chilson, Poucher, and Redgrove appeared in English; by Cerbeland in French; and by Winter in German. The chemistry of cosmetics even became an integral part of some science courses offered at universities.

Opposite: **JEAN HARLOW,**
30s ICON IN PLATINUM HAIR
AND WHITE SATIN SHEATH,
1934.
Photograph ©Archive Photos.

Above: **ELSA LANCHESTER IN**
THE CLASSIC HORROR FILM
THE BRIDE OF FRANKENSTEIN,
1935.
Photograph © Archive Photos.

In summary, the look of the 1930s was a polished, perfectly symmetrical face that, with its sculpted surfaces and clearly defined forms, corresponded to the canon of beauty established by the film and fashion industries. Its image of a sublime, untouchable femininity aligned with theories of makeup that involved the methodical study of bone structure, skin color and texture, exalting the face and giving it new importance, and above all, individuality.

Makeup that produced a more natural result altered the way women viewed cosmetics. Makeup could transform a face—render it more "perfect"—by creating the illusion of symmetry without the obvious artificiality of the 1920s painted face. Beauty thus acquired gave women new stature and strength. "Every woman can be powerful with her beauty, and beauty belongs today to every woman who desires it," stated Dr. Nadia Gregoire Payot in her introduction to the 1936 edition of *Maquillage, Dictionnaire de la Beauté*. (Payot's own beauty parlor opened on the Rue Castiglione in 1930, offering improvement via creams and lotions, like her classic astringent La Pâte Grise, to eager clients.)

It was a learned skill. In practice, women of the thirties spent long hours putting on their makeup and didn't seem daunted by complicated explanations or methods of application. "A lovely girl is an accident; a beautiful girl is an achievement," commented Hoyningen-Huene. American *Vogue* described what a typical reader wore on her face: "In the country: Arden's Ultra Amoretta foundation cream, powder, a little brilliantine over eyebrows and lashes, Coty's Origan, and Guerlain's pale lipstick. In town, she wears Helena Rubinstein's sticky foundation called Crème Gypsy, applied with a pad of cotton wool wrung out in cold water and dyed to a light ochre. A little grease rouge, and two powders, first a light rachel and then a deeper shade. A blue or brown pencil line drawn on the eyelid and followed by a touch of Vaseline. Black mascara, brushed with a clean brush when still wet to take off excess, eyebrow pencil and darker lipstick."

The cosmetics companies suffered less from the economic hardships of the Depression than most industries. According to an article in *Beauty Fashion*, "Toilet goods emerged from the Depression stronger than they went into it....In 1930, when consumer expenditures dropped from $78 billion to $46 billion, cosmetic sales in department stores only showed a 14% decline." Due to clever marketing efforts, such as the introduction of smaller, less expensive sizes and less luxurious containers, as well as greater publicity and increased acceptance of makeup, public support increased. "Individual consumers bought more cosmetics when it was over than they had purchased during the presumably lush years that led up to 1929," *Beauty Fashion* concluded. Despite this bright prognosis for the industry, as the forties approached, the dark cloud of war loomed overhead.

PRODUCTS

NAILS

NAIL POLISHES GAINED POPULARITY IN THE THIRTIES AS IMPROVED PRODUCTS AND NEW SHADES BECAME AVAILABLE. IN THE EARLY THIRTIES CUTEX INTRODUCED LIPSTICK THAT MATCHED NAIL POLISH. IN 1932, THE REVSON BROTHERS (CHARLES AND JOSEPH) FORMED THE REVLON COMPANY, WHICH FIRST SPECIALIZED IN NAIL POLISHES, AND SOON AFTER DEVELOPED THE "CREAMY NAIL," AN OPAQUE POLISH RATHER THAN A TINTED TRANSPARENT FILM. FINGERNAILS WERE PAINTED ONE COLOR OR WERE GIVEN "PLATINUM TIPS" BY APPLYING OPAQUE SILVER POLISH TO THE TIPS OF RED ENAMELED NAILS. THE COLORS THAT WERE AVAILABLE INCLUDED GREEN, OCHRE, VIOLET, BLACK, AND BLOOD RED. CUTEX INTRODUCED A WHITE PENCIL TO BE USED UNDER THE NAIL TO IMPROVE NAIL COLOR AND TO GIVE THE ENDS OF THE NAILS AN OPAQUE APPEARANCE. A NEW TREND IN SCENTED NAILS WAS STARTED, ALSO BY CUTEX: "PERFUMED NAIL POLISH," AVAILABLE IN CORAL, CARDINAL, AND GARNET.

EYES

EYE MAKEUP WAS CONSIDERABLY REFINED DURING THE THIRTIES, AS NEW PRODUCTS WERE DESIGNED AND TECHNIQUES PERFECTED. EYEBROWS BECAME IMPORTANT TO GIVE BALANCE AND STRUCTURE TO THE FACE. THE WIDE SPACE BENEATH THE BROW WAS EXAGGERATED BY PLUCKING STRAY EYEBROW HAIRS, AND THE ARC WAS RE-CREATED WITH AN EYEBROW PENCIL. THE BROW WAS LEFT FULLER AND MORE NATURAL THAN IN THE TWENTIES, BUT IT WAS STILL SHARPLY DESIGNED IN A SEMICIRCLE. LIQUID EYEBROW DARKENER WAS SUGGESTED TO PERMANENTLY DARKEN HAIR, AND WHEN NEEDED, FALSE BROWS—TUFTS OF HAIR GLUED ON THE FACE—WERE RECOMMENDED BY THE *DICTIONNAIRE DE LA BEAUTÉ*. SHADOW WAS OFFERED IN VARIOUS COLORS FROM BLUE TO VIOLET TO BLACK AND BROWN. THE MOST SIGNIFICANT TREND, HOWEVER, WAS THE INTRODUCTION OF PURE GOLD OR SILVER. ALONE, OR MIXED AS BLUE SILVER, BROWN GOLD, OR MAUVE GOLD, THESE GAVE A "MYSTERIOUS" QUALITY AND A NEW SHEEN TO THE LIDS. AMERICAN *VOGUE* SUMMED IT UP BY SAYING, "AT ANY RATE, YOUR EYELIDS AND EYEBROWS SHOULD BE SHINY, AND VASELINE, GLAND CREAM, OR BRILLIANTINE IS VERY GOOD FOR THE PURPOSE." EYE SHADOW APPEARED IN CAKE FORM TO BE RUBBED ON WITH THE FINGER, OR IN THE NEWLY LAUNCHED EYE SHADOW STICKS. EYELASHES WERE MASCARAED (RATHER THAN COVERED WITH THICK EYE WAX) AND OFTEN DONE IN TWO COLORS—ONE ON THE INNER LASH, AND ANOTHER, BLUE OR GREEN, ON THE TIPS. FALSE EYELASHES, CUT INTO SMALL BITS AND APPLIED INDIVIDUALLY WHERE NEEDED, WERE SUGGESTED FOR EVENING. MAYBELLINE OFFERED A SOLID FORM OF MASCARA, AS WELL AS A CREAM FORMULA, ALONG WITH EYELINER PENCILS AND CREAM SHADOWS.

FOUNDATION

"A TRANSPARENT QUALITY IS THE EFFECT TO STRIVE FOR IN YOUR SKIN," ADVISED AMERICAN *VOGUE*, AND THE LOOK OF SHEEN ALL OVER THE FACE

WAS SAID TO BE PARTICULARLY "LUSCIOUS." REFINING LOTIONS, FOLLOWED BY FOUNDATION POWDER, WERE SUGGESTED. STARTED BY FRENCH CHEMIST ARMAND PETITJEAN, LANCÔME WAS LAUNCHED IN 1935 WITH A CLASSIC MULTI-USAGE CREAM, CALLED NUTRIX. COSMETICS DEVELOPED FOR THE CINEMA BEGAN TO APPEAR IN THE EARLY THIRTIES AND EACH MAJOR COSMETIC COMPANY MADE THE THIN BASE OF COLOR THAT WOULD LATER BE REFERRED TO AS "FOUNDATION." MAX FACTOR DEVELOPED HIS REVOLUTIONARY PAN CAKE MAKEUP, THE FIRST WATER-SOLUBLE, MATTE MAKEUP, IN 1938. FACTOR USED THIS NAME BECAUSE HE CREATED THE DRY, ROUND CAKE IN PANCHROMATIC COLORS TO BE USED WITH THE NEW COLOR MOVIE FILM. THE PRODUCT HAD IMMEDIATE SUCCESS AND WAS SOON OFFERED TO WOMEN EVERYWHERE IN NEW SHADES. FOUNDATION WAS MATCHED TO SKIN TONE AND USED TO HIGHLIGHT OR SHADE PARTS OF THE FACE. POWDER WAS OFFERED IN A LARGE VARIETY OF COLORS FROM WHITE TO MAUVE TO GREEN, THEN APPLIED TO THE SKIN TO EVEN THE COLOR. THE FASHION FOR OCHRE OR DARK BEIGE COLORS WAS LESS PROMINENT AS IT HAD BEEN IN THE LATE 1920S. ELIZABETH ARDEN'S EIGHT HOUR CREAM, INVENTED IN 1930 TO PROTECT THE ENTIRE BODY—FACE, BODY, NAILS AND HAIR—BECAME A LEGEND, ESPECIALLY AFTER IT WAS TESTED IN 1953 BY EDMUND HILLARY, WHO WORE IT CLIMBING MT. EVEREST.

ROUGE

ROUGE WAS PRESENTED IN THE SAME FORMS AS IN THE 1920S, BUT SHADES WERE MUCH MORE SUBTLE AND VARIED. TANGEE CONTINUED TO OFFER MATCHING LIPSTICK AND ROUGE IN ONE SHADE, WHICH APPEARED ORANGE IN THE CONTAINER BUT WHEN APPLIED BECAME BRIGHT CORAL. ALL MAJOR COSMETICS COMPANIES CONTINUED TO OFFER ROUGE IN CAKE, LIQUID, AND GEL FORMS, ALTHOUGH THE GEL BEGAN TO GAIN POPULARITY BECAUSE IT COULD BE APPLIED MORE PRECISELY. A SIGNIFICANT CHANGE IN ROUGE WAS THE USE OF TWO DIFFERENT COLORS—ONE TO SHADE AND ONE TO HIGHLIGHT THE FACE. THE GREAT VARIETY OF COLORS (SOMETIMES AS MANY AS TEN) OFFERED BY THE MAJOR COSMETIC COMPANIES WAS ALSO A REMARKABLE NEW EVOLUTION.

LIPSTICKS

LIPSTICKS CONTINUED TO BE EXTREMELY IMPORTANT, EXISTING IN MYRIAD COLORS RANGING FROM BRIGHT RED TO MAUVE TO RUSSET TO LIGHT PINK. SCHIAPARELLI LAUNCHED NEW TINTS, SUCH AS THE BRIGHT PINK SHOCKING; INCARNAT, A TRUE RED; SCHIAP, A BRIGHT YELLOWISH RED; FRAGILE, A BLUISH-PINK, AND PRUNEAU, A DEEP PURPLE TONE. IMITATION OF HOLLYWOOD STARS WAS URGED IN APPLYING LIPSTICK WITH A BRUSH, RATHER THAN DIRECTLY FROM A TUBE. BRUSHES WERE SOLD FOR THIS PURPOSE, AND MARTHA LORRAINE OFFERED A ROLL-TOP MODEL WHICH WAS PARTICULARLY HANDY. A BRUSH CALLED CINEMA SABLE WAS ANOTHER COMMERCIAL SUCCESS, SUGGESTING THAT ITS USE WOULD TRANSFORM ANY MOUTH INTO A STAR'S MOUTH. OUTLINE PENCILS FOR THE LIPS FIRST APPEARED IN 1938, ALONG WITH ANOTHER INNOVATION (BY VOLUPTE), THE LIP KIT CONTAINING A LIPSTICK, PENCIL, BRUSH, AND SIX STENCILS OF ASSORTED SHAPES, WHICH FIT OVER THE MOUTH TO AID OUTLINING. THE CUSTOMER CHOSE A STENCIL AND ORDERED A BOXFULL OF THAT SHAPE.

Preceding page: **PHOTOGRAPH BY LOUISE DAHL-WOLFE.** *Courtesy Keith de Lellis Collection.*

Left: **AUTOPORTRAIT, TAMARA DE LEMPICKA, PARIS, 1932.** *Oil on canvas, 35 x 26 cm.*

Above: **COLETTE PHOTOGRAPHED ON OPENING DAY IN HER MAKEUP SALON, PARIS, 1932. HER INSCRIPTION READS: "ARE YOU FOR OR AGAINST THE 'SECOND PROFESSION' OF THE WRITER?"**

Right: **MAX FACTOR'S BEAUTY CALIBRATOR, A MACHINE THAT MEASURED THE FACE AGAINST "IDEAL" PROPORTIONS, 1932.** *Courtesy The Max Factor Museum of Beauty.*

VOGUE

WOMEN IN DEFENSE
America Trains for 18 Skills

·

LONDON PORTFOLIO
Lady Reading's Message
R.A.F. Flyers

·

MID-SUMMER FASHIONS
for "More Taste Than Money"

JULY 1, 1941
PRICE 35 CENTS
40 CENTS IN CANADA

ADVANCE
RETAIL
TRADE
EDITION

see section facing page 74

THE PERIOD BETWEEN 1937 AND 1946 WAS DOMINATED BY THE REALITIES OF WORLD WAR II, ARRESTING DEVELOPMENTS IN THE ARTS, FASHION, AND BEAUTY FOR NEARLY A DECADE. THE PURSUIT OF BEAUTY DURING WARTIME PRESENTED A PARADOX FOR THE TWENTIETH-CENTURY WOMAN, AS SHE CONFIRMED HER EQUALITY WITH MEN WHILE WORKING ALONGSIDE THEM, WHETHER IN FACTORIES, IN BUNKERS, OR IN WHITEHALL. AS WOMEN ENTERED INDUSTRY IN RECORD NUMBERS, REDEFINITION OF THE FEMALE ROLE BECAME A UNIVERSAL PREOCCUPATION.

Preceding page(detail): **WOMEN ASSIST IN THE WAR EFFORT IN FACTORIES AT HOME.** *Photograph © Archive Photos.*

Opposite: **AMERICAN** *VOGUE* **COVER, JULY 1941.** *Photograph by Toni Frissell.*

Right: **SHISEIDO ADVERTISEMENT, CIRCA 1940.** *Courtesy.Shiseido.*

Women were expected to be "competent," "mature," yet "nurturing" for affection-deprived soldiers. An advertisement by Britain's Yardley cosmetics expressed the confusion: "We cannot leave men to fight this war alone. We asked for equal rights and we cannot have it both ways. It is only fair that we should face the music side-by-side with our men. Total war makes heavy demands on us. The slightest hint of a drooping spirit yields a point to the enemy. Never must careless grooming reflect a 'don't care' attitude. Now that leisure and beauty aids are limited we must never forget that good looks and good morale are the closest of good companions. Put your best face forward!"

Cosmetics, therefore, became a secret weapon of war. The United States government acknowledged for the first time the psychological value of physical appearance, and beauty products were subjected to investigative research, legislation, presidential commentary, and military inquiries. Studies proved that makeup served as a morale builder, helping to "combat fatigue," and one official report by the Office of Civilian Supply to the U.S. Director of Economic Stabilization in 1943 recommended that factory dressing rooms in which beauty products were provided might "improve efficiency by as much as 10–15 percent." Veronica Conley, in an article in 1951, described lipstick as the "most missed" among the shortages of war, adding: "Navy nurses evacuated from submarines included lipstick among the few personal items they took with them." Nevertheless, Britain's Limitations of Supplies Order of 1940 slashed available cosmetics materials—like petroleum and alcohol—to their nadir. Yardley's factory switched to manufacturing aircraft components and seawater purifiers, while Cyclax changed over to producing special sunproof creams for desert fighting.

The products that did appear in the forties reinforced the image of brave women holding fast the home line. Harriet Hubbard Ayer created a perfume duo that consisted of two bottles and scents—one called *Je Chante* (I Sing) and the other *Malgré Tout* (No Matter What). Ciro, a French perfume manufacturer, issued *Danger* in 1940, while his competition, Pierre Dune, created *Près du Coeur* (Close to the Heart), dedicated to any women who were alone in 1941. In 1943 a perfume/powder combination called *Attente* (The Wait) appeared, and the couturier Bruyère followed with a variation, *En Attendant* (Waiting).

And while they were waiting (and in greater numbers than World War I), women assumed jobs formerly held by men. In England, over six and a half million women were engaged in active war duties; in the United States, as early as 1942, two million female volunteers—rapidly becoming four million paid workers—undertook a vast array of duties, from telephone operator to clerk, driver, draftswoman, cook, mess-hall orderly, engineer, radio operator, machinist, policewoman, and factory worker. The services of women in the labor force became essential to the successful functioning of the economy, and their participation was as assiduously cultivated during the war as it had been shunned during the Depression. The U.S. agitprop image of "Rosie the Riveter," sporting dungarees and tool belt, nonetheless showed her working in lipstick and mascara.

"Womenpower" was now a catchword inextricably connected with cosmetics and, as one Tangee ad of the period, entitled "War, Women, and Lipstick," made clear: "For the first time in history women-power is a factor in war. Millions of you are fighting and working side by side with your men....It's a reflection of the free democratic way of life that you have succeeded in keeping your femininity even though you are doing a man's work....No lipstick—ours or anyone else's—will win the war. But it symbolizes one of the reasons why we are fighting....the precious right of women to be feminine and lovely under any circumstances."

However, few products were available to this vast, newly moneyed female public. *Beauty Fashion* magazine estimated in 1943 that "a sizable proportion of the new workers represent an entirely new market for cosmetics—women and girls who hitherto have not had funds for more than the barest essentials in beauty."

Cosmetics, despite shortages, remained marginally available throughout the war, but their use changed significantly, accommodating a reserved, "responsible" attitude toward makeup. As British *Vogue* remarked in a 1940 article: "Today you want to look as if you thought less about your face than about what you have to face; less about your figure than about how much you can do. You want to look as if you cared about your looks, yes, but cared more about being able to do a full day's work—whether it be in a factory, on the land, coping with a day nursery, or just managing your home single-handed as so many of us do today. You want to look beautiful, certainly—what woman in what age hasn't wanted to?...but you want it to be a beauty that doesn't jar with the times, a beauty that's heartlifting, not heart-breaking; a beauty that's beneficial, but not beglamoured, and a beauty that's responsive—not a responsibility."

Wartime fashions in beauty corresponded to the idea of propriety in crisis as in this 1942 article in *Revue*: "What's wrong with those exquisitely tapered nails? They couldn't do a hand's turn without breaking. For the face, no makeup, but a non-greasy all-purpose cream, dusted with powder....save your cosmetics for evenings out...."(Interestingly, this attitude changed at the war's finish, when the boys were en route home. A 1948 article on career choices for women appeared in American *Vogue* alongside a Jergens ad encouraging these same women to "Wear your man-captivating shade of New Jergens Face Powder, and find surprise, new loveliness, that Pin-Up Girl Look that all the boys adore.")

"Saving" makeup for an evening out was to some extent a wartime necessity, and as early as 1940 women began hoarding their favorite products. A March 27, 1942, decree ordered the recuperation of cut hair in America's beauty salons. The nation's shorn locks were thereafter washed, sanitized, and mixed with fibranne (the name for rayon before 1971) to create thread, principally used for making articles of clothing. Cosmetics that did survive in the straitened market, such as Ricilis mascara, were sold through advertisements that admonished buyers to use it sparingly so that other women might also profit from the products.

Some new beauty articles that were tailored to the lives of working women appeared. Elizabeth Arden made the Busy Woman's Beauty Box, which contained, along with a large stand-up mirror, Ardena Fluffy Cleansing Cream, Velva Cream, Orange

Above: IN WORLD WAR II,
STOCKINGS WERE IN SHORT
SUPPLY. THIS RESOURCEFUL
WOMAN PAINTED HER LEGS
WITH A "STOCKING" SHADE
OF BODY MAKEUP. LONDON,
1941.
Photograph © Hulton Deutsch.

Right: MARLENE DIETRICH
BEING PAINTED WITH GOLD
LEAF BY MAKEUP ARTIST
EDITH WILSON FOR MGM'S
FILM, *KISMET*. FOUR COATS
WERE APPLIED—EACH HAD
TO DRY COMPLETELY.
DIETRICH ALSO STARTED THE
FAD OF SPRINKLING GOLD
DUST IN HER HAIR.
HOLLYWOOD, 1944.
*Photography courtesy Marc
Wanamaker/Bison Achives.*

Skin Cream, Cameo and Illusion Powders, Ardena Skin Lotion, Lille de France, Elizabeth Arden smooth lipstick, and Divine Eye Sha-Do—all for $6.50. Arden also featured a new Book Box, which contained these necessities cached in a book-shaped container. Maybelline also aggressively sold eye makeup to working women, prefiguring the 1970s' trend of "dressing for success" with their ad: "Bright Girls use Maybelline....the Eye make-up in Good Taste. Perhaps one business woman in a hundred realizes the power of lovely intelligent eyes. And she's the one who inspires confidence—who gets ahead. Why not discover the full potential of your eyes?"

The war witnessed other significant changes, including the appearance of full-page color cosmetics ads. Popular themes included exotic women and bright, luxurious, international settings, foreshadowing the commercial style of the postwar period. Air Spun makeup by Coty, Three Precious Sapphires nail enamel by Chen Yu, and Revlon's Windsor, Scarlet Slipper, and Bright Forecast were all product lines that initiated this new tradition in cosmetics image.

Few new magazines emerged in wartime. French *Vogue*, under the direction of Michel de Brunhoff, ceased production, and *Marie Claire*'s editorial and production facilities moved outside Vichy France to Lyon. British and American *Vogues* continued, but with reduced staffs. Articles shifted their emphasis to concerns of women in wartime rather than fashion. Remedies for household problems, wartime recipes, patterns, renovations, and creative child care solutions occupied pages normally filled with haute couture. The immediate effect of the war was to increase magazine costs dramatically. British *Vogue* jumped in its newsstand price from one to two shillings in 1940, and to three shillings by 1942. Its circulation, ironically, also increased, from 52,000 in 1941 to 106,000 in 1949. Clearly the need to dream, to experience the fantastic and frivolous, was even more essential in wartime. But the magazines shied away from predicting the future. James Laver, invited by British *Vogue* to hypothesize about the look to come, replied, "Fashion has reached one of those turning points in history when everything may happen, just because anything may happen to the world. Neither in politics, nor in social life, nor in dress, are the lines yet laid down."

Despite shortages, cosmetics sales in 1940 gained seven percent over 1939 figures; in the United States alone, sales of

Above right: FATAL APPLE **NAIL COLOR ADVERTISEMENT, 1945.** *Courtesy Revlon.*

Below right: **FRENCH ADVERTISEMENT FOR CHANTAL BEAUTY PRODUCTS, 1945.**

Opposite: **STUDY FOR A SOAP ADVERTISEMENT, CIRCA 1949.** *Photograph by Ruzzie Green. Courtesy Keith de Lellis Collection.*

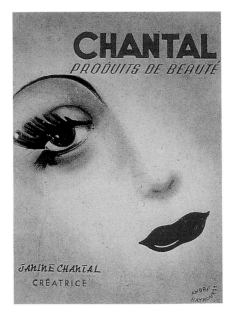

CLEARLY THE NEED TO DREAM, TO EXPERIENCE THE FANTASTIC AND FRIVOLOUS, WAS EVEN MORE ESSENTIAL IN WARTIME

beauty products totaled an unprecedented $450 million. In 1941, *The New York Times* found, twenty million dollars' worth of lipstick was purchased in America. The article commented on this expenditure, with opinions ranging from a soda jerk's startled "That's an awful lot of lettuce to spend on a woman's face!" to C. A. Willard of the Cosmetics Branch of the War Production Board's dismissive "Most of it doesn't do any good anyway," to a flight instructor's ingenuous observation that "every girl in his shop wore makeup, and it gave him a lift every time he went in." A seaman thought girls ought to taper off, "especially on smeary lipstick," while a Coast Guard lieutenant admitted that he "had no desire to find out how women would look without makeup."

By 1942, important restrictions were levied on cosmetic production, and the supply of beauty items in Europe dropped to one quarter of peacetime levels. The United States War Production Board attempted to ration cosmetics by limiting production according to necessity, but the law was rescinded two months later when it was deemed impossible to arbitrarily distinguish which items (i.e., lipstick or powder) were essential. The board reversed its judgment and legislated the control of supplies of basic ingredients instead, declaring cosmetics "necessary and vital products" contributing to the morale and well-being of women engaged in the war effort. The shortages created by the war first necessitated curtailing the raw materials and supplies used for packaging: aluminum, brass, glass, and cellophane were all requisitioned for the war effort. In Paris, women dressed in shoes with hinged wooden soles (leather was requisitioned) and imaginative hats made out of wisps of tulle, and formed long lines on the Champs Elysées to bring their bottles to Guerlain or Caron to be refilled. Hairdressing salons in Paris were ordered to recover clippings for forwarding to textile manufacturers, to be recycled as clothing. Paper and cardboard were also rationed, and since makeup was usually removed with tissue paper or softened cardboard, a substitute was called for. The French magazine *Votre Beauté* in 1940 suggested that women use butter, oil, or margarine—or any shortening normally available in their kitchen—to remove dirt and makeup with a paring knife or letter opener, just as men used a razor.

Shortages of primary ingredients included glycerin, alcohol, talc, and fats, as well as perfume essences from occupied France and Italy. Castor oil, a key component of lipstick, was so hard to come by that when a chemist at Revlon heard of a warehouse-full in Tennessee, he raced south to arrange a purchase. Devising a quick quality check, he wound up sticking his finger into each of dozens of forty-gallon drums, sniffing and licking. He bought out the whole stock—and spent the rest of his trip

on the toilet (reported Andrew Tobias's book on Charles Revson, *Fire and Ice*). Manufacturers developed unorthodox methods of replacing these ingredients, such as supplementing the dwindling supplies of nitrocellulose for nail enamel with film scrap, and using old family recipes for colorants. Packaging proved most difficult, with metal commandeered by the military, plastic in short supply, and glass too expensive.

English women invented numerous solutions to the shortage: boot wax served as mascara, shoe dye as eyebrow darkener, and rose petals and ribbons dipped in wine for two weeks produced a liquid blush reminiscent of the Victorian age. A bizarre mix of skin cleansers like lemon juice, potato flesh, fruit-parings' juice, and egg whites were recommended to tone British complexions. Artist Françoise Gilot remembers that in France, real gold powder was rather grandly substituted as eye shadow, as were the more mundane soot and charcoal.

An English welfare officer at a munitions factory remarked, "Cosmetics are as essential to a woman as a reasonable supply of tobacco is to a man; 1,000 pounds worth of cosmetics distributed among my girls would please them more than 1,000 pounds in cash." The insatiable demand created an opportunity for cosmetic bootleggers, who supplied a "black market" with beauty products created under unsanitary conditions and sold on the streets. To thwart such activity, in 1943 British Paramount News made a film entitled *Bootleggers*, which illustrated the difference between production of quality items and the dangerous conditions under which contraband cosmetics were made, in a vain attempt to dissuade women from purchasing these products.

Another side effect of the war, the disappearance of stockings, proved even harder to accept than dress restrictions. The alternative of leg paint, which originated in the twenties, was still "thoroughly unsatisfactory, with some kinds turning yellow in daylight and others rubbing off on skirts and leaving indelible marks," said British *Vogue*. Women used various tricks and homemade products, or the occasional available cosmetic. In France, chicory juice was applied with cotton or a sponge. For the lucky few, Elizabeth Arden's Fin 200, a lotion that covered the skin and purportedly resisted water, mud, and snow, or Cyclax's Stockingless Cream were used to replace stockings. Industrious women around the world drew lines down their legs with eyeliner pencil to imitate seams. The practice was so common that women's magazines felt compelled to pass on practical advice for leg painting to their readers. *Good Housekeeping* in 1943 offered the following hints:

1. Before you begin, rub your fingernails over a cake of soap so that the tips of the nails won't be filled with brown.

2. To avoid splashing makeup around the bathroom, stand on a newspaper and put one foot on the tub.

3. Cup your hand, pour out enough to cover the entire leg, and press hands together. Starting at the foot, spread the color with a round-and-round motion of both hands.

4. Work fast, concentrating on covering the surface before the makeup dries. Use a light touch; heavy pressure makes streaks.

5. When the leg is covered, lightly pat it with the fingertips of both hands, paying special attention to spots where color is uneven. When the makeup seems to stick to the fingers, stop patting.

6. Never try to patch spots after the makeup is dry. The results will be streaky.

7. If you dress before the leg is dry, pin up your skirt with pinch clothespins to keep it from rubbing off the color.

8. If you get caught in the rain and the makeup spots, wait until the skin is dry, then rub the skin briskly with your hands or with tissues to blend the color.

Makeup was on the offensive as a weapon of war, as Major Peter Rodyenka, a military tactician, defined it in a 1943 article in American *Vogue*: "Offering concealment and confusion of identity, makeup became a preoccupation of all servicemen." Japanese soldiers in the Pacific theater were especially talented at using makeup and colors that blended perfectly with the scenery. Camouflage, hardly a new military strategy, was nonetheless refined in World War II by new products. From early on, it became a military priority: Hollywood makeup artists like Max Factor, Jr., were commissioned to create products that would approximate the colors, terrain, and foliage of three specific ecosystems—snow, desert, and jungle. These kits, with three or four wax-based colors to be applied liberally to the face, were distributed to ground troops. Camouflage creams (one brand aptly called Commando Make-Up) and anti-sunburn lipsticks were also first employed on the battlefield.

Techniques of plastic surgery were also considered of great military interest, and the ability to alter identity, from features to fingerprints, became an effective weapon. One English secret service agent was reportedly transformed into the "twin" of a commanding general of the Eighth British Army through plastic surgery. The transformation was so complete that the ruse was never detected, even by the general's closest aides. For the agent in question, however, the disguise became a deeper problem. Once his mission was ended, he was unable to regain his original personality. He died in a psychiatric clinic, still attempting to resolve the dilemma of his double identity, reported Josette Lyon in her 1970 book, *Beauté et Jeunesse*.

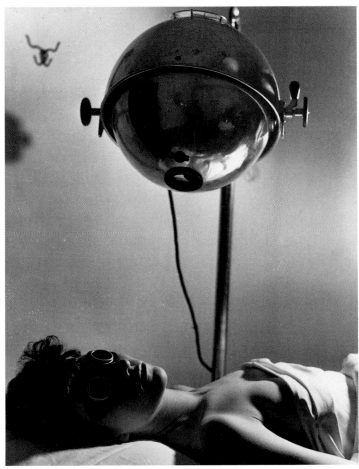

Top: **BEAUTY MASKS, 1941.**
Photograph © UPI/Bettmann Archive.

Above: **FOUNTAIN OF YOUTH LAMP RADIATES ULTRAVIOLET RAYS, SAID TO WORK WONDERS IN ROUTING SUPERFICIAL SKIN BLEMISHES. THEY WERE ALSO SAID TO HAVE A BENEFICIAL EFFECT ON THE HAIR, CIRCA 1945.**
Photograph by Hans Reinhart/
© Bettmann Archive.

Left: JACQUES-HENRI LARTIGUE REMARKED TO HIS WIFE, FLORETTE, HOW FUNNY HE THOUGHT HER PAINTED NAILS LOOKED. SHE THEN PAINTED HER ENTIRE FINGER BLUE, FOR AN ESPECIALLY DRAMATIC EFFECT, PARIS, 1947.
Photograph by Jacques-Henri Lartigue.

Opposite, above: YARDLEY'S OLD ENGLISH TALCUM POWDER WAS PACKED IN WAX DURING WORLD WAR II, SINCE TIN, GLASS, BAKELITE, AND OTHER MATERIALS WERE SCARCE. LONDON, CIRCA 1943.
Courtesy Yardley of London.

Opposite, below right: RITA HAYWORTH, TITIAN-HAIRED PINUP OF THE WAR YEARS, REPRESENTED THE HEIGHT OF HOLLYWOOD EROTICISM IN A POSTER FOR THE FILM *GILDA,* 1946.
© Archive Photos.

Opposite, below left: POSTER FOR DIRECTOR BILLY WILDER'S CLASSIC FILM *SUNSET BOULEVARD,* WHICH STARRED GLORIA SWANSON, WILLIAM HOLDEN, AND ERICH VON STROHEIM, 1950.
© Archive Photos.

Maintenance of armies in the Far East theaters prompted exhaustive studies of the properties of insect repellents—over four thousand compounds were consequently researched. Other military uses of makeup and cosmetics became essential to soldiering. In the fields of military and naval aviation and in naval warfare, efficacy and safety of sun-screening agents became a concern, since men marooned on life rafts or in the desert were often subject to severe solar exposure. New flashburn creams designed to protect exposed skin surfaces were distributed to tank crews and flame-throwers by the U.S. Army.

The safety of Allied agents behind enemy lines was also a priority for military organizations. The use by secret agents of perfumed soap or powder, shaving creams, perfume, makeup, or lipstick of foreign origin would inevitably have led to suspicion. Spy agencies studied these products, and preparations that simulated those available in the enemy country were made.

In America and England, special toilet soaps and barrier creams were developed for use in shell-filling factories and, used in conjunction with suitable protective clothing and hygienic measures, proved to be of value in reducing the incidence of tetryl dermatitis, a skin irritation resulting from contact with the corrosive chemicals employed in making ammunition.

American innovations included the development of precision forms of measurement for the isolation and restructuring of various chemicals. American Cholesterol Products, Inc., of Milltown, New Jersey, manufactured cholesterol by isolating it from lanolin—using a process that had been specifically designed for cosmetic and pharmaceutical production. The use of glycerol monostearate esters as cosmetic emulsifiers was first developed and commercialized in Germany in wartime, by Goldschmidt.

Cosmetics manufacturing plants were requisitioned for wartime production, which often posed problems with chemical expertise and safety. Revlon made first-aid kits, hand grenades, and dye markers in a factory owned by the Vorset Corporation in Oxford, New Jersey. Charles Revson chose this facility because it was divided into eighteen separate buildings, so that a mistake in one would "not necessarily obliterate all the others." Chemical formulas given by the government needed verification, and in this process, trial and error was often used. As Tobias noted in *Fire and Ice*, "Dye markers are not as easy to make as they sound, given, for one thing, the varying

THE WAR FORCED THE DEVELOPMENT OF A STABLE MANUFACTURING AND DISTRIBUTION STRUCTURE CAPABLE, BY THE FIFTIES, OF LARGE-SCALE PRODUCTION

"Donne-moi tes lèvres
je te rendrai la beauté"

Rouge à lèvres
Guerlain

colors and temperatures of water in different parts of the ocean, and given—as Charles later demonstrated to the Navy—that he had been given faulty specifications. He had to come up with his own recipe for dye markers. There is a story that, in the course of the trial and error this effort entailed, the Vorset plant one day turned the Raritan River green."

A telling episode occurred when Revson was in Washington, where a procurement officer asked him whether he knew anything about "powder" (meaning gunpowder). Charles, thinking of make-up, grandly assured him that he knew absolutely everything about powder, and so was given a plummy wartime contract.

Although the years 1939–1944 caused a serious disruption in the cosmetics industry, it was nevertheless a watershed period for it. The war forced the development of a stable manufacturing and distribution structure capable, by the fifties, of large-scale production. By controlling the availability and quantities of primary ingredients, the manufacturers were forced to formulate their products wisely and economically. Methods of manufacture were streamlined by the pressures of wartime production and were for the first time regulated and accurately worked out. The cosmetic industry workers also came out of the war more secure; guaranteed wages and working conditions were finally established.

The war also changed the international structure of the cosmetics industry. As a result of the conflict, France not only lost face but also lost, to the United States, dominance of the fragrance and cosmetics industries. Germany lost its long-established lead in the chemical and dye business. Most of Europe and the Orient lost impetus for cosmetics development (understandable in economies where feeding the population was the primary concern), and overall, cosmetics manufacturers required a considerable time period to make up the five to seven years lost to the war and postwar recovery.

The U.S. during this period took the role of leading cosmetics innovator and eventual exporter. In an attempt to fill the void in Western Europe, the Middle East, and the Orient, U.S. companies rushed in with subsidiaries, licensees, even production in captive plants. It was in this immediate postwar period that companies such as Max Factor, Helena Rubinstein, Revlon, Bristol-Myers, and Avon were able to gain a huge share of overseas cosmetics business.

During the war, the immense Hollywood machine remained at full throttle, for the government recognized it as a prime means of maintaining morale. Actors and actresses joined the armed forces in record numbers. Makeup artists, such as the Westmore brothers, were spared the draft but did their part,

including staging a permanent makeup show at the USO's Hollywood Canteen, making up stars to look like other stars. On one memorable evening, Perc Westmore converted Mickey Rooney into a miniature Clark Gable, and Bette Davis into Bela Lugosi as Dracula. In addition, Waves and Wacs (female Army and Navy personnel) were given patriotic free beauty treatments and makeup advice at the House of Westmore.

The Office of War Information suggested that Hollywood build its movie formula around one or more of six basic principles: 1. The Issues (what are we fighting for, and the American Way of Life); 2. The Nature of the Enemy; 3. The Allies; 4. The Production Front (supplying materials for victory); 5. The Home Front (sacrifice and civilian responsibility); 6. The Fighting Forces. From *Yankee Doodle Dandy* (1942) to *Casablanca* (1942) to *A Bell for Adano* (1945), profits soared as the public sought out cinema to escape the harsh realities facing them. British film, despite the Blitz, rose to the drama of the occasion, producing film after serious film, like Noel Coward's *In Which We Serve* (1942), *Millions Like Us* (1943), starring Patricia Roc; and the romantic comedy on homecoming, *Perfect Strangers* (1945), starring Deborah Kerr. Italian cinema's neorealist movement took root during the war, with films starring the earthy and sensual Anna Magnani, culminating at the war's end with *Roma Città Aperta* (1945) by Rossellini, which caused a furor abroad. In occupied France, escapism was the watchword, with 1942's *Les Visiteurs du Soir* and the supreme evocation of the past, *Les Enfants du Paradis* (1945), both starring the exquisite actress Arletty, playing respectively a devil and a courtesan. German appreciation of film as a powerful propaganda device as well as entertainment led to booming wartime production, including the mesmerizing films of Leni Riefenstahl, *Triumph des Willens* (1935) and *Olympiad* (1938); actresses like Pola Negri and Paula Wessely were also popular.

The urge for entertainment in Hollywood film introduced a newly rounded, sensual, accessible woman. Dorothy Lamour, Rita Hayworth, Lana Turner, Betty Grable, Hedy Lamarr, and Lauren Bacall were beauty icons during the war, playing island paramours, tinsel glamour queens, and adventuresses with hearts of gold. Character dramas also became popular with movies like *The Great Man's Lady* (1942), in which the young Barbara Stanwyck's portrayal of an elderly woman represented a triumph of makeup as disguise.

The intersection of makeup with real life in wartime was perhaps best expressed in an anecdote from Helena Rubinstein's autobiography, *My Life For Beauty*. "I asked President Roosevelt what I could do to be of help in the war effort. He had just been

reading a London newspaper, he told me, and he was much impressed with the story of a woman who was carried out of a blitzed building on a stretcher. Before she would agree to take a sedative she pleaded with the ambulance attendant to find her lipstick and give it to her. 'It does something for me,' she said. 'Your war effort,' President Roosevelt assured me, 'is to help keep up the morale of our women. And you are doing it splendidly.'" It would not be long before the whole world had changed, and the beauty industry would be reconfigured along with it.

PRODUCTS

HELENA RUBINSTEIN LAUNCHED HER HEAVEN SCENT LINE OF PERFUME AND POWDER WITH A SPECTACULAR 1940s PROMOTION FEATURING THOUSANDS OF BALLOONS OVER NEW YORK'S FIFTH AVENUE. PRICES OF RAW MATERIALS SOARED, WITH ATTAR OF ROSES CLIMBING FROM 4 TO 40 DOLLARS AN OUNCE. THE FOOD DRUG AND COSMETICS ACT WENT INTO EFFECT IN 1940 AND IN 1942 THE WAR BOARD ISSUED A DECLASSIFICATION OF COSMETICS AS "AN ESSENTIAL COMMODITY," CURTAILING PRODUCTION, ONLY TO REVOKE THE ORDER THREE MONTHS LATER. IN 1943 A YOUNG AMERICAN OF AUSTRIAN ORIGIN LAUNCHED THE COMPANY THAT BEARS HER NAME: ESTÉE LAUDER, AND IN THE SAME YEAR HELENA RUBINSTEIN LAUNCHED THE FIRST MEN'S LINE IN COSMETICS, GOURIELLI.

FOUNDATIONS AND POWDERS

IN 1941 CYCLAX'S STOCKINGLESS CREAM OFFERED A SKIN DYE TO REPLACE WAR-RATIONED STOCKINGS. THE FIRST COMPACTED POWDERS APPEARED IN 1949, AND INCLUDED MAX FACTOR'S CREAM PUFF, WHICH BECAME A HOLLYWOOD MUST. LANCÔME UNVEILED THE FIRST CREAM TO ENHANCE THE SKIN'S NATURAL PROTECTION, IN 1947, CALLING IT PROGRÈS. THE NEXT YEAR, IN 1948, HELENA RUBINSTEIN INVENTED FOUNDATIONS BASED ON PULVERIZED SILK FILAMENTS: SILK FILM AND SILK TONE.

LIPS

GALA'S LIPLINE INTRODUCED A HIGHLY SUCCESSFUL, LONG THIN LIPSTICK FOR OUTLINING AND FILLING CONTOURS. RIMMEL'S LIP PALETTE IN 1948 INCORPORATED A RANGE OF COLORS, PACKAGED WITH MIRROR AND BRUSH.

NAILS

PEGGY SAGE, DESPITE ITS AMERICAN-SOUNDING NAME, WAS LAUNCHED IN 1942 AS A 100 PERCENT FRENCH COMPANY FAMOUS FOR ITS NAIL POLISHES. IN 1948 PRODUCTS LIKE DURA GLOSS AND LUSTRE COAT (TRANSPARENT HELPERS THAT BRUSHED UNDER AND OVER NAIL ENAMEL), EXTENDED THE LIFE OF VARNISHES.

Preceding page: **APOCALYPTIC THEMES INSPIRE A FRENCH LIPSTICK ADVERTISEMENT, CIRCA 1948.** *Courtesy House of Guerlain.*

Above: **MANNEQUIN AND LIVE MODEL, 1945.** *Photograph by Erwin Blumenfeld.*

Opposite: **STUDY FOR AN ADVERTISING PHOTOGRAPH. NEW YORK, 1948.** *Photograph by Erwin Blumenfeld. Courtesy Staley-Wise Gallery, New York.*

The

Dream Contained *1950s*

THE 1950S WOMAN ASPIRED TO ELE-GANCE: TRADITION HAD RETURNED, AND WITH IT THE DESIRE FOR CONSERVATIVE IDEALS, FOR ASSURANCE IN TIMES OF INCERTITUDE AND GROWTH. THE 1950s FACE, WITH ITS ARTIFICIAL PALLOR AND GRAPHICALLY DEFINED FEATURES, PER-PETUATED AN IMAGE OF WOMAN AS AN ENSHRINED CREATURE—A GODDESS OF THE HOME, CONTENT IN HER ROLE AS ACCESSORY AND IMPECCABLE SOCIAL FASHION OBJECT.

Preceding pages: **COLGATE-PALMOLIVE-PEET CO. ADVERTISEMENT (DETAIL).** *Photograph by Ruzzie Green. Courtesy Keith de Lellis Collection.*

Opposite: **VEILED CHANEL HAT IN** *HARPER'S BAZAAR,* **1958.** *Photograph by Lillian Bassman.*

Right: **CLAIROL MADE ADVERTISING HISTORY WHEN IT EARMARKED A RECORD $1 MILLION FOR THE ADVERTISING AND PROMOTION OF MISS CLAIROL, ALONG WITH A SLOGAN: "DOES SHE...OR DOESN'T SHE? HAIR COLOR SO NATURAL ONLY HER HAIRDRESSER KNOWS FOR SURE!" 1956.** *Courtesy Clairol.*

The sculptural aesthetic of the prewar era was replaced by a formality that again suggested the artificiality of a mask. But this mask was an expression of conformity, not of provocation and independence, as it had been during the 1920s. The heavily applied foundation, eyeliner, browliner, and powder created a new fifties look of aloof, contained, "doe-eyed" femininity.

The cosmetics business during the postwar period evolved from a loose association of motivated entrepreneurs into a burgeoning multimillion-dollar industry comprised of multinational corporations. Using the new scientific advances gained in the war to create an ever-wider array of beauty products, astounding growth was fueled by sophisticated advertising and marketing techniques, which sold products with increasing fervor. The dominant individual in this postwar expansion was undoubtedly Charles Revson of Revlon, of whom it was said (in Andrew Tobias's 1971 biography of Revson, *Fire and Ice*), "While his social impact was obviously not as great, nor as practical, as that of Henry Ford, he nonetheless changed the appearance of women throughout the world—both in how they looked to others and how they looked to themselves. He injected a little excitement into what [his brother] Martin, borrowing from Thoreau, liked to call the 'quiet desperation' of the average housewife's daily life."

The tremendous growth of material culture the United States enjoyed in the period from 1945 to 1965 was unparalleled anywhere else in the world. While Europe and Japan were still rebuilding from World War II, the United States focused its energies on the conversion of factories and the manufacture of consumer products. In the process, cosmetics expanded their market well beyond the rate of population growth, fueled by several developments that climaxed during the 1950s. Among these were the steady expansion of the middle class (marked by rises in per capita disposable income and education levels), increased social mobility, more women entering the work force, and not least, the rise of television.

With the return of peace, the social and economic roles of women again became controversial, and a period of testing and transition resulted. Anxious soldiers wondered whether the war had permanently changed their wives. Parents waited to see if their daughters would come home and settle down in a nearby community. And social scientists speculated about the war's impact on marriage, the family, and morals.

Women were becoming confused and frustrated by the growing conflict between traditional ideas about woman's place and the reality of increasing female involvement in activities outside the home. Before, women had been required to make only one big decision: choosing a husband. Thereafter, their life revolved exclusively around the duties of the household. The fifties woman, however, faced a more complicated set of options: marriage and children, certainly, but also participation in a world beyond the home, especially after the childrearing years. Articles like a 1947 *Life* magazine feature on the "American Woman's Dilemma" appeared frequently to weigh in on the "trouble with women," the "manners of women." "Choose any criteria you like," wrote Margaret Mead, "and the answer is the same; women—and men—are confused, uncertain and discontented with the present definition of women's place."

These deepening schisms prompted an inevitable backlash. In hindsight, the 1950s were indelibly marked with an intense preoccupation with conformity, and the climate was imbued with a new Puritan ethic. A combination of social repression and sexual exploitation characterized attitudes toward women in the 1950s. It was a decade remembered culturally for the swelling orchestral sounds of big bands yielding to the yowls of rock and roll, for tightly structured couture clothing alternating

with Capri slacks and gingham crop tops as "leisure" took hold as a concept.

Makeup in the 1950s joined ritual to social convention. Magazines suggested spending special time to perfect one's look, and the acts of putting on makeup, drinking coffee, lighting up a cigarette, and chatting on the phone became part of a much publicized stereotype of 1950s feminine behavior. Makeup was even celebrated in a 1958 *Time* magazine cover story on feminine beautification in America. "With a clink of vials and a wafting of odors, the rite begins. It is 6:45 a.m. and her husband is still abed, but pretty Mrs. James Locke sits before a mirrored table in her three-room San Francisco apartment, her blonde hair covered by a filmy nylon cap. Over an array of multi-scented bottles, sticks, and tubes, Jean Locke hovers like an alchemist. She cleans her skin of night cream, anoints it with icy water—and for one brief moment shows her true face. Then, slowly, comes the metamorphosis. Over her face she spreads a foundation cream, creating a pale and expressionless mask. She caresses her cheeks with a liquid rouge, slowly adding color to her face, tops it off by gently patting on a flesh-colored powder. She shadows her eyes with turquoise, dabs a few drops of perfume behind her ears, at her elbows, temples, and wrists. With a dark pencil she shapes her eyebrows to give an artful lift to her expression, brushes her eyelashes with a penlike wand to emphasize her blue eyes. Finally, twenty minutes later, she spreads on the finishing touch—an orange lipstick to match her fingernail polish." Ready to face the world, this model of fifties womanhood then went off to her job—as a secretary in an advertising agency.

The Mrs. Lockes of the United States spent about four billion dollars on the makeup "ritual" in 1957, and it was estimated that 95 percent of women over the age of twelve used at least one beauty product. The consumer army was growing. Along with postwar Europe and Japan, the United States experienced a "baby boom," and the population increased by twenty-eight million in ten years, a birthrate superior to India's. The marriage age steadily dropped, until three quarters of American women were marrying by the age of twenty-five, and nearly half of English brides had been married by the time they were twenty. And for these postwar brides, the "business" of attracting, and retaining, a husband was seen as a major function of cosmetics.

The decade witnessed a substantial exodus to the suburbs: between 1950 and 1968 towns and villages within commuting distances of large cities grew more than five times faster than urban areas, with the number of people living in such communities increasing from 24 to 35 percent of the total population. The

suburban way of life added a new dimension to woman's tradition-al role, both isolating her as a homemaker and creating an exag-gerated need for social organizations, for meeting grounds, country clubs, and private bars, that was reminiscent of the Victorian era.

Ironically, the pace of female employment quickened rather than slowed during the postwar years. In 1960, twice as many women as in 1940 were at work and 40 percent of all women over sixteen held jobs. Although the jobs were often con-sistent with traditional ideas of what women should do (work in the secretarial sector increased the most during this period), their sheer numbers did point to a real modification in women's activities. Whether women worked or not, the conversion to a peacetime economy, the tensions of the Cold War, and the popularity of antifeminist Freudianism created, in the now famous phrase of American author Betty Friedan, a "feminine mystique" that enforced domesticity and motherhood, in an overall context of sexual subordination to men. (Friedan in turn acknowledged her debt to French intellectual Simone de Beauvoir, whose seminal *The Second Sex*, published in France in 1958, had profoundly influenced her.)

Another postwar paradox emerged: statistics showed that employed women had a universally higher usage rate of cosmetics than women of the same age group who did not hold a job. The higher the disposable income, the more upwardly mobile the envi-ronment, the greater was the consumption of makeup.

Whatever the reason, the fifties image of women differed from their reality, affecting cosmetics and all other aspects of life. While the cloistered woman was the image, the actuality of an active public life-style called for makeup to bridge the gap. That dichotomy was visible in fashion, too, as women discovered with vehement enthusiasm the pleasures of new-found peace. Long held in check by fabric restrictions and utilitarian functionalism, fashion as expressed by a young generation of couturiers became extravagant, excessively "feminine," almost neo-Victorian. Balmain, Rochas, Balenciaga, and Givenchy launched lines that appealed to an international audience dominated by cash-rich Americans. But it was Christian Dior, an unknown assistant from the house of Lucien Lelong, who embraced the truly different spirit of style of the postwar period.

On February 12, in the glacial winter of 1947, his collec-tion was presented at Dior's new offices at Avenue Montaigne in Paris. It was received in utter silence, followed by ear-splitting applause. Overnight what influential *Harper's Bazaar* editor Carmel Snow dubbed "The New Look" created a worldwide com-motion. The devastating beauty of the mannequins who took the

audience's wild response with aloof expressions was as legendary as their dresses. Jacques Rouët, who worked with Dior, had this to say about it: "The lack of makeup products during and after the war had created a forced naturalism. When the exquisitely made-up models appeared, the women in the audience immediately understood the new refinement—the precision, the conformity of the 1950s beauty."

Dior had, in one fell swoop, rendered obsolete the princi-ples of modern dress and makeup so painstakingly established during the earlier decades of the century. His "Femme Femme" (Womanly Woman) silhouette restored an impression of luxury and frivolity, of cloistered "woman-object." A woman made to please, to be seen, forever elegant, spoiled, and impractical—this would be the basic beauty image of the decade. In one fateful moment, prewar style vanished. Skirts dropped twenty centimeters to below calf-level and were made to float in the wind with the help of petticoats, whose charm had been rediscovered. Lips and eyebrows were again well defined. Shoulders shed their square padding to become soft and delicate. Straight lines were replaced by a wasp waist that set off the bust and hips, which assumed a fullness that skillful stiffening of material emphasized even further. Undergarments, like the newly invented bustier (by Marcel Rochas), bound the body in a modern version of the Victorian corset. During the day, women wore girdles known as "minimiz-ers," while for the evening, they wore boned merry widows. The uplift caused breasts to appear as large as possible, further enhanced by padding constructed to come to a point that accentu-ated nipples. The sophisticated, extreme lines of this new shape demanded eyebrows and mouths just as exaggeratedly linear.

Dior's "New Look" proved extremely controversial, with its overtones of social repression and sexual exploitation. "Dior go home," cried the American feminists who judged a hem lower than the knee retrograde. "Scandal!" protested the French working women who could not acquire the masses of material needed to create the look, as fabric rationing was still in effect. The British Chancellor of the Exchequer, Sir Stafford Cripps, publicly expressed indignation at the new fashion for promoting excess when the rigors of the postwar economy demanded moderation—at a time when soap was scarce, food not yet universally abun-dant, and privation still omnipresent. But the revolution had begun, and makeup again followed fashion's flag. Frustrated throughout the war by the scarcity of beauty products, women uniformly reacted by adopting the new, haughty style in cosmetics with as much enthusiasm as they had embraced the exaggerated haute couture shapes.

By 1949, the *oeil de biche* (doe-eyed) look credited to cosmetologist Etienne Aubrey, created by shadow, eyebrow pencil, mascara, and, most importantly, eyeliner, was in vogue. Aggressively unreal, it was nonetheless an overnight success, introducing the overtly painted, formal approach that would mark beauty well into the 1960s.

In the fashion collections of 1950, according to American *Vogue*, makeup tended toward lighter skin, darker lips, and no rouge. Cake powder compacts were back, and an emphasis on packaging prevailed. Rimmel introduced a lip-color palette with mirror and brush included, while Gala was equally inventive with Thick and Thin, two lip pencils joined by a delicate chain. The importance of the eyes resulted in the creation of a plethora of reformulated products and shades—mascara, eye shadow, and lining pencil. Color was essential: Revlon, for example, in 1950 suggested Fresh Violet eye shadow with Blue Frost eyeliner, Titian mascara with Green Frost eye shadow and Walnut eyeliner.

In a direct departure from the prewar 1930s, fashions in clothing and makeup were designed to coordinate. Eye shadows, mascara, and lipsticks complemented the color of a dress (rather than the wearer's hair or complexion), regardless of their appropriateness for the woman who wore them. Hollywood makeup artists objected to this arbitrary rule, protesting as well the style touted by the fashion magazines for little black or colored lines around women's eyes, which they termed "the Dracula look." There were other detractors: *Mademoiselle* reported the results of a nationwide poll in which men, finding their wives transformed, expressed ambivalence at the appearance of frankly painted women and said they preferred the outdated, but more natural, look.

The need for extravagance, for a sense of life far removed from the privations of the war, had another avenue of expression: a renewed interest in the "Beau Monde." Recalling the Belle Époque's fascination with aristocracy, the 1950s saw the rise of a social precursor of the "jet set," whose existence was consecrated to the pursuit of elegance, liberty, and sybaritic enjoyment.

The 1947 marriage of Princess Elizabeth to the Duke of Edinburgh introduced a decade of fairy-tale alliances, of self-willed transformations through the mediums of makeup, hairstyle, and clothing, where the chrysalis-to-butterfly evolution took place in the public eye. Offering a dream of hope to an audience hungry for it, the marriages of Prince Rainier of Monaco to the American actress Grace Kelly, the Shah of Iran to the exquisite Sorayah, the Aga Khan to the American actress Rita Hayworth, and King Baudoin of Belgium to diminutive Fabiola were highlights on the fifties social calendar. As commoners became queens, images of a fantasy world

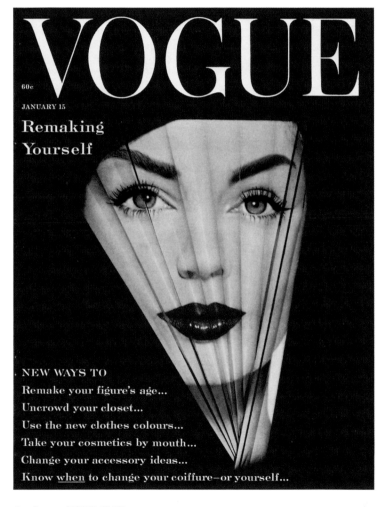

Preceding page: **MODEL JEAN PATCHETT IMMORTALIZED THE *OEIL DE BICHE* (DOE-EYED) LOOK, 1950.**
Photograph by Erwin Blumenfeld.

Above: **AMERICAN *VOGUE* COVER, 1959.**
Photograph by William Bell.

attainable by any woman blessed by beauty, capable of refinement, and deserving of luck was marketed to the curious masses.

Makeup played its important part as well. The twenty-first birthday party of the English Princess Margaret was photographed (and reported on) by Cecil Beaton in *Royal Portraits*: "The dress by Dior was disappointing—stern and without originality, but her color was marvelous. She had applied a remarkable makeup—

EYE SHADOWS, MASCARA, AND LIPSTICKS COMPLEMENTED THE COLOR OF A DRESS, REGARDLESS OF THEIR APPROPRIATE-NESS FOR THE WOMAN WHO WORE THEM

bright lips, rosy cheeks, and black mascara...and she had an extraordinary vivacity of spirit." According to coiffeur Alexandre de Paris, preparation for Margaret's wedding some years later to the photographer Antony Armstrong-Jones required a communal makeup table, on which Margaret had placed rose-tinted *fards* (rouge) so that all the ladies-in-waiting could wear the same tone of lipstick and powder.

Such grandiose occasions (where women would sometimes change twice in a single evening) afforded unprecedented opportunities to the new generation of couturiers and hairdressers. Alexandre, who coiffed such notables as Brenda Fraser, Jacqueline de Ribes, Barbara Hutton, and Marie-Hélène de Rothschild from his Avenue de Matignon salon, qualified the new extravagance, saying, "Women wanted spectacular hair but they knew how to use their own makeup. Many would go to Guerlain or another salon in the afternoon and have a beauty treatment, and be made up by the technicians there, and then just adjust it at night."

Television and the fashion magazines did their part to disseminate fifties social values, with coverage of the rich and famous generated to satisfy their increasingly avid fans throughout the world. Suddenly, girls who had once aspired to fame, fortune, and independence à la Hollywood dreamed instead of an enshrined life of luxury and refinement, a princely husband and a royal wardrobe—and the means by which they would become "queen for a day" was in attentively re-creating the beauty rituals of the regal rich.

As images of the "good life" introduced a fashion for the allusive signs of international chic, makeup, always in season even for relaxed, weekend occasions, played a major part in determining the look. Immediately identifiable accessories, like an Hermès scarf and "Kelly" handbag, and products such as Stormy Pink lipstick, eye shadow, and powder, served as clear indicators of social standing.

Left: **FULL DRESS MAKEUP WAS EQUALLY APPROPRI-ATE FOR LEISURE TIME ON THE ROAD, 1959.**
Photograph by John Rawlings.

Below: **AVA GARDNER POSES AS ONE OF THE POPULAR VARGAS "PIN-UP" GIRLS, 1950.**
Illustration by Alberto Vargas.

Top left: **THE 1950S WERE A DECADE OF FAIRYTALE MARRIAGES. HERE, GRACE KELLY AT PRAYER DURING HER WEDDING TO PRINCE RAINIER II OF MONACO, 1956.** *Photography © UPI/Bettmann.*

Top right: **QUEEN ELIZABETH II WEARING THE IMPERIAL STATE CROWN, AND HOLDING AN ORB AND SCEPTER AFTER HER CORONATION IN WESTMINSTER ABBEY, 1953.** *Photograph by Cecil Beaton,* © Bettmann Archive.

Above: **JACQUELINE LEE BOUVIER AND SENATOR JOHN F. KENNEDY'S WEDDING IN NEWPORT, RHODE ISLAND, 1953.** *Photograph by Frank Jurkoski,* © Bettmann Archive.

The beauty secrets of the princesses were detailed in fashion magazines, and the mastery of applying makeup to achieve a flawlessly painted face signified social and sexual success. Some women even changed the color of the walls of their homes to complement the tint of their face powder—as the Duchess of Windsor had done in her Paris residence. They read the suggestions in *Queen*—like wearing "Coronation pink" colors of rouge and lipstick during the 1953 ascendance of Elizabeth II of England to the throne. They copied; they conformed.

Fashion photographs of the 1950s were a dominant instrument in this manipulation of the consumer. Print had not yet been supplanted by television as the major source of information and cultural iconography, and it portrayed a socially and fashionably correct woman who exuded an aura of sleek self-confidence. An immaculately groomed accessory, the model was only one element in these pictures, which illustrated a life-style rather than sold products. The image and its chic (not the clothes or the makeup alone) were the primary determinants of fashion. This idea gained currency through the influence of art directors Alexey Brodovitch and Alexander Liberman and photographers Richard Avedon, Irving Penn, and William Klein, as well as through the clout of Carmel Snow. With important consequences on the commercial, cultural, and aesthetic standards of the period, the representation of fashion as a cultural activity, rather than a product, created an entirely new emotional symbiosis.

Beauty pictures that formerly had set a product or a model against a defined, static background were replaced by photographs featuring perfectly made-up women, bathing in a Moroccan palace, playing roulette in Monte Carlo, reading *The Life of Picasso* in the grass during a private moment. The apparent new candor was, in fact, an elaborately created illusion: beauty as artificial formality. Women throughout the occidental world would remark, as they put on their makeup to go gardening, that they felt "naked" without their foundation, mascara, and lipstick.

Richard Avedon's work underscored the provocation implicit in 1950s fashion photography, wherein, as Brodovitch preached, "the subject of the photograph in some ways mattered less than the audience for it." Playing on tension between women's liberty and the alienation it caused, Avedon portrayed the mask of the 1950s beauty ideal, which at once protected, made passive, and insulated the woman who wore it. Avedon, in particular, was quick to assimilate new cultural phenomena in his work. After Japanese Kabuki theater became popular in Paris in the mid 1950s, he experimented with a favorite model, Dovima, in an oriental look. Dovima accentuated the slant of her eye make-up, and the white of her skin, and adopted a formalized expression that suggested the structural rigor of the Japanese theater. This look was a major aesthetic influence for a fashion industry that needed increasingly exotic locations and dramatic situations to attract an audience. But while the genre of fashion photography was first defined in the fifties, the fashion shoot was not yet the elaborate production it later became. Instead, the photographer, his assistant, the editor and her assistant, and the model would be the only ones present. Though editors often served as hair and makeup aids, journalist Babs Simpson reported, it was the model who was chiefly responsible for creating her own image. Eileen Ford, who opened the dominant Ford modeling agency in 1946, recalled: "There were few makeup artists during the 1950s, and they worked chiefly in salons; so at fashion sittings, the girls needed to bring everything, and to know what to do. They were true professionals, and took their jobs quite seriously, often spending hours to develop the look wanted. The good models, like Sunny Harnett, or Jean Patchett, or Lisa Fonssagrives, instinctively knew how to present themselves—how much makeup to wear, and where to put it."

Bettina, the quintessential fifties Parisian model, said of the period: "Other models taught me how to put on my makeup. Makeup styles were dictated by the current fashions, by the couturiers. Jacques Fath, for instance, liked to be surprised; he enjoyed innovation, and would allow us great liberty. But our makeup was much more natural than it became during the mid-1950s. From the runways, the look filtered down to the fashion magazines, after being interpreted by the models, the editors, and often the photographers. By the time the look arrived on the street, it had often been exaggerated out of proportion."

Photographic models became significant fashion personalities in the 1950s. By mid-decade, modeling was such a highly paid profession that the hourly rate could be as much as the weekly wage for girls in ordinary jobs. Because it looked so easy and glamorous, it became the dream of a new generation of young hopefuls who knew little of the rigors of the job. The new attention to models had an impact on the world of makeup. Cosmetics companies naturally gravitated to favorite faces, prefiguring the advent of exclusive contracts for mannequins. Charles Revson, at Revlon, favored three women during the 1950s—Dorian Leigh, her sister Suzy Parker, and Barbara Britton. Leigh was employed to incarnate Eve for Revlon's first color print ad, a highly successful full-page launch of the Fatal Apple line of cosmetics in 1945. Raven-haired, swan-necked, Leigh was thereafter considered "lucky," and Revson used her in promotion after promotion.

Top: **BETTE DAVIS SHAVED
HER HEAD FOR HER ROLE
AS ELIZABETH I IN THE FILM**
THE VIRGIN QUEEN, **1955.**
Photograph © Archive Photos.

Above: **THE 1954 FILM** *ON THE
WATERFRONT* **RECEIVED
SEVEN OSCARS, INCLUDING
BEST PICTURE AND BEST
ACTOR FOR MARLON
BRANDO, SEEN HERE APPLY-
ING HIS OWN MAKEUP.**
*Courtesy Marc Wanamaker/Bison
Archives.*

Barbara Britton, a striking blonde with perfectly proportioned features, was the spokesperson for Revlon's live television
commercials for twelve years. Personifying integrity, grace, and
beauty on television, Britton's classic commercial appeal to an
audience weaned on Grace Kelly's cool looks was only equaled in
staying power by the darkly glamorous Suzy Parker's ascendance.
The younger sister of Dorian Leigh ("They don't make combos like
that anymore," Revson regretfully said of the sisters), Parker was
perhaps the most well-known print model of her time, and
Revson's undisputed favorite.

Alongside these changes, the advertising sector became a
social and economic power in the postwar era, as agencies swelled
to accommodate the plethora of goods and services that assisted
the American public in taking advantage of its prosperity. The role
of advertising in selling makeup increased apace. Earlier advertising's central task was simply to achieve recognition for the brand
names that were rapidly replacing the unlabeled bins of pink powder in pharmacies. But by the 1950s, competition for mass markets had become intense, and cosmetics companies were spending
up to 80 percent of their budgets on publicity (although the norm
was closer to 25 percent).

New cosmetic products were introduced at an even faster
rate, and advertisers and agencies struggled to find some claim to
uniqueness that would set their product apart from the rest.
Agencies employed the services of psychologists, sociologists, and
market research studies to maximize the impact of their product
message. They attempted to control the desires and taste of the
consumer—to persuade the reader that "what she was looking at
was what she was looking for."

Advertising adopted the "editorial look," deliberately
designing ads to look like magazine editorial content. Instead of a
simple product shot that might have been lost among others featured in a magazine, the new advertising philosophy created a
wholly unexpected and arresting pictorial fiction.

The full-scale, double-page color promotions of cosmetics
in major fashion magazines that appeared for the first time after
the war were particularly good at selling "class to the masses"—or
the chance to be fashionable for the price of a lipstick. The cosmetics company Chen Yu, launched in 1946, was particularly
effective at this approach, selling their Cloudsilk Make-up with a
luxurious picture of a model dressed as an Indian princess in silks
and gold, and a text that said, "Out of a dream world into yours
comes a veil of cloud silk to cover your skin with a new, more perfect kind of beauty, a beauty impossible to achieve until now. It's a
totally new makeup as smooth to the eye and to the touch as a

rare piece of Chinese silk." Revlon introduced their version of matching lipstick and nail polish with an ad that invited readers to "Pick up a tea-cup, light a cigarette, draw on a glove. Your slightest gesture delights the eye...with lips and fingertips accented vitally, fashionably, by Revlon nail enamel."

These promotions allowed for a total media and marketing approach. In 1950, Revlon introduced a new color with a full-page promotion in *The New York Times*. Smoke curled from the burning edges of a hole in the center of the page and, at first glance, the hole and the smoke looked real. The print that accompanied the illustration said, mysteriously, "Where's the Fire?" Controversy ensued. Shortly thereafter, the color Where's The Fire? was introduced as Revlon's new shade.

Helena Rubinstein also went to great lengths to publicize the launch of a new product. When the fragrance Heaven Scent was introduced, she let go hundreds of pale blue balloons over Fifth Avenue, each bearing a sample of the fragrance.

Great emphasis was placed on the psychological aspects of advertising. Now "empathy," or the use of unconscious suggestion, replaced an obvious story line. The so-called Freudian approach to publicity was formalized in the 1950s, although it was by no means nonexistent before. Norman P. Norman, a public relations figure known as "Mr. Madison Avenue," had been trained in psychology and advocated involving customers with the advertised products at subliminal levels, using in ads the real reasons why people buy certain products. "Since his orientation was Freudian, and a large part of his agency's business had been in cosmetics and lingerie, these real reasons were often sexual," reported a former colleague.

By 1952, intuiting the new sensuality of the decade, Revson threw off restraint and introduced the most effective campaign in the history of cosmetic publicity for his new makeup line, called Fire and Ice. *Business Week*, in the fall of 1952, reported that "Fire and Ice marked a new height in an industry where advertising is an all-important ingredient." The double-page ad showed a beautiful girl in a silver sequined dress and red cape, followed by a headline—"Are You Made For Fire and Ice?"—and a questionnaire. Eight of fifteen possible positive answers indicated a consumer ready for the experience.

The response to the promotion was sensational. Nine thousand window displays were devoted to Fire and Ice. Every newspaper and magazine wrote about it and every radio announcer made reference to it, it seemed. Fire and Ice beauty contests were conducted around the country. "There is a little bit of bad in every good woman," the company executives crowed. None were as

delighted as Revson, who was widely quoted as saying he wanted his models to be "Park Avenue whores—elegant, but with the sexual thing underneath." The Fire and Ice copy was nearly as suggestive: "What is the American Girl made of? Sugar and spice and everything nice? Not since the days of the Gibson Girl! There's a New American beauty...she's tease and temptress, siren and gamin, dynamic and demure. Men find her slightly, delightfully baffling. Sometimes a little maddening. Yet they admit she's easily the most exciting woman in the world! She's the 1952 American Beauty, with a foolproof formula for melting a male! She's the Fire and Ice girl. (Are you?)"

Named the Best Ad of the year by *Advertising Age*, Fire and Ice's runaway success in print was equaled only by its phenomenal baptism in the fifties' defining new medium: television. Advertising's "education value" was quickly subordinated to its use as a competitive weapon. It was widely accepted that advertising could and did exert influence on the cultural standards of its audience—it begot changes in public taste. The image of glamorous motherhood was frequently favored. A Revlon ad summed up the pitch, showing a bejeweled woman with her two handsome children, under which the text read: "Designed to lift a woman's good looks to their absolute peak. The woman who uses 'Ultima' feels a deep sense of fulfillment...beyond it there is nothing."

As a verbal and visual persuader, the first purpose of advertising was to catch the attention of the consumer, and then to manipulate him or her into buying the product. Yet during the 1950s, wrote Daniel Bell in *The New Leader*, advertising concentrated "on arousing the anxieties of consumers to coerce them into buying." The very use of the product, whether it worked or not, would be sufficient to quell anxieties, the advertising companies argued to justify their strategies. A product that satisfied was one that offered that high order of subliminal value. Ruth Waldo, a vice president of the J. Walter Thompson agency, explained with a preposterously expensive cosmetic: "The advertising says there's turtle oil in it, and the royal jelly of the queen bee. Well, turtles live forever. And the royal jelly is what the queen bee has that makes her that very special and highly delightful kind of bee." (In fact, royal jelly was the hottest "new" cosmetic ingredient in a number of companies' preparations. It was also among the priciest.) Another advertiser pointed out that "Two identical lipsticks, marketed under different brand names, may have very different values for a teen-age girl. Wearing one of them, she feels her ordinary self; wearing the other, which has been successfully advertised as the highroad to romance, she feels a beauty—and perhaps she is."

Left: **MODEL DORIAN LEIGH IN REVLON'S LANDMARK CAMPAIGN FOR FIRE AND ICE, 1952.**
Photograph by Richard Avedon. Courtesy Revlon.

Below: **REDS AND PINKS RANGING FROM CREAMY PASTELS TO FUCHSIAS SWEPT THE 1950s MARKET, 1954. Courtesy Revlon.**

In terms of marketing, you've got to have the will to win. You've got to see the blood running down the street. You've got to be able to take it. If you're not, you're nobody. You never will be.

—Charles Revson, in *Fire and Ice*

In 1950, cosmetics in America topped $400 million in retail sales, an impressive increase over Depression figures. But only two years later, by 1952, cosmetics had become a billion-dollar industry. Product research, crude and inaccurate in the 1930s and 1940s, had become a science in the 1950s. Motivational analysis (showing why people chose one brand over another) became essential information when launching a cosmetic, and the demand for psychological classifications inspired the development of research centers to define consumer trends. These centers, in turn, created a new emphasis on the marketing approach.

The Institute for Motivational Research, directed by Dr. Ernest Dichter, was one such center where marketing information was analyzed and furnished to cosmetics companies and advertising agencies. Dichter, in an interview with Betty Friedan for *The Feminine Mystique*, described his findings: "Properly manipulated...American housewives can be given the sense of identity, purpose, creativity, the self-realization, even the sexual joy they lack—by buying things. Fortunately for the producers and advertisers of America and also for the family and the psychological well-being of our citizens, much of this gap may be filled, and is being filled, by the acquisition of consumer goods." Cosmetics companies therefore began to pattern their development after successful multinational industrial giants like General Motors or Ford. The distinction between a commodity and a differentiable product—between a utilitarian cosmetic such as talcum powder and an imaginatively conceived and marketed beauty aid—became a cornerstone in the strategy of the most successful companies.

Though Dior was credited with renewing new symbiosis between cosmetics and fashion, it was Charles Revson who actually implemented the change. Close association had existed during the twenties, when Chanel, Patou, Coty, Schiaparelli, and other French companies sought to launch prestigious perfume and makeup products, but the liaison had been downplayed during the following decades. As the postwar decade witnessed a return to enthusiastic interest in haute couture, cosmetics were once again positioned as fashion accessories. Women were tempted by the latest "fashions in makeup," and this had the effect of automatically broadening the makeup market. A woman who before would not have bought a new bottle of nail enamel until the old one was empty now might keep a half dozen on her dresser. Revlon was

credited with instituting this planned obsolescence, bringing out a new color every fall and spring. By the mid-forties, its semiannual shade promotions were as much of an event to women as Detroit's new-car introductions were to men.

The cost of producing and packaging a cosmetic was the fundamental number in Revson's business. According to Andrew Tobias in his biography of Revson, the cosmetics king preferred products that cost little to make yet could be sold at a 300 percent markup. "If his cost of goods was enough," Tobias continued, "he could advertise heavily; he could afford severe quality standards; he could operate his impressive research facility; and he could still make a good profit." Revson even created training think tanks, dubbed "Psycho-Revlons," where salesmen would act out selling scenarios in front of a group and have their performances criticized. Satirized at first (even parodied in *The New Yorker*), the sessions were soon imitated by other companies.

If prospects for growth in the cosmetics industry were particularly promising after the war, competition was also much greater. A whole new generation of entrepreneurs came up: Germaine Monteil, a French couture designer, began to make lipstick in 1936 when she found that she could not get existing makers to supply the right shades for the clothes she designed. In 1942, she closed her couture business and focused entirely on cosmetics, manufacturing Rose Skin Cream and a series of "Super" products, including Super-Glow foundation, Super-Moist lipstick, and Super Sheen powder, all directed at French tastes.

A company destined to become one of the giants of the late twentieth century was Estée Lauder, founded by an American of Austrian descent in 1946. Her four unique treatment products, including cleansing oil, skin lotion, a cream pack, and an all-purpose cream, were sold with an emphasis on their favorable quality-to-expense ratio. Once Saks Fifth Avenue started to sell the Lauder line, retail success soon followed. Lauder capitalized on this jump start in 1951 with the first (and instantly well received) Youth-Dew product, Estoderme Youth-Dew Cream, a face treatment whose formula included a whole egg. Lauder then developed a bath oil in 1953 that offered the same emollient benefits for the body, and after that, a fragrance also named Youth-Dew. Lauder's striking success illustrated the evolution in cosmetics marketing and philosophy. Eschewing the "salon route" taken by earlier entrepreneurs like Arden and Rubinstein (which required a large initial expenditure), she risked the high road of competition in retail stores, which could make a success of a new makeup line very quickly—and defeat it just as fast. Confining her line to the most exclusive stores, she relied on personal charisma, quality, and high price positioning to distinguish her products. One of her creams, Re Nutriv (which cost 115 dollars an ounce and contained turtle oil as one active ingredient), soon became known as the most costly product on the market.

Her personal appearances were carefully orchestrated to sell the image. "I spent money on one or two elegant outfits, which I wore everywhere, rather than on a whole wardrobe of mediocre clothes. I wore seamless stockings, unheard of at the time (I'd copied them from a model I'd seen)—my little Dior outfit of a black dress, and a brown hat encrusted with tiny black beads, and cocoa-brown gloves," said Estée Lauder in her biography, *Estée: A Success Story* (1985). Another Lauder innovation was to give free samples of cosmetics, initiating what is now the tradition of "free gift with purchase" that proved uniquely suited to the launching of expensive cosmetics lines. "The customer seemed to be getting more from her little extra parcel than she would if the product costs only a dollar or two," reported Marilyn Bender in her biography of Lauder, *At The Top* (1975). Lauder also started the custom of sending postcards to clients of department stores, inviting them to come to the Lauder counter and pick up their free gift. The strategy worked so well that eventually all the other companies, including Revlon, were using it.

Lauder's individualistic, elitist business rapidly became a dominant presence, albeit an anomaly, in this decade of conformity and mass production. Estée Lauder was the arch rival of Revson from the mid-1950s on, and their competition served to kindle both social and professional rivalries that would eventually benefit both companies—much as it had benefited Elizabeth Arden and Helena Rubinstein in the early twentieth century. Arden and Rubinstein, in all their years in business, never did encounter each other face to face, though employees often jumped ship to the other's establishment, and Rubinstein even hired Arden's ex-husband. As for Charles Revson, he was quoted as warning Lauder, "I don't 'meet' competition—I crush it."

Other talented cosmetics figures during the 1950s, however, floundered in the highly competitive market. Hazel Bishop, a brilliant chemist who formulated a new, improved version of the indelible lipstick, also attempted a direct introduction of her product into department and dime stores. During World War II, she had worked for Jersey Standard and Socony, where one of her jobs involved analyzing cosmetics that caused skin irritation. There she perfected the nonsmearing, nondrying lipstick.

The launching of a single product proved difficult, although a 1950s survey did show that "98% of women use lipstick versus 96% who brush their teeth." The established cosmetics

Top: **WOMEN RECEIVING INSTRUCTION IN COSMETICS APPLICATION, LOS ANGELES, CIRCA 1954.**
Photograph © Bettman Archive.

Above: **A COMPLETE MAKEOVER AT THE MAX FACTOR COUNTER IN A LONDON DEPARTMENT STORE, CIRCA 1956.**
Photograph © Hulton Deutsch.

houses were not interested in either Bishop's product or her approach, so she formed her own company, turned to television and, by 1954, with only three salesmen, had captured 25 percent of the nation's lipstick market. She aimed for a mass-market audience, as radical a choice as isolating the luxury market had been for Lauder. Bishop could not finance the development of her company, however, and went public in 1954, selling stock to her top executives and her advertising agency. As sales rocketed, the advertising agency bought out all the other shareholders and proceeded to oust Bishop herself from the company. The initial success of advertising inspired her partners to spend a million dollars on ads to

GIs RETURNED FROM EUROPE WITH A NEWLY LIBERAL VIEW OF COSMETICS AND WERE NOT EMBARRASSED TO BUY BEAUTY PRODUCTS FOR THEMSELVES

enter the three-million-dollar rouge market. It was a bad risk. Hazel Bishop, Inc., after posting a short profitable period, sank into years of deficits and, finally, bankruptcy.

Men's cosmetics became a point of contention in the 1950s, representing a profitable share of the ever-growing cosmetics market. GIs returned from Europe with a newly liberal view of cosmetics and were not embarrassed to buy products for themselves in department stores. In 1945 there were more than a hundred manufacturers of men's toiletries, grossing about fifty million dollars a year; by 1946, the numbers had doubled. In 1946, Dr. Herbert Rattner wrote in the trade magazine *Hygeia*: "War has given a real impetus to the sale of cosmetic sets for men—it was an excellent solution to the problem of what to send to the man in service. While the packages are designed to appeal to women, the scents used in these articles are designed to appeal to men. They are of heather and fern, grasses, and resins, so-called virile rather than delicate scents, the names suggesting the outdoors, tanbark, leather, athletics, fishing, or hunting. Even the soap is now made in large 'man-sized' bars."

Helena Rubinstein led the march to men's cosmetics after marrying Prince Artchil Gourielli in 1948, when she launched a cosmetics line named the House of Gourielli, a salon for men complete with a ticker-tape stock machine, and a line of clothing. Her effort proved premature, however, and she ended the enterprise upon the death of the prince. In 1957, an establishment called the Groom Shop appeared in New York, featuring skin care for men, including mud packs, massages, creams for home use, and hair tinting. By this time, American men were spending about twenty-seven million dollars a year for scented shaving lotions,

Above: **A WOMAN USES A** *NEMECTRON,* **A METHOD OF FACIAL REJUVENATION SAID TO BRING MUSCLES UNDERNEATH THE SKIN BACK TO LIFE WITH ELECTRICAL IMPULSES, THUS REDUCING SAGS IN THE SKIN. WEST BERLIN, GERMANY, 1952.** *Photograph by Werner Kreusch.* © *Bettmann Archive.*

deodorants, and colognes, just less than a third of what was spent by women. Even mustache wax, not seen since the twenties, was making a comeback. Revson, who also sought to capture the new men's market, launched a line called That Man—ironically, the epithet Elizabeth Arden had scornfully used to refer to him.

The war had left yet another legacy, namely a rudely competitive spirit that used the tactics of espionage, including wire tapping, in cold-war defense of cosmetics secrets. Companies frequently tried to steal their rival's names, formulas, advertising, and even packaging. Revson, by no means the sole perpetrator, was nonetheless known for his elaborate spying organization, Kay Daly reported in *Fire and Ice*: "Charles never innovated anything but color. He stole everything. He had a lab up in the Bronx with a spectroscope that would make the CIA jealous...a guillotine-like bottle drop, used to drop bottles to see if they break; a spice rack/perfumery, with vials of such ingredients as Bulgarian Rose Otto, at $4000 the pound; and a rabbit/rodent ranch where the rabbits wore mascara, and the rats were being force-fed Head and Shoulders, to see how much it would take to kill them." And Revson took extreme pains to protect whatever secrets the lab yielded.

The practice of piracy was so widespread that in 1955, the New York State Joint Legislative Committee met to study "the illegal interception of communications." Raymond Spector, president of Hazel Bishop, was convinced that someone was spying on the company after he noticed similarities in the advertising of Bishop's products and those of its competitors. In 1955, details of a company loan request, exposing Bishop's shaky finances, were printed in an industry newsletter, and private detectives confirmed that the telephones had indeed been tapped.

While no one was ever prosecuted, Revlon executives were subpoenaed at lengthy hearings. There, Revson disingenuously revealed that the phone company had been tapping phones in his own company, at his own instructions, for years. William K. Heller, secretary-treasurer of Revlon, assured the court that the practice was "extremely beneficial" and led to greater "efficiency, service, and courtesy." He denied, however, that Revlon would ever extend that benefit to their competitors.

Media became a more throughgoing, omnipresent social influence, and by 1959, in England alone, televisions were owned by almost twelve million people. The 1953 coronation of Queen Elizabeth, broadcast live, introduced the world to the exciting possibilities of the televised image, and TV's rise thereafter was phenomenal. The use of television in cosmetics advertising was pioneered during the 1950s, and it soon became one of the most profitable venues for selling cosmetics. A single program was the proof

of the new medium's effectiveness, recalled Norman P. Norman: "There was never a show that sold goods the way *The $64,000 Question* did." Revlon sponsored the quiz show (whose craze ended in notorious scandal in 1958), and their association with it had "raised Revlon sales, profits, and consumer awareness so dramatically as to put it miles ahead of its competitors." Sales at the company, which had been growing from 10 to 20 percent a year in the first half of the fifties, suddenly shot up 54 percent in 1955. Helena Rubinstein, Max Factor, Coty, and Hazel Bishop, which had all been within striking distance of Revlon before *The $64,000 Question* went on the air, were left in the dust.

The show's success took the cosmetics business by surprise. Helena Rubinstein had dismissed the medium, allegedly saying that "only poor people watch those awful machines." Hazel Bishop's company did take the plunge, with its sponsorship of *The Kate Smith Show* and *This Is Your Life*, but *The $64,000 Question* outsold all the others. "Some of the products featured on the show were experiencing 300 percent and 500 percent sales increases. One lipstick shade sold out in ten days. We could have sold urine in a bag," admitted Jay Bennett, one of the show's producers. At its peak, an unbelievable 82 percent of the television sets switched on around the country were tuned to *The $64,000 Question* and its latest Revlon promotion.

With these sorts of runaway profits, Revlon commercials became extravaganzas not unlike small-scale Broadway productions. No expense was spared. One typical ad included dry-ice fog, willow trees, and "slaves" all over the floor; the qualities of the object of this excess were announced by the cool blond beauty of Revlon spokesperson Barbara Britton, who would habitually wear a hundred thousand dollars' worth of jewels from Van Cleef & Arpels. The windfall came to an abrupt halt when the quiz show was exposed as having been fixed.

While television stole the march, creative expression in the 1950s slumbered. Movies reflected, rather than inspired, aesthetic trends, while the repressive view of women by fashion and society during the postwar period infiltrated the types of roles offered to actresses.

The prewar ideal of inner depth, mysterious spirit, and fiery sexuality yielded to the fifties' standard-issue voluptuary, baby-face bride, or revered housewife. The cinema presented two distinct images of women—that of innocent sweetheart-goddess, or of erotic, voluptuous temptress. The first was a wholesome image incarnated in its cool, high-caste version by Grace Kelly or Vivien Leigh, or in a less sophisticated, more accessible version of the same type by June Allyson, Doris Day, Debbie Reynolds, or

Sandra Dee, examples of the pristine "girl next door." Their make-up was natural, with accentuated eyebrows, light, frosted lips, and hair that framed their face, which was often adorned with a few adolescent imperfections, such as freckles.

Alongside this relatively asexual model of beauty existed the fleshy, earthy one. Rita Hayworth, Ava Gardner, Dorothy Lamour, and Hedy Lamarr portrayed temptresses "with a sensuality so florid that their films were often set in foreign climes, where they could portray fallen women outside the bounds of society," sociologist Lois Banner observed in *American Beauty*. Generally dominated by men (or at least waiting for men to rescue them), these femmes fatales were rarely granted the independence displayed by their 1930s counterparts, Carole Lombard and Jean Harlow. They were routinely costumed in tight blouses with low necklines that exposed the top of their bosom, made up to appear even larger by the darker foundation used to shade the space between the breasts. Their unkempt hair was usually dark and full. Lips were painted and glossed bright red to appear more voluptuous and fluttering false eyelashes completed the look.

Only one actress combined aspects of the two stereotypes in the staid 1950s. Marilyn Monroe, universal sex symbol of the decade, brought a child/whore eroticism to the screen. Appearing as nearly naked as possible, she seemed to enjoy, even relish, a healthy sexual appetite and made it obvious that she would satisfy it where and when she wanted—and on her own terms. She treated men as playthings, and the deepest emotions of Marilyn's screen persona were narcissistic, seeming to project that her true love affair was with the camera and with those flickering images of herself that so excited the public. Her self-involvement was, in a sense, a liberation and perhaps explains why so many women admired her, copied her, and envied her freedom of behavior.

Monroe's magnetism was beginning to challenge stereotyped female roles as early as 1953 with her comedy performance in *Gentlemen Prefer Blondes*, in which she used the obvious attributes of her physical appearance to parody as well as embody her cinematic role. Her hair was peroxided a light blond, the color belonging to adolescents, angels, and virtuous women. Her make-up, rather than hiding the natural tone of her skin, created the impression of glowing health. She wore light pink (not tanned or olive tints) to recall the skin of a baby. Her eye makeup looked more natural than that of the screen sirens, but it was more flattering than the girl-next-door's. She employed gossamer, often iridescent shadows, ample mascara, false eyelashes, and eyeliner to intensify her regard. Softly arched eyebrows framed her eyes and gave them expression without sophistication. Her lipstick, often

Preceding page:
BUBBLY CHARM, 1959.
Photograph by Sante Forlano.

Left: **THE "BILD LILLI" DOLL, INSPIRED BY A CARTOON CHARACTER APPEARING IN** *BILD,* **THE GERMAN NEWSPAPER DAILY, IS THOUGHT TO HAVE BEEN THE ORIGINAL INSPIRATION FOR THE BARBIE DOLL, 1955.**
Photograph courtesy Billy Boy.

reddish pink or gold, was lavishly shined with Vaseline to create a round, voluptuous lip.

Yet even for Monroe, unthreatening, adorable sexiness was unnatural. Simone Signoret, in her autobiography, *Nostalgia Isn't What it Used to Be*, observed that on breaks during the shooting of the movie *Let's Make Love* (1960), with Yves Montand, Marilyn rarely wore makeup, preferring to spend her nonworking hours in a rayon dressing gown. Monroe called her movie character her "Marilyn getup" and dreaded the ordeal, which required three hours to accomplish.

Youth gained its own identity during the postwar period, and its own label, "teenager," representing a large sector of the population from Japan to Germany to the United States as well as the most significant new market in the emerging industrial postwar society. The capricious taste of the youth market gave rise to compact, inexpensive, and easily applied products such as Helena Rubinstein's Mascaramatic, a semiliquid contained in a pen with a wand, a forerunner of the brushless mascara. New types of beauty products for home use abounded, from face masks to Toni perms to shampoos for different hair types.

In these conservative years, adolescent females dressed to imitate their mothers. They wore hats with tied veils and floating "follow me" ribbons, short gloves, tight-waisted princess skirts, and heels. Girls of fifteen often looked twenty-five, and they aspired to appear feminine through the use of cosmetics. The style, even for teenagers, was to appear as ladylike as possible, and this conformity also emphasized the gulf between classes. Through appearance alone, the debutante, decked out in her ball gown and matching accessories, was distinguished from the high-school prom queen. This rigid, superficial social hierarchy finally began breaking down during the late 1950s, a process of destruction that would occupy the sensibilities of an entire generation in the next decade.

Audrey Hepburn perfectly portrayed the new ingenue aesthetic. She incarnated the *gamine* whose style combined the conventionality of the 1950s with a new, lively energy. In 1954, American *Vogue* called her "Today's wonder Girl...who has so captured the imagination and the mood of the time that she has established a new standard of beauty." Cecil Beaton added, in British *Vogue* (1954), that "Nobody ever looked like her before World War II...now thousands of imitations have appeared. The woods are full of emaciated young ladies with rat-nibbled hair and moon-pale faces."

Hepburn combined the dictates of the fifties fashion—the white face, the red lips, the dark eyes—with a new trend toward the ingenue ballet style. Popular in Europe after the war, new dance companies were being established and American designers such as Claire McCardell were experimenting with clothes inspired by dancewear—leotards and ballet slippers. Hepburn's slender figure corresponded perfectly to the more youthful aesthetic, and she provided a model for the newly liberated young girl.

The youth boom generated great interest in business and the media. New magazines were directed at the burgeoning group: *Seventeen* and *Mademoiselle* in the United States, and *Elle* and *Marie Claire* in France appeared. Existing magazines were refocused, with *Glamour* evolving from a journal of "Hollywood glamour" during the thirties to a "for the girl with a job" guide in the forties, to the magazine for young women in the fifties, which is as it remains today.

At a time when Revlon and Max Factor were considered high-priced products for mature women, products just for teenagers, such as the line called Campus Makeup, were created. Gala directed their efforts to the youth market by introducing inexpensive lipsticks sold in Woolworth's with exotic names, such as Lantern Red and Sea Coral. In 1948, Gala had introduced a pencil lipstick called a "lipline" to younger buyers. Intended to be easy to handle and to provide a firm outline, it was also one of the first refillable lipsticks. Gala also catered to the new fashion for whiter lips created when Italian and French cosmeticians put titanium in their products to produce a pale gleam, and these frosted colors appeared in nail varnishes, including green and silver.

Media campaigns directed by the cosmetics industry suggested that a young girl became feminine through the use of makeup. From their early years, girls were bombarded with play cosmetics, and dolls that could be made up were sold at the same cosmetics counters where Mommy bought her makeup. According to a survey of American teenagers, this strategy worked: two thirds of them had been wearing lipstick and 90 percent nail enamel since they were fourteen; eighteen percent had started using nail enamel before they were ten.

The face of beauty was beginning to change, as the emergence of a youth cult in the late 1950s provided a new definition of beauty. The origins of the new counterculture were urban, street-based, and expressive. Made current by the American Beats, by the artists in Greenwich Village, and by café society in Saint Germain des Près, this new youthful energy would become the engine that fueled the upheavals of the 1960s. The brittle elegance of femme fatale womanliness and superficial chic that shaped the fifties icon was about to undergo a change of unparalleled proportion.

Right: **MARILYN MONROE, CIRCA 1955.** *© Archive Photos.*

Below: **BOOK JACKET FOR** *THE SEVEN YEAR ITCH,* **WHOSE FILM VERSION WAS DIRECT- ED BY BILLY WILDER AND STARRED MARILYN MONROE, 1955.** *Photograph © Michael Barson Collection/Archive Photos.*

PRODUCTS

THE RECOVERY FROM THE WAR IN EUROPE STARTED A FLURRY OF NEW ENTERPRISES. IN 1950 ROC BECAME THE FIRST COSMETICS COMPANY TO DEFINE ITS PRODUCTS AS HYPOALLERGENIC, LAUNCHING, IN 1957, THE FIRST SUN BLOCKS FOR DIFFERENT TYPES OF SKIN. BROTHERS HUBERT AND MICHEL D'ORNANO, TOGETHER WITH THEIR FATHER, CALLED THEIR NEW (1951) COMPANY ORLANE, WHILE JUVENA, THE FIRST SWISS MAKEUP COMPANY, CAME OUT WITH ITS INAUGURAL LINE IN 1954. IN 1952, SEVERAL DERMATOLOGISTS FROM MOLITG-LES-BAINS CREATED A COSMETICS LINE CALLED BIOTHERM, WHOSE SECRET INGREDIENTS INCLUDED PLANKTON. IT STARTED A TREND AS LANCÔME IN 1955 CREATED THEIR OCEAN LINE, BASED ON SEAWEED, AND RUBINSTEIN INTRODUCED SKIN LIFE AS THE SEQUEL TO HER POPULAR VITAMIN FORMULA OF 1954, CALLING IT THE FIRST "BIOLOGICAL" PRODUCT.

WITH GROWTH CAME DEMANDS FOR INCREASED COSMETICS REGULATION AND TESTING. CHARLES W. CRAWFORD, HEAD OF THE FDA IN 1952, PROPOSED THAT THE FOOD, DRUG AND COSMETIC ACT BE AMENDED TO REQUIRE PRE-TESTING PROCEDURES FOR COSMETICS AND LISTINGS OF ALL INGREDIENTS ON THE LABELS.

FACE

FOR THE SECOND TIME IN HISTORY, BEAUTY PATCHES WERE REVIVED. AVAILABLE IN BOXES OF ONE HUNDRED, IN THE FORM OF TRIANGLES, CIRCLES, HEARTS, STARS, AND DIAMONDS, THEY ENJOYED A BRIEF VOGUE. PRODUCTS LIKE POND'S COLD CREAM AND POND'S ANGEL FACE WERE AVAILABLE FROM SWEDEN TO SINGAPORE. MAX FACTOR'S CREAM PUFF (THE FIRST COMPACT POWDER, INDISPENSABLE FOR ASPIRING ACTRESSES, WITH AVA GARDNER AS SPOKESWOMAN) WAS LAUNCHED IN 1953. BOURJOIS BECAME RIMMEL'S MAJOR COMPETITOR IN FRANCE IN THE FIFTIES WITH ITS JOLICILS MASCARA, WHILE RUBINSTEIN'S RED HELLION AND TREE OF LIFE LINES, AS WELL AS NEUSHAEFER'S TORRID AND PINK PASSION REACHED THE WORLD VIA THE NEW GLOBAL ECONOMY. KEEPING UP WITH DEMAND MEANT THE FACTORIES WORKED OVERTIME: MILWAUKEE'S KOLMAR LABORATORIES ALONE PRODUCED 2800 SHADES OF LIPSTICK, AND EMPLOYED 20,000 FORMULAS FOR COSMETICS.

THE PERIOD OF EXPERIMENTATION CONTINUED, WITH REVLON EMPLOYING MORE THAN SEVENTY CHEMISTS IN AN ONGOING SEARCH FOR NEW PRODUCTS. RUBINSTEIN ADVERTISED THE EXOTIC INGREDIENTS IN HER COSMETICS, SUCH AS THE JUICE OF WATER LILIES (SUPPLIED BY NUNS IN PARIS AND LONDON) AND EXTRACT OF HUMAN PLACENTA. LILLY DACHÉ SOLD A FACE POWDER CONTAINING PULVERIZED PEARLS, AND MEARL DEVELOPED SYNTHETIC NACREOUS PIGMENTS, INCLUDING BISMUTH OXYCHLORIDE, THAT WERE ADOPTED BY THE COSMETICS INDUSTRY FOR SUCH APPLICATIONS AS EYE SHADOWS, LIPSTICKS, MAKEUPS, AND NAIL ENAMELS. YARDLEY, PONDS, AND ELIZABETH ARDEN ENJOYED PARTICULAR SUCCESS WITH ENGLISH COMPLEXIONS, WHILE GALA'S MUTATION MINK PRODUCTS EVOKED TIARAS AND BENTLEYS BUT CAME IN ONLY TWO SHADES: "ENGLISH ROSE" FOR FAIR SKINS AND A SWARTHIER HUE FOR THE "CONTINENTAL COMPLEXION." IN 1954, MAX FACTOR PRODUCED THE MAKEUP THAT IS STILL USED AS THE STANDARD ON COLOR TELEVISION, AND ALSO DEVELOPED ERASE, THE ORIGINAL COVER-UP COSMETIC.

EYES

EYES WERE THE FOCUS OF THE MOST INTERESTING NEW MARKET, AND A PLETHORA OF PRODUCTS TO ENHANCE THEM WERE DEVELOPED. THE MAKEUP COMPANY AZIZA (MEANING "DARLING" IN ARABIC), FOUNDED BY NINA SUSSMAN IN PARIS IN 1920, WAS REESTABLISHED IN NEW YORK CITY FROM A SAUCEPOT IN A WEST 22ND STREET APARTMENT IN 1940. BY 1950 SHE HAD BEGUN A LUCRATIVE EYE-MAKEUP BUSINESS IN THE UNITED STATES.

LIPS

FOR THE MOUTH, A PERFECTLY DEFINED SILHOUETTE WAS A NECESSITY. LIP COLOR IN RED OR PINK USING TWO OR THREE DIFFERENT SHADES OF LIP COLOR AT A TIME WAS NOT UNCOMMON. A DARKER ONE WAS USED ON THE BOTTOM TO OUTLINE THE LIP, THEN A LIGHTER VERSION OF THE SAME SHADE WOULD BE PUT ON THE UPPER LIP. IN THE MIDDLE OF THE LOWER LIP A PALE GLOSSY COLOR WOULD PROVIDE THE FINISH. BUCKING THE TREND TOWARD INFINITE CHOICE, DOROTHY GRAY OF LONDON INTRODUCED IN 1955 PINK MINK LIPSTICK AND ELATION MAKEUP FILM, PROMISING THEY WOULD "GO WITH ANYTHING."

NAILS

THE RAGE FOR LONG, GLEAMING SCARLET NAILS WAS A FIFTIES PHENOMENON, AND REVLON DOMINATED THE BUSINESS (RUBINSTEIN EVEN DUBBED REVSON "NAIL MAN"). OPAQUE SHADES WERE THE MOST POPULAR AND REDS WERE *THE* COLOR IN DEMAND. NAIL ENAMEL MADE FROM GROUND FISH SCALES ALSO BECAME FASHIONABLE.

BODY

FINALLY, MAN-TAN, A REVOLUTIONARY NEW COSMETIC FOR MEN, WAS INVENTED, COMPOSED OF A COLORLESS SOLUTION OF DHA, A FORM OF SUGAR THAT, WHEN COMBINED WITH SKIN PROTEINS, TURNED THE SKIN TAN AFTER A FEW HOURS. THE COLOR COULD NOT BE WASHED OFF BUT FADED GRADUALLY, AND WAS BOTH UNEVEN AND COULD RUB OFF ON SHIRT COLLARS. MAN TAN WAS QUICKLY FOLLOWED BY OTHER LESS EXPENSIVE VERSIONS.

Youthquake *1960s*

DAZZLING AND HYPNOTIC, THE FACE OF THE 1960s CAPTURED THE REVOLUTIONARY ENERGY OF THE ERA, DISCOVERING THE CHARM OF EXAGGERATION. FIFTIES NOTIONS OF CHIC WERE REPLACED BY THE SIXTIES PURSUIT OF EVERLASTING YOUTH. RICHARD GOLDSTEIN SUMMED UP THIS ICONOCLASTIC ATTITUDE IN AMERICAN *VOGUE* IN 1968: "NOW BEAUTY IS FREE. A FREAK GODDESS OF THE SIXTIES [WHO] EXHIBITS HERSELF, MAKES YOU NOTICE.

Preceding pages: **FACE AND BODY PAINT THAT FEATURED FLOWERS OR COLORED ABSTRACTIONS WERE A LEITMOTIF OF THE 60s. DETAIL FROM REVLON "FLOWER SHADOWS" ADVERTISEMENT, 1962.** *Courtesy Revlon.*

Opposite: **CANDICE BERGEN AS A SUN-KISSED, SPACE-AGE GODDESS, 1966.** *Photograph by Costa Manos/Magnum.*

Below: **GOLDIE HAWN, THE HAPPY GIGGLING DING-A-LING FROM TELEVISION'S HIT VARIETY SHOW—*ROWAN AND MARTIN'S LAUGH-IN—*IN FULL BODY MAKEUP, 1968.** *Photograph © UPI/Bettmann.*

Exhibitionism is the quiet side of violence; it aims to provoke if not to injure. No wonder it dominates the fashions of the 1960s....It is impossible to talk about something as insular as beauty without noting that the same turmoil and insurrection that provides the terror of our time also inspires its greatest achievements. The style of type 60s is creative anarchy." Theater critic Kenneth Tynan was even more oracular about the cataclysm: "England is complacent and the young are bored. There is the desire to hear breaking glass."

The concept of beauty first acquired its contemporary meaning during the 1960s, when it was given a value akin to material success. Diana Vreeland, editor of American *Vogue* and doyenne of fashion, coined the term "The Beautiful People" to describe this new estate. Beauty "passed," allowing its bearers to ignore the social thresholds of the fifties, and a youthful, healthy, sexy appearance was extolled. Other forces were at work dislocating class and age barriers. The sixties offered fame and fortune to individuals who, not many years before, suffered social exile for having the "wrong color" of skin or unacceptable speech.

Many of the Beautiful People, in fact, came from uneducated, working class, or disadvantaged backgrounds. The selling power of beauty now superseded everything, including the fifties requirement of "good taste." As beauty rose to top the scale of moral qualities in this new echelon of values, Britain's hottest magazine, *Private Eye*, referred to its advocates as the "new aristocracy of pop."

Makeup mediated this transition into the ever-expanding world of images. Best placed to exploit the era's new opportunities were the well favored in body and feature. Women graced with perfectly proportioned faces—Brigitte Bardot, Jean Shrimpton, Twiggy—created their own identities with extreme applications of eyelashes, liner, and lipstick. Barbra Streisand, Sophia Loren, and Veruschka exaggerated their unusual features through makeup for a look of exotic individuality.

Reflecting the loosening of social constraints, the sixties face became phantasmagorical. The new sixties lifestyle was comprised of many disparate sources, unlike the monolithic social order of the fifties. As Tom Wolfe, author of *The Kandy-Kolored Tangerine-Flake Streamline Baby* and *The Electric Kool-Aid Acid Test*, put it: "Once it was power that created high style, but now high style comes from low places, from people who are marginal... who carved out worlds for themselves, out of the other world of modern teenage life, out of what was for years the outcast corner of the world of art, photography, populated by poor boys."

The cultural transformations of the 1960s were international, and the impact of European lifestyles, especially those from Britain, were increasingly felt around the globe. The Twist arrived from France in 1962, preceded by a new film, *Jules et Jim*, with the been-there beauty of Jeanne Moreau incandescent on the screen. International pop culture, drawing much of its inspiration from black America and working-class Britain, became all-pervasive. In 1964, Rudi Gernreich, a California designer, said international youth style came from England. "It really started, I would say, in the late fifties in London. Young London people began to instinctively change their attitude in the way they dressed. Then all the young people from all over the world started to identify with what the British started."

The youth explosion played an essential part in the widespread importance of style. Well educated and moneyed, the "baby boom" generation rose to unprecedented power as they came of age. By the mid-1960s, one third of the population of France was under the age of twenty, and in the United States, half was under twenty-five. *House Beautiful* reported that "In 1965, the American teenager spent $3.5 billion on clothes alone."

Young women changed their style of fashion and makeup to correspond to this new idiom, Lois Banner, in *American Beauty*, postulated: "Because of their continued buying power, the commercial beauty culture was forced to incorporate their version of naturalness into its prevailing styles." Beauty products were developed that would best complement adolescent charm, and makeup enhanced the juvenile look with an abundance of eyelashes, false freckles, rosy cheeks, and glowing, unpowdered skin.

The ideal body was now adolescent—without the obvious feminine attributes of a well-endowed bust and a rounded posterior. The all-important girdle, garter belt, and stockings that had symbolized 1950s femininity were abandoned in favor of ribbed tights worn with new thigh-high fashions. A fragment of elastic served as a bra, and nipples reappeared as a normal part of the anatomy. A new "unisex" trend turned femininity into an attitude rather than a physical manifestation. Paradoxically, however, makeup remained gender-specific, accentuating sexual differentiation. Fashion's use of nudity announced a new audaciousness, as Rudi Gernreich's topless bathing suit showed, yet the model who wore it, Peggy Moffitt, was remembered as much for her excessive makeup as for her breasts. Diet and exercise instruction dominated the women's magazines (where underwear and home appliances had been emphasized in the previous decade). But it was the "London look" in New York, *"le style anglais"* in Paris, that led the pack. "London is a city for the young," Peter Laurie admitted in British *Vogue* in 1964.

The new naturalism was codified and packaged as child's play, as Mary Quant in *Quant on Quant* explained: "The interpretation of beauty changes just as clothes do. The look isn't just the garments you wear. It is the way you put your makeup on, the way you do your hair, the sort of stockings you choose, the way you walk and stand. Makeup old-style is out. It is used as expertly as ever, but it is not designed to show. The ideal now is to look as if you have a baby skin untouched by cosmetics. Lipstick is kept to a pale gloss and the only area where you can go to town is around the eyes. There you can use the lot...eyeshadow, eyeliner, and lashes of mascara plus false eyelashes—even false eyebrows, I should think, provided you've managed to master the art of putting them on and keeping them in place."

The rebellious attitude of pop culture originated in London, not New York or Paris. Within the poor working-class districts of Liverpool, Manchester, London, and other cities of Great Britain, a wellspring of creative talent spouted. David Bailey, Zandra Rhodes, Terence Stamp, Jean Muir, Graham Smith, Mary Quant and Tony Armstrong-Jones were among the new stars. Quant was a student when she opened a "Bazaar" with her

Top: **AWARD-WINNING BULLET LIPSTICK ADVERTISEMENT, 1962.** *Courtesy Yardley of London.*

Below: **LIPSTICK (ASCENDING) ON CATERPILLAR TRACKS, 1969–1974, CLAES OLDEN-BURG.** *Painted steel, aluminum, plastic, 24' x 10'11" x 13'1", Yale University, New Haven, Connecticut. Courtesy Pace-Wildenstein Gallery, New York.*

Right: **THE PRUSSIAN-BORN COUNTESS VERUSCHKA, WHOSE AMAZON STATURE AND EXOTIC FEATURES INTRODUCED NEW THEATRI-CALITY TO MAKEUP, 1966.** *Photograph by Franco Rubartelli.*

husband, Alexander Plunket Green, in the Chelsea section of London, where she sold inexpensive clothes for teenagers. Credited with the introduction of the miniskirt, the poor-boy sweater, the high boot, and the little-girl look, Quant soon exported her style worldwide: by 1965 to the tune of $12 million in annual retail sales.

Mary Quant's influence was immediate. As she remarked in her autobiography, *Quant on Quant,* "The clothes I made happened to fit in exactly with the teenage trend, with pop records and espresso bars, jazz clubs, the rejuvenated *Queen* magazine, *Beyond the Fringe,* and *Private Eye* coming out of the same spirit of adventure." The "Mods" and the "Chelsea Girls," who followed the makeup and fashions of Quant and other young designers, were youths who originally imitated the look and behavior of 1950s motorcycle gangs. The Mods were modern and daring, though the uninitiated found it hard to tell the sexes apart at first glance. Brilliant color was as permissible in menswear as it was in women's. Long and short haircuts were worn by both. Since the sexes lived much the same sort of lives, they wanted the same sort of clothes to live in. The style of the original leather-booted, black-stockinged Chelsea Girl, who looked like a contemporary counterpart of a gay musketeer, began to be copied by the rest of London and watched with interest by others all over the country, and around the world.

Left: **CORKSCREW HAIR AND RHINESTONES**, 1967. *Photograph by Penati.*

Quant introduced her own cosmetics line, produced by Gala cosmetics, in 1966. Like her clothing, her beauty products were based on the needs and tastes of the young, liberated, miniskirted generation of which she was a part. Quant revolutionized cosmet-

THE IDEAL BODY WAS ADOLESCENT, WITHOUT THE OBVIOUS FEMININE ATTRIBUTES OF A WELL-ENDOWED BUST AND A ROUNDED POSTERIOR

ics packaging and advertising. She eschewed classically "feminine" pastel makeup cases and introduced graphic black and silver, shiny plastic containers. Quant resuscitated the use of the cosmetic pencil after trying colored Caran d'Ache artist's crayons on her models' faces. She created witty names for her products, such as Come Clean Cleanser, Jeepers Peepers eye shadow, and the famous Paint Box—a small, square, black box that contained pencils, powder rouge, lip salve, a lip brush, pastel shadows, and instructions.

In 1970, Quant issued a new line advertised throughout the world as Makeup to Make Love In. It addressed the revolution in social mores with a frank response. "We wanted to produce a range in which a girl could kiss and cuddle without looking smudged and frightful. Normally if a girl goes to bed in her makeup, she gets up looking a hideous mess," said Sue Steward, the creative adviser at Mary Quant, as reported in Rosemary Simon's *The Price of Beauty*.

Designing intuitively, without the aid of traditional market studies, Quant chose true, bright colors such as hot pink, day-glo orange, tawny gold, green, and violet for her makeup collection, and used crayons anywhere on the face—to draw false freckles, or flowers on the cheeks. She used gels but no powder, so there was nothing to clog the pores. Quant cosmetics, available first in her clothing boutiques and subsequently in stores throughout the world, filled the need for inexpensive, novel cosmetics. They also quickly became status objects of the pop idiom, and the Quant compact was as treasured for transporting cosmetics as the Van Cleef & Arpels jeweled purse had been forty years earlier.

The Parisian couturier André Courrèges brought the same youthful look to the French haute couture collections in 1964, presenting plastic fashion-sculptures worn by "moon girls" in white and metal. In a 1987 interview in Paris with the author, Courrèges confirmed that he had "wanted to remove the obviously outdated sexual references—the red lips, red nails, black eyebrows...the arbitrary heaviness—[and celebrate] a new sex appeal that corresponded to the young, illuminated spirit of the modern woman. I was fascinated by the tint of the model's skin, by the freckles, real or painted, by the luminescence of pastel pink lips and rouge, by colors and light."

His short dresses of intricate construction and movement marked the best of Paris couture, yet their futurist shape and details produced a major revolution in the fashion world. As Courrèges skirts became shorter, his shoes became flatter, and boots higher. "A kind of gold-plated, space-age goddess was created, a walking contradiction in terms," Andy Warhol enthused in American *Vogue*, adding somewhat disjunctively, "Courrèges clothes are so beautiful—everyone should look the same. Dressed in silver. Silver doesn't look like anything. It merges into everything. Costumes should be worn during the day with lots of makeup."

Courrèges actively participated in designing the makeup and hairstyles used in his fashion shows. In the same interview in 1987 he recalled: "I was extremely concerned that the skin and hair colors of the girls complement their clothes. I used redheads with freckles, oriental models, and, when it became possible, black models. I tried to exaggerate their personal style—to put fake freckles on the redhead, to give the Japanese woman a more oriental look. I wanted each girl to be a unique person, and found the makeup which suited the individual types. This was more important than creating one basic image." Courrèges sought to offer women the possibility of wearing almost uniform clothing, with the paradoxical aim of allowing them to exaggerate their own personality. "I used wigs in the way most designers used makeup," he explained. "The colors were often brightly hued and obviously artificial. The shapes were geometric—to suggest a playful change of style or image," and complement his structured clothing. In fact, the craze for false hair reached a peak in the sixties, and those great mops of Dynel called out for eye makeup designed to be seen at one hundred yards. Black eyeliner alternating with white had a brief but memorable vogue; it went well with body paint that featured flowers or colored abstractions.

Paco Rabanne contributed to the refinement of the modern couture image. He employed metals, plastic, netting, and other artifacts of modern technology to create a style of clothing that, although resolutely futuristic, referred more to primitive and modern art than to classical modes of dressing. His models were also chosen for their individual style, and he was reputed to have been the first to use black women on the runways of Parisian haute couture. Donyale Luna, the formidable model from Detroit, Michigan, was his favorite; because of his challenge to the racial barrier, Rabanne's fashions were boycotted by *Harper's Bazaar* for a number of years.

Rabanne shared the belief that the new image required a carefully analyzed look. "It was no longer possible to simply derive the hair and makeup from what had been done before," he asserted. "I had to create a style for women which was consistent with the world around them, and that included new types of facial decoration. I tried to incorporate the feeling of primitive cultures in my makeup—to contrast cold futurist metal with the symbolic, almost magical makeup derived from the Aborigines or some African tribes. The effect was quite mystical—the women seemed strong, contemporary, protected by their armor, yet exposed and inviting through the primitive beauty of their skin, hair, eyes and mouth."

Pop music was taking the place of religion in 60s culture, and the Beatles were its contemporary gods. The phenomenal success of the Beatles' 1963 tour put anything British over the top. The second most-popular British export was the miniskirt. When it arrived in America in 1965 after the Fashion House Group held a show aboard the *Queen Elizabeth*, the seismic effect was noted immediately by Diana Vreeland (the editor-in-chief at American *Vogue* from 1963, who single-handedly arbitrated fashion in America in the decade). Lynn Sutherland, a model who was transformed by Vreeland in the late 1960s, remarked that "she wanted a particular style of girl, one who could wear a type of makeup and hair style, and still have a personality come through. I learned what style she wanted, and complied with her ideas, only to discover that I, too, had achieved my own individuality."

In Vreeland's *Vogue* there was a delicate tension between the exuberant spirits of makeup and coiffure, the apotheosized visions of street fashion that gave beauty its urgency and importance, and the serious expressions of the models. Penelope Tree holding a diamond up to her eye is poker-faced; Twiggy's black-rimmed eyes look wise; Marisa Berenson, bewigged, powdered and patched (adorned with fake beauty marks), is regally decadent. Vreeland provided the link between the banality of high fashion and the profound social movements that dominated the decade. She mixed celebrities with political figures, artists, demonstrators, and (in the pictures of Irving Penn) mud men from Peru. In glorifying influential individuals and rendering them fashionably current through makeup and fashion, she created pop culture heroes. While blacks and women marched in the streets and students barricaded college buildings, consumer-oriented publications were creating a new group of international celebrities.

Jacqueline Bouvier Kennedy was one such symbol of youth, style, and international chic for the early 1960s, in a nation torn by political strife and racial tension. Her career as an elegant First Lady elevated the 1950s ideal of domesticity to a more distinguished level. Her impeccable makeup—replacing the 1950s powdered, linear formality with 1960s' dewy freshness—indicated a new style for the American aristocracy. Jackie's photogenic look, a sophisticated youthfulness that was copied throughout the world, emphasized her eyes and eyebrows. Her dark lashes were highlighted with mascara, liner, and eyebrow pencil—but little else. Her flawless skin was seldom powdered, and her lipstick was tawny—never dark red. On formal occasions she projected an image of healthy, youthful charm. While her husband forged a unique social welfare program and identified himself with minorities and the poor, Jackie decorated with taste and discrimination, patronized the arts, looked ravishing, and lent moral force to the ethic of individual consumption that had gained strength in post-World War II affluence.

Among the Beautiful People and beauty influences of the 1960s were models like Jean Shrimpton, Twiggy, Penelope Tree, and Veruschka. British-born Shrimpton was discovered by a film director while sunning herself in Hyde Park between classes at a London secretarial school. Her "gawky looks just happened to fit the fashion trend," as she said modestly in her autobiography, *The Truth About Modeling.* Shrimpton epitomized the Chelsea Girl: sexy, sportive, and relaxed. Her long legs, fine-boned face, and floating hair made her look a young mother one minute and a wanton siren another—yet always recognizably herself. Her startlingly

Above: **MAKEUP TURNED ASTRAL WITH INTIMATIONS OF SPIRITUAL TRANSCENDENCE. MOONDROPS ADVERTISEMENT, 1969.**
Courtesy Revlon.

wide-set eyes attracted the camera lens, and her perfectly proportioned features, pouting mouth, and arched eyebrows embodied a new aesthetic, both vulnerable and detached. Journalist Eugenia Sheppard said of "Shrimp" in *Newsweek* in 1965: "She has the face every woman would like to look like this very minute."

Even at the beginning of her career, Shrimpton paid great attention to her makeup. To prepare for the camera, she would spend forty minutes putting on cosmetics at home and arrive at the studio with her face impeccable. "She had exquisitely fine skin, which was kept practically makeup free, except for pale pan stick by Max Factor, or Mattefilm by Guerlain. She did use some rouge on her cheeks. But no one understood how she made up those exquisite eyes, and she kept her secrets well," commented makeup artist Olivier Échaudemaison. Later, in *Mademoiselle*, she revealed the truth: she defined her eyes with liquid eyeliner often in black, brown, or the newly introduced navy blue, and also used shading and highlighter. Lighter powder shadow went on the lower part of lids, and she always added a darker line in the crease of the lid to give her trademark wide-eyed expression. Eyelashes were heavily mascaraed, and often augmented with fake lashes. She preferred tawny lipsticks such as Lancôme's youthful Bois de Rose. Shrimpton, in her autobiography, concedes, "[T]he aim of going to so much time and trouble is to look as natural as possible, to look as if you have no makeup on at all. These artifices merely cover up your blemishes."

By 1965, Shrimpton had appeared on thirty fashion magazine covers in Paris, London, and New York. Revlon, Max Factor, Yardley of London, and Ponds were all using her as their official model. Her association with Yardley greatly increased the venerable firm's popularity, giving it a completely revolutionized sixties image.

By 1966, with Jean Shrimpton already established, the fashion world looked for a fresh new exemplar. Twiggy, a.k.a. Lesley Hornby, was discovered at the age of fifteen by photographer Nigel John Davis (or Justin de Villeneuve, as he came to call himself). And it was the unisex look of Twiggy that came to truly personify the youth revolution of the time.

Twiggy met Villeneuve at the hairdresser's and he immediately recognized her potential. She was not, however, an overnight success, because she was too small to fit the requirements of normal models of the period. To create her own mold, it was necessary for Twiggy to submit to a complete make-over, which was orchestrated by the well-known London hairdresser Leonard. Leonard gave her a new, trendy, short hairstyle that perfectly complemented her delicately formed features. After the transformation, all the clients at Leonard just turned and gasped.

"There was this little Cockney girl in a little white gown, with her long neck and her huge, huge eyes; she looked like a fawn. I knew then that she really was going to make it," concluded Villeneuve in his autobiography. Twiggy added her own, exceptionally effective beauty mark: lower lashes that were painted like those of a doll that Twiggy had. The effect was incendiary. Twiggy became a pop icon and immortalized the look of the middle 1960s. She had made her image with makeup, and she capitalized on it by marketing such products as Twiggy eyelashes, which became a best-selling sixties accessory.

The face of '66—"Twiggy the Cockney Kid With the Face to Launch a Thousand Shops," as the *London Express* canonized her—became the cover girl of virtually every magazine in the world. By the time she made her first visit to New York in 1967, even truck drivers were reported to have recognized her on the street. Twiggy is credited with introducing the emaciated androgynous look criticized by later generations, and models certainly adopted her style and attitude. American *Vogue* noted her influence on model Penelope Tree: "What makes her a sensation is not her impeccable background but the way in which photographers can transform her little girl lost appearance into bizarre high style elegance. She attended Truman Capote's masked ball with her mother. She was spotted in the cloakroom by Richard Avedon, who asked her to pose. The lashes which she pastes on in clumps are a Twiggy trademark, and she has become so adept at putting them on that it takes her only fifteen minutes a day. The 1967 Twig has become a tree."

The unconventional beauty of Prussian-born Countess Vera Gottlieb von Lehndorff, commonly known as Veruschka, also had its moment. Six feet four inches tall, with a dramatic mane of blond hair, and an ability to transform herself through makeup which introduced a whole new theatricality in fashion, Veruschka was the real-life goddess the 60s sought. Veruschka's tinseled lashes were unequaled: long, feathery, overtly decorative. French and Italian fashion magazines celebrated her freely interpreted makeup, first as costume, subsequently as camouflage. French *Vogue*'s August 1968 cover extolled her "Jungle Look," as Veruschka and the designer Giorgio di Sant'Angelo created what the editors called a "revolutionary manner to be made up." It advocated changing the form of the face with light and shadow, urging readers to avoid creams or foundations and use instead ultralight powders over a base to cover the pores of the skin. "Don't use pencils," the article cautioned, "only fingers, to give a more natural and blended look. The eyebrows should be fixed with false-eyelash glue applied with a toothbrush. The effect will be was one of ethereal, feline beauty."

Above: **ELIZABETH TAYLOR, WHOSE WHOLESOME INGENUE MAKEUP HEAD-LINED THE 50s, BECAME AN OUTRÉ 60s ICON IN ORIEN-TAL EYELINER IN THE FILM** *DR. FAUSTUS,* **1968.**

Right: **LESLIE HORNBY, A.K.A. TWIGGY, WHOSE HUGE EYED, LITTLE-LOST-GIRL CHARM WAS IMMORTALIZED WORLDWIDE ON MAGAZINE COVERS. AMERICAN** *VOGUE,* **1967.**

Photograph by Richard Avedon.

Veruschka didn't stop at the face, either: she was famous for being photographed with her entire body painted in a mixture of gold powder and paraffin.

Fashion editors and models were primary inventors of their own images, until Pablo Manzoni, a makeup artist from the Elizabeth Arden Salon in Rome, came to New York and began to create makeup of such extraordinary exoticism that the fashion world realized there was a dramatic new potential in beauty images. Manzoni's series of eye fantasies for *Vogue* and *Harper's Bazaar* were embellished with peacock feathers, sequins, lace, flower petals, even diamonds. Several of these magazine

VERUSCHKA DIDN'T STOP AT THE FACE, EITHER: SHE WAS FAMOUS FOR BEING PHOTOGRAPHED WITH HER ENTIRE BODY PAINTED IN A MIXTURE OF GOLD POWDER AND PARAFFIN

covers earned Manzoni special notice, including the coveted Coty Award, and he became, in a sense, the first makeup celebrity. An article in *Newsweek* described his mastery as having "the touch of a miniaturist, the steadiness of a demolition expert."

Fashion photography itself underwent a dramatic change during the 1960s. Frank Horvat, a French photojournalist whose work in fashion began in the early part of the decade, brought a new energy and decisive edge to his work by using the small, silent, sharp-lensed Leica camera, more commonly used for real-life action than for fashion, to capture women in "natural" situations. As Martin Harrison remarked in his 1993 book, *Appearances*, "he led the reaction, with Jean-Loup Sieff, against the excessive amount of makeup it was then de rigueur to apply to models." When the results of Horvat's first big shoot, on location in Yorkshire, were published in British *Vogue* in 1960, it had a profound effect on London fashion photography (attested photographer David Bailey in an interview in *Photography*); not only because of the naturalism of the images, but also because of the models, "whose freshness represented a radical break with the 'tea-time' gentility which was still the norm." Bailey had his own revelation to add: "Make-up is important and it should be used with the utmost discretion. Skin must look like skin...you are helping people see women as something real—not as mere dolls."

It was an attitude that evolved as the decade continued. The work of photographers Terence Donovan, William Klein, Franco Rubartelli, Richard Avedon, and Irving Penn used the medium of the model to send a message of what fashion was about. As British *Vogue* summed it up, "[Top models'] hair, and makeup, down to the last flick of eye pencil, are copied around the world...."

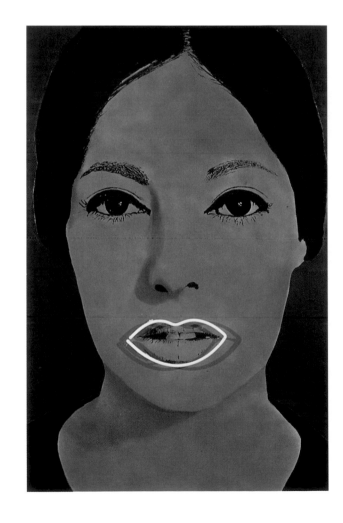

Opposite: PAINTING UNDER HIGH TENSION, **1965,** **M. RAYSSE.** *Courtesy Visual Arts Library, London.*

Above: **NUDE # 57, 1964, TOM WESSELMANN.** *Acrylic and collage on board, 48" x 65". The Whitney Museum of American Art.*

Right: **BERLIN, LIPSTICK, 1964.** *Photograph by Bernard of Hollywood.*

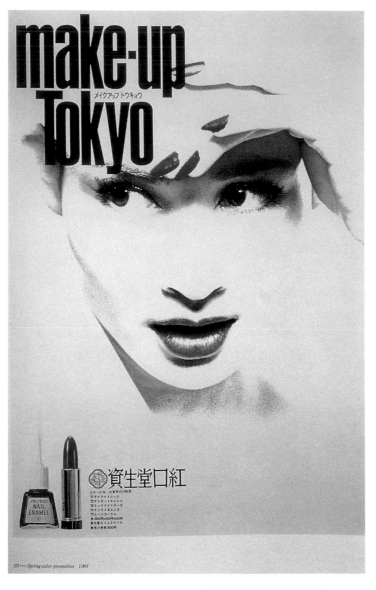

**SHISEIDO SPRING MAKEUP
PROMOTION, 1964.**
Courtesy Shiseido.

During the 1960s, movies ceased to be a seminal influence on women's beauty. Sixties radicalism had an aversion to the prescribed dogmas that informed the cinematic world, where proportion and classical beauty still reigned. Television instead became a major arbiter of fashion and makeup, and fashion magazines were read more avidly than ever.

Lois Banner argues in *American Beauty* that, in fact, "The last female film star to have a direct, personal impact upon standards of physical appearance was the French film actress Brigitte Bardot who starred in *And God Created Woman* (1957), the first film shown in neighborhood theaters to include a nude scene." Blond and voluptuous, Bardot embodied the ideal appearance of the 1950s, but her long hair, light lipstick, and nudity foreshadowed the rebellious 1960s and how apparently liberal sexuality indicated the future. Bardot's beauty was also sixties bohemian, as she disclosed in French *Elle* in 1967: "I spend about five minutes. Three movements of the pencil, *pif paf*, and it is finished. When I work, the process lasts a little longer, about one half-hour."

According to BB, as she was known, the most important aspect of makeup is the treatment of the eyes. She consistently used a black crayon to line the inside and top of her lid. "With my pencil, I draw a line in the middle of the eyelid. The *banane*, as it was called. Then, I cover the entire eyelid, and spread the black shading with my finger. No lines under the eye—that makes the look extremely heavy—then mascara." On her face Bardot used neither foundation nor powder for everyday wear, but for the movies, which still required elaborate cosmetic treatment, she used a very pale color, spread with a sponge, and a little powder rouge on her cheeks. She outlined her lips with brown pencil but she used no lipstick, "just a colorless base to give the lips brilliance." This use of makeup to gain a sultry look revolutionized the image of the 1950s sex queen. Bardot symbolized an aspect of sexual liberation that an entire generation had waited for, perhaps without knowing it.

Movies during the 1960s, from *Cleopatra* to *Fellini Satyricon*, from *Blow-Up* to *The Graduate*, from *Goldfinger* to *Bonnie and Clyde*, from *Barbarella* to *Breathless*, all presented women who conformed to the Beautiful People aesthetic. No longer starring classical, perfectly proportioned female beauties, these movies accentuated the extraordinary, and praised the excessive.

Cleopatra was the first of the films that defined a new image of beauty. Elizabeth Taylor, the wholesome ingenue known

BEAUTY TOOK ON POWER AS A POLITICAL STATEMENT, AND STYLE AS PROVOCATION

during the 1950s for her violet eyes and her perfect features, became, through her taste for heavy eye makeup and oriental liner, an outré icon of the 1960s. Taylor's romance with actor Richard Burton increased her status as a celebrity and all major cosmetics companies launched "looks" inspired, like hers, by Egyptian goddesses.

Movies like *Blow-Up* and *Darling* extolled beautiful eccentricity rather than classical glamour. In *Blow-Up* (perhaps the defining film of sixties style) fashion models Veruschka and Jean Shrimpton wore the most eccentric makeup and fashions of the period. Makeup was an essential expression of fragile youth, innocent spontaneity, revolutionary spirit. Beauty here took on power as a political statement, and style as provocation.

Goldfinger, the James Bond film in which makeup first became a murder weapon, also launched a trend. Sean Connery's colleague, a female secret agent, was suffocated when her skin was entirely covered with gold paint. Fashion magazines sardonically called this the "gold phenomenon" as cosmetics companies began the "gold rush"—launching new series of lye-tinted cosmetics that exploited the exquisitely sadistic—though beautiful—image from the movie.

The decade climaxed with *Fellini Satyricon* (1969), some of whose characters reached the apex of excessive beauty and exoticism. The stunning black model Donyale Luna appeared as a goddess, complete with gold makeup and sapphire contact lenses. *Satyricon* was the last milestone in a sixties breakthrough, as for the first time non-European models were also featured in fashion magazines. Before then, black women had difficulty finding cosmetics. As Barbara McNair comments in her book *Beauty for The Black Woman* (1972): "White girls had a world of makeup to choose from; we Black girls had to settle for a darker shade of makeup intended for whites, and hope for the best."

Ebony magazine, founded in 1945 by John H. Johnson, was aimed at this increasingly significant and sophisticated black population. Owned by a black family and produced by a mixed staff on which blacks were the majority, the lavish periodical sold three quarters of a million copies and reached a total of five million readers. In the early years *Ebony* took strong political stands, espousing black civil rights and putting forth a powerful vision of black achievement. Yet personal appearance posed a consistent problem. Beauty articles initially discussed how to appear as "white" as possible, and advertisements for hair straighteners, skin whiteners, and other such beauty aids were common.

As the push for civil rights grew more insistent in the 1960s, articles that firmly tied personal appearance to political statement began to appear. Nineteen sixty-six emerges as the fulcrum year in the development of a truly black aesthetic and *Ebony* for the first time featured a cover showing a black woman with a naturally curly coif and makeup that didn't try to hide her ethnic features. Bannered "The Natural Look; New Mode for Negro Women," the article inside cut right to the issue: "Many Negro Women Reflect White Standards of Beauty." The author pointed out the contradiction bluntly: "[T]he straightening comb and chemical processes seemingly offered the only true paths to social salvation. Not so today, for an increasing number of Negro women are turning their backs on traditional concepts of style and beauty by wearing their hair in its naturally kinky state....We, as black women, must realize that there is beauty in what we are, without having to make ourselves into something we aren't."

A black woman also appeared in a mainstream magazine in 1968, when Naomi Sims, on the cover of *Life* magazine, was touted as a new image of American beauty. "Black is beautiful" had finally penetrated white consciousness. By the end of the decade, black was not only beautiful but fashionable, and models such as Pat Cleveland, Grace Jones, Bethanne, and Toukie Smith appeared on the runways of Paris and New York. Radical chic embraced other black images: Black Panther members like Huey Newton, the assassinated heroes Martin Luther King Jr., Malcolm X, and Medgar Evers, and sign and symbol of black beauty at the barricades, Angela Davis and her defiant orb of hair.

Visual abstraction marked the explosive iconography of the times. Pop artists Roy Lichtenstein, Robert Rauschenberg, Tom Wesselmann, and Andy Warhol interpreted the painted face as self-definition and explored the act of transformation through makeup. The popular subject matter of the comic strip, printed fan magazines, or tabloids yielded serial images cannibalized by the contemporary aesthetic.

Makeup also intersected with the phenomenon of "Happenings," first witnessed in 1910–17, again in the 1950s, and returning with a vengeance in the 1960s. Artists Allan Kaprow, Red Grooms, Yves Klein, and the Japanese Gutai group were all specialists of the Happening, which could be defined as a "staging of sensations," in which paint and the act of painting a body, or rolling bodily on a canvas, were a method of artistic expression—in a way, using makeup to actively create a work of art. La Monte Young and Charlotte Moorman's performance, in which she played the cello with bared breasts, was one such art landmark, along with William Klein's fashion film, *Qui Êtes-Vous, Polly Maggoo?*

The nervous stimulation of the mid-sixties gave rise to an alternative society of idealists, the "flower children," who used

Top: JEAN SHRIMPTON, THE GRAY-EYED, WILLOWY MODEL WITH THE "LONDON LOOK," 1965.
Photograph by David Hurn/ Magnum.

Above left: NATALIE WOOD, EPITOME OF THE SMOLDER-ING SEXUALITY OF REBEL-LIOUS AMERICAN YOUTH, 1961. *Photograph by Ernst Haas/Magnum.*

Above right: BRIGITTE BARDOT, FRENCH ACTRESS AND SUL-TRY BOHEMIAN BEAUTY, CIRCA 1960.
Photograph by Bernard of Hollywood.

words like "love" and "freedom" in a new way. Ethnicity was in vogue in the search for meaningful references outside Western culture which led hippies and Mods to the far corners of the earth. Makeup followed. It soon became evident that this gentle libertinism was as ripe for exploitation as any other movement. Flower power was turning ugly in the heat of anti-Vietnam War agitation and amidst a burgeoning drug culture.

Despite its aura of iconoclasm and novelty in beauty and fashion, the decade was characterized as much by a continuation of the consumer-oriented culture of the 1950s as it was by a radical overturning of those values. Youth culture was preempted by formidable forces already deployed by the cosmetics companies and fashion magazines, who quickly appropriated Mod idioms to promote sales.

The accelerated expansion of cosmetics in the 1950s had caused overdistribution, increased government regulation, and a stultifying sameness in merchandising. It also created a similarity in product development and domination of the industry by a few companies, with the loss of the special creative flourish heretofore characteristic of pioneers in cosmetics manufacturing. The industry in the 1960s grappled with the problem of how to couple a new mass image (and the opportunities it presented) with its once prevalent snob appeal. That aura of glamour had helped boost the business into the billionaire class and was an indispensable ingredient of its success. "If we keep up the way we're going, we'll end up a mechanized business like breakfast food, and you can't sell cosmetics that way," lamented Frazer Sinclair of *Drugs and Cosmetics Industry*, and *Beauty Fashion*, both trade publications.

Mass distribution brought other complications to cosmetics selling. A woman picking up a package of makeup or hair color in a self-service outlet had no one to advise her. One wrong selection, and quick disenchantment with a whole line might follow. Peter Ribs of Helena Rubinstein described the situation as "the price that's paid for substituting consumer convenience for cosmetic authority."

The impressive growth of Avon (long the sales leader in the industry with an exclusive house-to-house operation of over 100,000 field representatives) was further indication that service continued to be vital to cosmetics sales. Avon's effectiveness—accounting for 20.7 percent of all industry sales—attracted others to that kind of operation. Helène Curtis launched Studio Girl, a house-to-house operation with over 5,000 representatives, and Bristol-Myers began a new initiative with Luzier, a small door-to-door organization.

Biba, a Mod shop in London, provided another example of the new techniques for marketing makeup. Its founder, Barbara Hulanicki, began a mail-order business in 1964 and a boutique (called Biba after her sister) in undistinguished two-room premises off Kensington High Street. Spectacularly different, however, was Biba's dark, exotic, glittering interior, with jumbled clothes, feathers, beads, and Lurex filling the counters. All items were extremely inexpensive, and Biba Cosmetics, in snazzy, simple black square plastic containers, were on display for all to try. Women would spend hours trying the products. Biba, a sixties success, finally closed at the end of the decade. Changed styles, higher prices, and charging for overhead proved antithetical to Biba's freewheeling spirit. Its fifteen minutes in the spotlight of makeup had come and gone.

From futurist to romantic, from the crackle of plastic and the clink of metal to ethnic fantasies of gypsy, backwoodsman, and highwayman, from Afghan coats and Peruvian ponchos to velvet ruffles and matching ringlets, style in the sixties meant multiple choice in identities, mirrored by makeup in all its guises. The effect is still felt today.

PRODUCTS

IN 1962 HELENA RUBINSTEIN PIONEERED (FOR $35) HER DAY OF BEAUTY, BEGINNING WITH A WEIGH-IN, EXERCISE SESSION, BODY MASSAGE, LUNCH, FACIAL, SHAMPOO, HAIRDO, MANICURE, PEDICURE, AND AS ONE LAST FINISHING TOUCH A MAKEUP SESSION. THE TOTAL TIME INVESTMENT FOR THIS REGIMEN: SIX HOURS. THE FIRST PROTECTIVE HYDRATING CREAM WITH COLOR WAS BIENFAIT DU MATIN, DEVELOPED BY LANCÔME IN 1969. CRÈME B21 OF ORLANE, AN ANTI-WRINKLE CREAM BASED ON AMINO ACIDS, WAS LAUNCHED IN 1968, AND PROPELLED ORLANE INTO A WIDER ARENA. CRÈME ABRICOT BY CHRISTIAN DIOR, A 1963 NIGHT CREAM FOR TIRED NAILS THAT REPAIRED AS YOU SLEPT, WAS AN IMMEDIATE SUCCESS. IN 1964 HELENA RUBINSTEIN INVENTED LONG LASH WATERPROOF, A LONG-STEMMED, TECHNICOLOR APPLICATOR OF MASCARA THAT CONDITIONED AND DIDN'T STREAK. IN 1962 THE FIRST MODERN BUST CREAM, TENSUR BUST, WAS RELEASED BY CLARINS.

THE BIG NEWS IN 60S MAKEUP CAME FROM LONDON. MARY QUANT'S CLEVER PACKAGING AND WITTY PRODUCT NAMES CAPTURED THE ATTENTION OF A GENERATION, AND HER FAMOUS PAINT BOX—WITH PENCILS, ROUGE, LIP SALVE, LIP BRUSH, SHADOW IN FLOWER-POWER PASTELS—QUICKLY BECAME A CLASSIC. BIBA APPEALED TO THE SAME AUDIENCE WITH INEXPENSIVE, WELL-DESIGNED COSMETICS SOLD INITIALLY FROM A LONDON SHOP, BUT SOON DISTRIBUTED WORLDWIDE.

From Street to Elite

1970s

BY 1970, A WHOLE GENERATION OF BABY BOOMERS HAD EXPLODED IN AN OUTCRY OF VIOLENCE THAT WAS HEARD THROUGH-OUT THE WORLD. DISSATISFACTION WITH TRADITIONAL VALUES AND SOCIAL STRUCTURES CREATED POLITICAL UNREST, WHETHER CONCERNING THE WAR IN VIETNAM, THE CIVIL-RIGHTS MOVEMENT, OR WOMEN'S EQUALITY. STUDENT INSUR-RECTION WAS RAMPANT FROM MILAN TO BERKELEY, FROM PARIS TO NEW YORK, AND A REFORMIST IDEALISM REPLACED, FOR A TIME, THE DRIVE TO PROSPER AND SURVIVE IN THE COMPETITIVE TWENTIETH CENTURY.

Preceding pages: **OUTRAGEOUS AMERICAN ROCK GROUP 'KISS', KNOWN FOR THEIR LEATHER STUDDED COS-TUMES AND BLACK, WHITE, AND SILVER MAKEUP, 1976.** *Photograph ©Archive Photos.*

Left: **HARD-EDGED SEXUAL ANDROGYNY COLORS THE VERY FEMININE MAN'S SUIT BY YVES SAINT LAURENT, PARIS, 1975.** *Photograph by Helmut Newton.*

Right: **LAUREN HUTTON, WHO BECAME THE HIGHEST-PAID MODEL IN AMERICA (FOR PERSONIFYING REVLON'S ULTIMA PRODUCTS), CIRCA 1974.** *Photograph ©Archive Photos.*

The general political climate changed the way people viewed themselves. Daily photographs of the unrest, dissent, and protest qualified what was considered important, newsworthy, and even attractive. The heavily camouflaged soldiers in Vietnam who appeared in media images of the late sixties introduced a new ref-erence for the meaning and use of cosmetics. Infantrymen with their faces painted black, green, and orange, and protesters with obscenities, peace signs, and crossbones painted on cheeks and foreheads came to represent the face of sobering reality: full of anger, fear, and pride in equal measure.

Makeup in this context was imbued with new purpose—during the 1970s it became a means of camouflage, enabling women and men to fit in to different situations and environments. No longer only a ritual or province exclusively of femininity, make-up defined whatever new personae people chose to don as politi-co-social statements. For the first time since the turn of the centu-ry, women—and men—chose their faces according to situational needs, not just the dictates of fashion. Makeup became a schizo-phrenic affair—women would "dress for success," in the business world, wearing serious, polite makeup with an androgynous polish in order to play down the sexual or personal definition; then they would "dress for seduction" in the discos, with exotic, kohl-lined eyes and glossy lips appropriate to the bell-bottoms, platform shoes, bright lights, and pounding music.

American *Vogue* described the duality: "A 1970s woman can make herself a different face for each passing mood, each fantasized role, even each time of day. At the office, she can sport the fresh, 'natural' look of the career woman, by using a dozen shades and tints, from eye liner to translucent lip gloss, all supposed to make her appear as if she were wearing no makeup at all. Then, in the evening, she can switch to smoky mauve eye shadow and dark red lipstick touched with midnight blue, calculated to give her a mysterious aura that will stand out under disco lights and smite her dancing partners with an advanced case of 'Saturday Night Fever.'"

The highly painted faces worn by rock and roll stars such as David Bowie and Mick Jagger joined stylized movie images like those from *A Clockwork Orange* and *Barry Lyndon*, in a referential parade of faces of the future and past. The decade ended with the emergence of the punk movement, reigned over visually by Vivienne Westwood and Malcolm McLaren. Punk's look of urbane savagery was even more of an outcry against the political system than the angry music itself.

Beauty was no longer considered uniquely in aesthetic terms, but also for its ability to affect social and cultural traditions. The power of the psychological aspects of appearance became relevant as a suitable subject for academic investigation. Between 1920 and 1970 only ten scholarly articles had been published concerning beauty. In the 1970s some forty-seven articles suddenly appeared. Not only was the question "What is beautiful?" tacitly posed in these studies, but far removed from the excitement and confusion of the fashion world, beauty as a concept and discipline was clearly evaluated.

One of these academic studies involved sixty U.S. college students (thirty males and thirty females) who were asked to predict the personality and life changes of persons represented to them in photographs. The researchers had prepared twelve sets of three pictures, half showing women and half showing men of differing levels of physical attractiveness. Half of the students were given female photographs to respond to, half male photographs (so that some people were rating subjects of their own sex, some of the opposite sex). The experiment unambiguously

Above: **NO. 7, A LINE OF PRODUCTS DESIGNED FOR THE BOOTS DRUGSTORE CHAIN IN GREAT BRITAIN, 1977.**
Courtesy Boots Cosmetics.

Opposite: **FRENCH FILM POSTER FOR** *A CLOCKWORK ORANGE,* **DIRECTED BY STANLEY KUBRICK, WITH MAKEUP BY BARBARA DALY, AND ADAPTED FROM THE NOVEL BY ANTHONY BURGESS, 1972.**

A 1970s WOMAN MAKES HERSELF A DIFFERENT FACE FOR EACH PASSING MOOD, FOR EACH FANTASIZED ROLE, FOR EACH TIME OF DAY

showed that both male and female students, no matter which gender they were considering, assumed that physically attractive persons possessed more socially desirable personalities than unattractive ones, and predicted that their lives would be happier and more successful, both socially and professionally. The researchers entitled their report "What is Beautiful is Good," though the study seemed directed instead toward establishing that "What is beautiful is successful."

Some studies simply concentrated on the long-held suspicion that beautiful female students in an essentially male-dominated world were likely to have advantages over less beautiful ones. One university study suggested that, even in large classes where it was difficult for the instructor to know students individually, beautiful girls received higher grades. (The conclusion suggested that this was because their faces and names were better retained in the minds of instructors.)

Researchers went on to study the relevance of beauty in the workplace, discovering, not surprisingly, that "beautiful men were thought to be the most masculine, and the most physically attractive women to be the most feminine; that beautiful men seemed to have an advantage in so-called 'masculine jobs,' and beautiful women in 'feminine jobs.'" Beautiful people routinely received higher salaries, since attractive applicants were seen to have more occupational alternatives (as well as social advantages), so that higher salaries were necessary to attract them. Research like this gave cosmetics companies new pragmatic arguments to attract customers interested in the pursuit of beauty.

While the social scientists were busy proving the power of beauty statistically, it became evident, as the decade continued, that women's world, and men's to some extent, had been turned upside down by the radical changes that had transpired in employment, sexuality, divorce, and family relationships. The divorce rate soared from 35 per 1,000 in 1960 to 121 in 1984. Sexuality had also altered dramatically. During the early 1960s, nearly 50 percent of American women had delayed having sexual intercourse until marriage. By the early 1980s, in contrast, 75 percent became sexually active prior to marriage. One of the results was a significant increase in births to unwed mothers; another was a much more tolerant and expressive attitude toward sexuality generally, including a much wider acceptance of homosexuality.

Extraordinary changes were occurring in the family and workplace, too, resulting in giant strides forward for women who, two decades earlier, would have been unable even to conceive of some of the choices they now had. In the U.S. the Equal Rights Amendment (ERA) was brought before Congress, where it received enthusiastic support, going to the states for ratification in 1972 (where it subsequently failed). Politicians developed new enthusiasm for women's issues and enacted the Education Amendments Act, which barred sex discrimination of any kind by colleges and universities. The number of women delegates to political conventions soared from 13 percent in 1968 to 40 percent in 1972, and many of those delegates played an essential role in supporting feminist causes. Court decisions proceeded in tandem with other political trends, and in 1973, Roe v. Wade, concerning the hotly debated abortion issue, guaranteed a woman's right to control her body. Women's integration in certain male-dominated institutions became of paramount importance to the growing numbers of educated, culturally mature women of the 1970s, and male-only bars were stormed, clubs were breached, and locker rooms invaded.

All of these changes were accompanied by an employment rate among women that continued to skyrocket. By the early 1980s, nearly two thirds of all women from twenty to sixty-four in the United States were employed, 250 percent more, proportionately, than had been employed at the beginning of World War II. Furthermore, the growth of the communications and service industries, and the entry of greater numbers of women into areas hitherto dominated by men, further altered the employment scenario. The evidence was overwhelming that women competing in the job market felt even greater pressure than ever before to pay the most meticulous attention to their personal appearance. "Good grooming" was essential, and, where it was important for a man to be at least personable, it was imperative for a woman to be beautiful.

Fashion and makeup styles expressed the overall uncertainty that women felt in the midst of such monumental changes. Designers no longer dictated the trends but rather attempted to intuitively predict the needs of the post-1968 generation of women. These needs would reflect the sharp internal conflict that most women felt—between the dominant, aggressive, independent businessperson and the "other half" in a man's world. That dichotomy became the identity crisis in the seventies, especially in the United States and Great Britain. But repercussions were felt everywhere, as women found themselves increasingly uncertain of, and challenging, their place in the world.

Fashion culture was, more than ever before, definitively divided into couture and ready-to-wear. Yves Saint Laurent set the couture tone for the decade with his androgynous pantsuits and formal "smoking" attire for women. He responded to the schizophrenic roles of the modern woman: active and affirmed one minute; sensual and submissive the next. The femme fatale complete with high heels and red, glossy lips returned to the runways

wearing menswear and short, slicked-back hair—a reference to the woman liberated by feminism but possessed of a bisexual energy. He introduced the fabulously successful fragrance Opium to international acclaim in the biggest launch in cosmetic history. His cosmetics line (designed by two astute women, Chantal Roos and Catherine Canovas) followed the same pattern.

In an interview with the author, Chantal Roos explained, "Contrary to when the businesswomen aesthetic—the business suit, business hair, business face—was the current trend, we recognized women needed a true choice. We decided to propose a sophisticated version of femininity, giving women the possibility of presenting themselves as sexy, sensual beings as well as responsible, capable females. We chose colors from each collection and used them in a pure, undiluted sense. We gave numbers to the lipsticks, like Saint Laurent No. 19, a pure fuchsia tint used by all the makeup artists. It caught on like wildfire because nothing so violent, so ripe had existed as pure color before." (The lipstick was banned from the United States by the FDA, because it contained a potentially cancer-causing colorant, which added to the legend.) Jose Luis, a brilliant South American makeup artist, worked with Loulou de la Falaise, Roos, Canovas, and Saint Laurent to help polish the final look. Roos continued: "It was a question of letting a woman experience everything, at least visually, that she could. Once there, women understood immediately. Somehow we had created something exquisitely naughty."

The ready-to-wear movement prospered in the seventies, redefined by a new generation of women designers, namely Sonia Rykiel, Dorothée Bis, Emmanuelle Khanh, and Jean Muir. The mid-seventies also spotlighted the influences of *créateurs* like Jean-Charles de Castelbajac, Claude Montana, and Thierry Mugler, whose cutting-edge fashion was more theatrical than that of the classic couturiers, yet more expensive and unique than most prêt-à-porter. In their hands, clothes were put together, layered on, taken off, and accessories (bearing labels that advertised status) gained new importance.

Mugler's sirens slinked down the runway in razor-straight skirts, teetering on four-inch heels and flaunting a hard attitude. Montana re-created the working woman's suit with large shoulders and leather trimmings, while Castelbajac brought urban chic and creativity to sportswear with blanket coats and down outerwear. The modern life-style of the seventies woman had informed the concept of fashion as never before. In the hands of the new designers the fashion show itself was also transformed into a full-scale media event. The collections were presented in front of 3,000 international spectators and broadcast on television. Dramatic

makeup was essential on the runway, even for sportswear. Makeup shined with iridescence, kohl-encircled almond eyes became popular again, and elaborately drawn, glossed, and polished lips were commonplace. As a harbinger of the decades ahead, models of the 1970s began to be seen increasingly on television, in life-style interviews, and in society columns no longer restricted to magazines' fashion pages. Their new-found celebrity overshadowed the cloistered, luxurious world of couture.

In contrast to this European extravagance, American designers introduced the neutral look. Calvin Klein revolutionized American fashion by repositioning the understated components of classical chic: cashmere, beige, and pearls. Makeup followed suit, and gloriously soft skin colors were propounded to underline the style's subtle appeal. Ralph Lauren proposed his version of this trend with the "country look," or "American princess"—blond hair, natural makeup, and casual style. Uncontrived, it modernized the clean-cut image of American youth. The outdoorsy look also helped focus attention on diet, physical fitness, and a healthy appearance. In a natural outgrowth, there was new interest in the proletarian uniform of jeans worn with T-shirts of choice, now recast by designers as the status uniform of the decade. Gloria Steinem, with her scrubbed minimalism, was the look's serious feminist icon; Cheryl Tiegs' blue eye shadow and ranginess marked the apex of its California golden girl type; Diane Keaton in *Annie Hall* represented its quirky iconoclast/individualist variety.

Fashion magazines were as ambivalent as the fashions themselves. Retailers complained to French *Vogue* that their arty layouts and haughty models no longer showed their clothes to advantage. In the first three months of 1971, American *Vogue* lost 38 percent of its advertising pages, and *Harper's Bazaar* dropped 37 percent. Grace Mirabella, considered very much the modern American woman—sporty, witty, charming, and strictly business—took over at American *Vogue*. Acutely aware of the newly liberated attitudes of women, tuned in to the popularity of the more practical style in slacks and shirtdresses, she changed the *Vogue* point of view overnight. She first reduced its page size to create a more compact, less esoteric magazine and to decrease costs. The medium was indeed the message, affirmed Mirabella: "The pages began to look more charged, less concerned with aesthetics and massive fashion statements. They were cropped, speedy and communicative, an intimate integration of words and pictures....Everything we do now is with the constant idea of *real*. We discuss real clothes for real people."

Beauty necessarily became a more substantial part of the magazine. *Vogue* ran more "makeovers" and chronicled more makeup trends, venturing into subjects such as the psychological effects of color or analyses of different beauty ideas. It also discussed the new androgyny and turned its focus toward urban women readers—including working women who didn't have time to go to the beauty parlor every day.

Other magazines, geared to the interests of working women, enjoyed new success, such as *Glamour* and *Mademoiselle*. French *Vogue*, however, remained an artistic and photographic leader in the world of fashion. It stayed loyal to the tradition of extraordinary fashion photography and consistently supported haute couture as well as the work of the new *créateurs*. Almost in defiance of the inroads into international style made by the bourgeois, the extraordinary balls of the Baron de Rede, Helen Rochas, and other members of the jet set were covered by French *Vogue* as important fashion events.

Meanwhile *Interview* magazine, published in New York by Andy Warhol and Fred Hughes, became the seventies' standard bearer of international chic, and mainstream readers' introduction to the underground and disco worlds. Using an oversized format, it deified the culture of gossip, paparazzi, and pop art, chronicling the nightlife of glitz and escapism practiced by denizens of 70s watering holes like Studio 54, Regine's, Les Bains Douches, Club Sept, and Annabelle's.

Although celebrities had been used to sell cosmetics throughout the century, the idea of models specifically contracted to represent a company or product was an innovation of the decade. Although Estée Lauder's advertising had always featured one model to present a unified image, the exclusivity of the model's commitment was never contractually formalized until Lauren Hutton was hired by Revlon to become the face of Ultima II. Charles Revson (who had adamantly opposed the idea of paying models for their exclusivity) was convinced by photographer Richard Avedon that Hutton should be signed. Under the terms of the contract, Hutton could advertise no other products, whether cosmetics or clothes, but she could continue to do editorial work. Guaranteeing the unheard-of fee of about $175,000 a year (for thirty-five days of work), her contract also stipulated that she would be photographed uniquely by Richard Avedon. The Ultima contract made Hutton a sudden celebrity—and also proved an exceptionally effective media ploy. It had a tidal effect among advertisers, who realized anew that their products' image needed forceful molding. By 1977, Hutton was earning $250,000 to advertise Ultima, CHR, and Cerissa products, and had increased her territory to include television in addition to print. Revlon executives considered her highly effective: "When we picked her, we

Top: **NATURAL STYLE AND CASUAL MAKEUP DEFINED FARRAH FAWCETT, KATE JACKSON, AND JACLYN SMITH, THE THREE "ANGELS" OF THE TELEVISION DRAMA** *CHARLIE'S ANGELS,* **1977.** *Photograph © Archive Photos.*

Preceding page: **THE FANTASY OF FLESH—RAW, REAL AND DAMAGED—WAS PART OF THE SPECTACLE OF THE 70s. TEXAN MODEL JERRY HALL, 1974.** *Photograph by Helmut Newton.*

Bottom: **DAVID BOWIE AND ANGIE BOWIE AT A ROYAL PREMIERE OF A JAMES BOND FILM, 1973.** *Photograph © Archive Photos/Express Newspapers.*

were looking for more than a typical beauty, we wanted someone a woman could identify with, something accessible. And Lauren certainly is that, because of all her well known imperfections, notably her gap-toothed smile."

Estée Lauder, which had been using the model Karen Graham since 1970, followed suit, engaging her exclusively for $200,000. Graham's image as photographed by Victor Skrebneski, became so inextricably linked with that of the company that some shoppers actually confused her with the founder.

Other model and celebrity endorsements in the cosmetics world quickly followed. The 1978 film by Louis Malle, *Pretty Baby*, made the bushy eyebrows of Brooke Shields a hallmark of beauty. Thick, dark, and wild, the unwieldy big-brow look fit the natural style also emblematized by Margaux Hemingway, who signed in 1975 to represent the Babe line of cosmetics. Fabergé's Richard Barrie explained her appeal, saying, "I think she represents what other girls want to be." Hemingway's much-touted $1 million contract was based on a complicated set of options that covered a two-to-four-year period and involved both advertising and personal appearance commitments.

Catherine Deneuve, the classically beautiful French actress, had worked for Chanel since 1972; now photographed by Richard Avedon, she was paid $250,000 on contract. Candice Bergen, Cheryl Tiegs, and Farrah Fawcett, whose blonde, healthy "California-girl" good looks were especially popular, also signed to represent various cosmetic products, and the list of models as minor celebrities grew as the seventies continued.

Rolling Stone magazine, founded and edited by Jann Wenner, chronicled the essential world of rock and roll—providing a record of the glamorous and often outrageous lives of musical icons such as the Rolling Stones, Lou Reed, and the Grateful Dead. It printed the information and images necessary to confirm the exceptional cultural influence of rock musicians during this decade, in the context of a new, color, gazette-style format that was easy to read. The proponents of Glam or Glitter rock were far removed from the clean-cut, blue-eyed blondes of Cover Girl fame. Outrageous and ultra-individualist, Glam rock spawned a potent, much-followed fashion. Marked by extreme theatrics, its demigods were personalities like Alice Cooper, Lou Reed, Elton John, and David Bowie, who used the trappings of transvestism and decadence. Bowie's music was about transformation, and fashion and makeup were part of his method. The shock value of his appearance was essential to his work's popularity. Affected, dandified, purposely camp, Glam rock's blasé sophistication developed in reaction to the sixties' prevailing aura of naiveté and sincerity.

Glam helped to disseminate one of the dominant cultural movements of the decade, the rise of androgyny. Hair was long or short no matter what your sex. The notion that all males possess female qualities and vice versa (known as psychological androgyny) had even spread to scholarly disciplines, especially art history and psychology.

Fashion and beauty photographers of the 1970s faced daunting challenges, as the exciting and exotic themes that earlier fashion photographers had at their disposal were no longer the subject of magazines. Instead, the prevalent sportswear, business suits, and knitwear needed a more matter-of-fact vision, and a corresponding makeup to make them comprehensible.

Grace Mirabella, then editor-in-chief of American *Vogue*, remarked, "Photographers like Arthur Elgort introduced a spontaneity in the seventies that had never existed in fashion photographs. The split second where the light, the shape of the figure, the energy, the movement, and the model's expression were perfect created the picture, and with it, the statement." The message was one of human potential: the models themselves seemed to live the lives they portrayed on camera. Grace Mirabella added: "Photography was more on the streets requiring the models to *act*. In the seventies, instead of a picture of a girl simply sitting in a car, she is now a girl sitting in a car, about to leave for somewhere special, having been someplace interesting." Patti Hansen, Rosie Vela, Rene Russo, and Lisa Taylor were often photographed portraying the "day-in-a-life" activities of Everywoman. But there was a difference. "These girls have the looks," remarked *Vogue* in 1978, "that are changing the whole meaning of beauty today. The glorious charge of health and vitality and fitness....The clear, clean skin. The thick shiny hair. The strong wonderful bodies. The high of health. It's what American good looks are all about."

As audiences became accustomed, through new license in films and television, to more sexual, violent, or explicit images, fashion felt the pressure to shock its audience equally, to work hard to retain and attract interest. Photographers portrayed worlds and ideas more connected with sexual fantasy than with the reality of fashion, and the term porno-chic entered the vocabulary. Particularly in French and Italian *Vogue*, where extravagant haute couture was still commonly featured, photographers like Helmut Newton showed fashion in violent, sexually explicit tableaux. Women were strident in stiletto heels, flashed long, red nails, fought other women for men, for dogs, or for other women. Accessories such as whips, sunglasses, and metal accoutrements increased the atmosphere of violent menace. Newton, according to Francine Vormese, an editor who participated often on his fashion

Left: **ALL-AMERICAN RED-HEAD PATTI HANSEN, WHOSE ATHLETIC BODY AND TOMBOY FRECKLES ENERGIZED FASHION SHOOTS, 1976.**
Photograph by Arthur Elgort.

Bottom: **KAREN GRAHAM'S COOL, ARISTOCRATIC COMPOSURE WAS GIVEN AN ACCESSIBLE, SPORTY LOOK IN THIS ESTÉE LAUDER ADVERTISEMENT.**
Photograph by Victor Skrebneski.
Courtesy Estée Lauder.

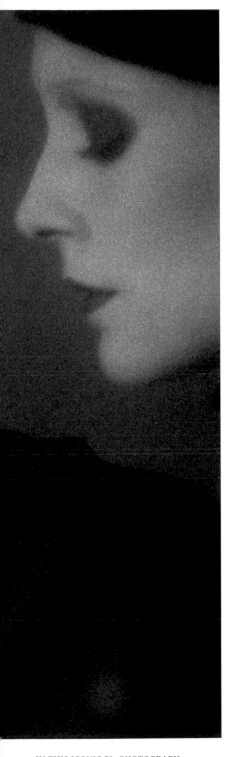

IN THIS ICONIC 70s PHOTOGRAPH
ENTITLED *PERFORMANCE*, VEILED
AND LANGUOROUS MODELS
(DRAPED BY JEANNINE MONTEL
UNDER THE DIRECTION OF KARL
LAGERFELD WITH MAKEUP BY
HEIDI MORAWETZ) SHARE
ENIGMATIC INNER SECRETS, 1973.
Photograph by Sarah Moon.

shoots, would require the makeup artist to use blood-red lipstick and red nail polish with a high shine, and black eye makeup. Finally, Newton would supply a set of false breasts or nipples if the models needed more shape under their clothes. This seventies image of provocation, with a chic of its own, sent a sinister message about the cool, impeccably corrupt, woman of the decade. "I think," remarked Newton in an interview with the author, "that the greatest enemy of fashion is boredom. Big women fascinate me, muscular types, the Germanic woman, and I prefer to photograph blondes rather than brunettes because their hair produces a gleam." Elusive, undefinable femininity—a direct result of make-up, coiffure, and situation—had the starring role.

Guy Bourdin, working for French *Vogue* in the 1970s, used cinema makeup to create the slick-surfaced perfection for which he was noted. According to Heidi Morawetz, a makeup artist who, as a Viennese art student in the early 1970s, worked with Bourdin to create some of the defining photos of the decade, the photographer specified matte white foundation with pure pink tones, to adjust for the brilliant white lights (of a type often used for the movies) he favored. Rose blush and violent fuchsia lipstick were sometimes added to give the models a hard, yet coquettish, quality. Bourdin used models as props to tell a story, and in his images women looked frantic, even mad, but perfectly put together, and sensually controlled. Their icy edge created a chilling, if compelling vision of women.

Women photographers offered a completely different though equally provocative vision of beauty and fashion. Deborah Turbeville, one of the most successful photographers of the decade, declared her antipathy to the work of male photographers

I THINK THAT THE GREATEST ENEMY OF FASHION IS BOREDOM

in an interview with the author: "Newton and Bourdin—while their photographs may be exciting and brilliant—put women down. The models looked pushed around in a hard way. For me there is no sensitivity in that. I don't feel the same way about eroticism and women. Women can be vulnerable and emotional; they can be insecure and alone; but that is the psychological tone and the mood that I work for." Turbeville used evocative settings of decaying or cavernous rooms to set her groups of women in. They radiated something delicate and disturbing as they congregated in their odd environments. Oblique glances were enigmatic, dislocated. The models' surroundings seemed dreamlike and insubstantial, but their bodies said one thing and their clothes another. The makeup followed suit, creating a surreal effect. That ambivalence spoke directly to many women.

Sarah Moon, a Paris-based photographer, produced some of the decade's seminal images, portraying a baroque environment painted with a rich palette in which women seemed caught in time, moving within the boundaries of feminine imagination. Like Bourdin, she lit and composed her photographs much like a movie set. As the image creator for Roc cosmetics, Moon worked closely with makeup artists of the period, particularly Naik le Fur (who was to become the artistic adviser to Cacharel), Jacques Clemente, and Barbara Daly, to create an expressive, almost feline femininity. Moon's elegant images—at once vulnerable and engrossing—used makeup with an otherworldly aura, drawing the viewer into the intimacy of women's sensibilities. "She brought together the different images of this century's fashionable women—the society beauty, the maid, the fashion model, the movie star—and the sum of these parts became the new Aesthetic Heroine," said Martin Harrison, summing up Moon's contribution.

Printwork had a significant influence on movies of the period. Barbara Daly, the brilliant makeup artist who conceived the face of the characters in some of Stanley Kubrick's films, stated in an interview with the author: "Achieving a character's image was an extraordinary procedure. Stanley Kubrick would collect and open fashion magazines, and use the photographs to inspire his work. For Malcolm McDowell's character in *Clockwork Orange* we worked for two weeks trying to come up with a face that was appropriately aggressive, yet not contrived. When you put a false eyelash on a strong, virile man you begin to see the strength of the creative violence that is possible. When Stanley Kubrick saw it he knew immediately that we had found the face." For *Barry Lyndon* Daly researched the makeup of 18th-century England and used products similar to those of the period. She attempted to replicate the style of the time yet produce something "extraordinary and creative at the same time—not just a period documentary."

Francesco Scavullo, an American photographer, became synonymous with the 1970s' commercial look of feminine success with his sophisticated covers for *Cosmopolitan*. He worked with the same makeup artist, Way Bandy, and hair stylist, Maury Hobson, throughout the decade, and their collaboration could be said to have singlehandedly created the seventies' "natural look." In his book, *Designing Your Face*, Bandy refers to the art of makeup as making a "sculpture portrait," suggesting that by analyzing photographs of oneself, one could deduce what was necessary to create a personalized "ideal" face. Recalling the thirties' concept of sculptural perfection, Bandy saw makeup as a means not just to create a decorative mask, but to fundamentally alter perception and proportion. His advocacy of this idea had a decidedly seven-

ties' New Age ring to it. "To be able to change identity as well as our appearance is a basic human wish," said Bandy in his 1976 book *The Way of Beauty*. "We should allow ourselves to be different...to fully realize his or her [sic] importance as an individual, by expression of personal fantasy or a spirit in visible style."

Antonio Lopez, the renowned illustrator, was also influential in creating beauty images that brought a fresh vision to fashion's parochial context. He colored the decade in extravagant, multidimensional beauty illustrations. Using fashion models like Texas-born Jerry Hall as inspiration, he transformed his subjects from awkward American teenagers into sophisticated visions where makeup was an essential accessory to the atmosphere.

The brilliant partnership of Vivienne Westwood and Malcolm McLaren helped create the punk movement, which, towards the seventies' end, effectively expressed a moment of excess and political upheaval. Using a deliberately artificial, aggressive aesthetic to provoke reactions in urban London, the young rebels creatively used makeup, tattooing, and body piercing to fascinate the beholder by horrifying him; to dispense with facile enticements in order to bring into play more secret and dangerous impulses. The punk responded to the savage political spirit of the times and prided himself (or herself) on outdoing it. He flaunted the new tribalism, painted his face in day-glo colors, and dyed his hair fluorescent shades to prove that the Peace and Love slogans of the hippies and their music were not reflected in reality.

Like urban bushmen, punk aesthetic was based on sex and violence. Westwood, in an interview with the author, described the beginnings of the punk movement as a fantastic search for a vision that corresponded to the realities of the late 1970s. She and McLaren experimented with numerous possibilities in their boutique, Sex, on King's Road in London before settling on a vision through a process of elimination—urban guerrillas. "It was a slow process," remarked Westwood. "We had been looking for something which would symbolically correspond to what we were feeling and seeing in London at the time. The tribal influence was introduced by a salesgirl named Jordan who one day arrived with no makeup, but with a line of brown on her face. The next day she arrived with a book by Leni Riefenstahl, held it up, and with poster paints, imitated the [face painting of the] indigenous peoples that Riefenstahl had photographed. Makeup became a composite of vivid colors and frightening body piercing, a provocation rather than an accepted aesthetic."

Hard, purist, anarchic, punk challenged the conventions; black became the color of the moment. As a cultural movement, it was reactive, as though people increasingly exposed to a culture of

brutality felt a need to reclaim it as the new icon of the late twentieth century. But these anti-beauty visions were sexy, interesting,
rather than inhuman. The connection to the future seemed more
visionary than anything that couture design, and even science fiction, could offer to the cultural consciousness.

Punk occurred in the wake of a crisis in beauty, after
recession had hit the fashion world like a hammer. The fantastic
beauty of the 1960s vanished, made obsolete by harsh economic
realities. The outlook was sobering; the Vietnam war and its consequences had deeply affected the U.S.A., and the mood was no

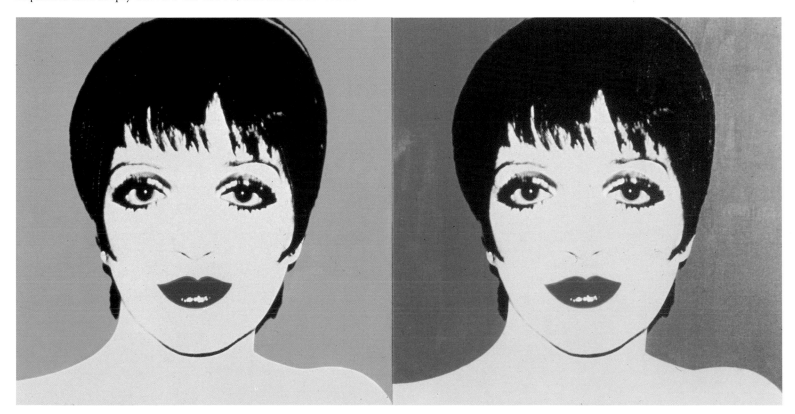

Above: LIZA MINNELLI, **1978,**
ANDY WARHOL. *Synthetic poly-*
mer paint and silkscreen ink on
canvas, two panels, each 40" x 40".
©The Andy Warhol Foundation, Inc.

longer propitious for dreaming, extravagance, or permissiveness.

Several Wall Street firms expressed concern about the
health and future of the beauty business, which had, since the
early 1900s, been virtually recession-proof. Until 1972 the cosmetics and toiletries industry had sales that grew 50 percent faster
than total personal spending. But 1974 proved this once recession-proof industry was no longer invulnerable. Personal spending
had grown 10.5 percent, but cosmetics and toiletries had trailed at
a more sluggish 8 percent.

In an article entitled "Cosmetics Shows Its Age," *W* magazine observed in 1979: "The cosmetics and toiletries industry has
not aged gracefully in the last decade. After weathering modest
volume increases, greater price sensitivity, considerably higher
marketing and advertising costs, and stiffer competition, it seems
to have lost its glamour."

Several factors were at play. The cosmetics industry was

considered middle-aged and cyclically oriented, uncreative and dogmatic. It had relied on price increases for profitability for too long without developing truly novel, modern products. Credibility posed another important concern. Consumers began to challenge cosmetics' claims, including use of the words *natural* and *organic* to describe products that were essentially chemical. Litigation involving at least five widely used color additives in makeup that had been found to cause cancer in laboratory animals created a groundswell of negative publicity.

New products were duly introduced into the market to help remedy the situation, and skincare and sunscreen lines became increasingly important. The U.S. Commerce Department, in its report of industry highlights for 1978, noted that cosmetics manufacturers were putting new emphasis on cost controls, improving quality and productivity under government guidelines; adopting more effective materials management; and exercising better selectivity in choosing new product projects to increase return on research and development. The climate, however, remained difficult, as the industry's free-wheeling entrepreneurial organization was fast giving way to a more formalized, structured type of management, which dampened innovation.

Ethnic markets, which had an estimated $500 million in sales potential per year, were studied and developed by companies. Male cosmetics became another area of growth, with sales of $340 million for the year 1977. The teen market, already a force during the 1960s, became even more important, with companies such as Love cosmetics directing new products to the young.

Cosmetics giant Revlon, transformed by new president Michel Bergerac, the former head of ITT's European division, moved into specialty health-care products, acquiring smaller cosmetics firms and pharmaceutical companies, such as Armour and Biomedical, during the 1970s.

Cosmetics companies were themselves the object of numerous takeover attempts, as many traditional smaller companies were incorporated into larger business conglomerates. Max Factor was acquired by Norton Simon; Elizabeth Arden, which after the death of its founder was left without efficient leadership, was purchased by the Eli Lilly company. Helena Rubinstein, also left in managerial disarray, was sold to L'Oréal (which even purchased her renowned Paris townhouse).

As cosmetics companies adopted a more personalized approach to the sale of beauty products, presentation was also reconsidered. High-priced European lines such as Lancôme and Lancaster recommitted themselves to the customer. Carol Phillips, who developed the Clinique line, put it bluntly: "Service and

Above: **COVER OF THE LIMITED EDITION BOOK, MAQUILLAGE (MAKEUP), BY DEBORAH TURBEVILLE,** 1975. *Photograph by Deborah Turbeville.*

OPPOSITE PAGE:

Top right: **PUNK STREET FASHION, LONDON, 1979.** *Photograph by Steve McCurry/ Magnum.*

Right: **BROOKE SHIELDS, WHOSE THICK, DARK, AND WILD BROWS WERE A COUNTERPOINT TO HER INNOCENT FACE, STARRED AS A CHILD PROSTITUTE IN FRENCH DIRECTOR LOUIS MALLE'S FILM** *PRETTY BABY,* 1978. *Photograph © Archive Photos.*

appearance at the point of purchase are the key elements in putting product performance across to consumers." Clinique's gleaming counters, with their hospital-green products and white-coated personnel in attendance, radiated an aura of scientific authority, as did the computers the company placed at the retail level to help the customer determine which skin-care products were appropriate for them. Clinique based its philosophy on the authenticity of its products, its treatments, and its formulas. Their skincare process had three parts: washing with soap, exfoliation with lotion, and moisturizing. Makeup preparations were touted as simply keeping up the good work: there was a base that functioned as a pore minimizer, and a foundation called Continuous Coverage, which contained sunblock.

Meanwhile, small, consumer-oriented cosmetics companies were established by independent businesswomen who viewed the giant conglomerates as lacking credibility. Adrien Arpel began her cosmetic and salon lines at age eighteen, with a four-hundred dollar loan from her father. She offered women mini-facials and makeovers at her store locations. Her products used strong, pure colors, and were moderately priced. By 1977, she had developed a company that grossed $800 million a year.

Suzanne Grayson, while a director of product marketing at Revlon, helped develop such successful products and lines as Face Gleamer, Blush On, and Ultima II. With her husband, Bob, she opened the first Face Factory in New York in a strategic location across from Bloomingdale's in 1974, employing an idea that originated during a visit to a Baskin-Robbins ice cream parlor. "Instead of trying out flavors, I imagined women trying out lipstick colors," Grayson explained in a *New York Times* article in 1977. "We then developed 229 lipstick colors, 105 eye-shadows, 23 makeup shades, 60 nail enamels, and 43 coloring pencils."

Madeleine Mono, another cosmetics entrepreneur, founded her company in 1974. An actress and antiques dealer by profession, she became interested in the cosmetics business when so many acquaintances asked her how she made up her eyes. A salon owner sought her out and suggested she give lessons to the clients. In 1974 Mono decided to import the product that was the basis of her own makeup, *kajal*, from India, which, although it had existed in commercial form in the Occident during the 1920s, had not been available in commercial markets since. Mono sold black and brown kajal labeled Indian Eyes to Henri Bendel, at that point one of the most avant-garde points of sale in the world. Three years later, she had a business worth $1 million.

Makeup has a nasty way of revealing the soul's secrets, telling tales of temporary social quiddities mixed with eternal

Following page: **UNPUBLISHED PHOTOGRAPH OF AMERICAN MODEL NAOMI SIMS FROM THE *NEW YORK TIMES* MAGAZINE FASHION SUPPLEMENT, 1970.** *Photograph by Gösta Peterson.*

verities. The 1970s' natural look gave way to glittering, bruised, hard-edged makeup by as early as 1980. But the pendulum would immediately start to swing again.

PRODUCTS

SKINCARE AND FOUNDATIONS

STATISTICS SHOWED THAT THE HEAVIEST USERS OF COSMETICS WERE WOMEN IN THE TWENTY-FIVE TO FORTY-TWO-YEAR-OLD RANGE, AND PRODUCTS THAT PROMISED ANTI-AGING INGREDIENTS THEREFORE BECAME INCREASINGLY IMPORTANT.

COUNT AND COUNTESS HUBERT AND ISABELLE D'ORNANO CREATED A NEW BRAND OF COSMETICS, SISLEY, IN 1976, BASED ON HIGH-TECH CARE OF THE SKIN THROUGH PLANT-BASED EXTRACTS. IN 1978, UNDER THE AUSPICES OF A FAMOUS SWISS CLINIC STARTED IN THE 1930S, PIONEERING REJUVENATION TREATMENTS GAVE BIRTH TO ANOTHER NEW LINE, LA PRAIRIE, WHOSE FORMULAS HAD A CELL-EXTRACT BASE. ESTÉE LAUDER LAUNCHED A MASS-MARKET LINE CALLED PRESCRIPTIVES IN 1979 WITH A CLASSIC DESIGN THAT SUGGESTED SERIOUS AND RIGOROUS MAKEUP, AND SKIN-CARE, AND OFFERED RELATED BEAUTY PRODUCTS. WOMEN WEARING LIGHTER MAKEUP NEEDED BETTER SKIN BENEATH IT AND THE RANGE OF PRODUCTS TO HELP ENSURE IT EXPANDED EXPONENTIALLY. IN CHICAGO IN 1973, FASHION FAIR, A COMPANY SPECIALIZING IN MAKEUP FOR WOMEN OF COLOR, LAUNCHED A LINE OF LIGHT FOUNDATIONS AND WARM MAKEUP SHADES. IN 1971 THE LABORATORIES OF PIERRE FABRE OFFERED A SLIMMING CREAM PACKAGED WITH A MASSAGE GLOVE, REINTRODUCING AN OLD CLASSIC, ELANCYL, TO FIGHT CELLULITE. BIOTHERM CREATED A LOTION THAT WAS ACTIVE AS WELL AS PREVENTIVE, CALLED ANTI-WRINKLE CREAM, FOLLOWING ONE YEAR LATER WITH A LINE OF PRODUCTS BY THE SAME NAME. IN 1974 ELIZABETH ARDEN LAUNCHED VISIBLE DIFFERENCE, A CREAM THAT PENETRATED CAPILLARY CELLS, PRESENTING SCIENTIFIC DOCUMENTS TO PROVE THE PRODUCT'S EFFICIENCY. CLINIQUE LAUNCHED ITS SKIN CARE FOR MEN LINE IN 1977. MAX FACTOR IN 1971 CAME OUT WITH A PRODUCT CALLED SELF DEFENSE, TO APPEAL TO URBAN WOMEN FIGHTING GUERRILLA WARFARE AGAINST WRINKLES. FACTOR'S GEMINESSE LINE ALSO CAME OUT WITH AN ANTI-WRINKLE CREAM, CALLED LIVING PROOF, IN 1977. CHANEL INTRODUCED ITS BEAUTY LINE IN 1975 AND OFFERED FOUNDATIONS MORE MATTE AND WHITER THAN BEFORE, AS WELL AS PURE BRIGHT PINKS AND VIOLETS. THEY ALSO CREATED CRÈME NO. 1, A PRODUCT THAT CLAIMED TO STIMULATE CELLULAR RHYTHMS AND TO OXYGENATE CELLS.

ROUGE AND BLUSH

OUTRAGEOUSLY COLORED PRODUCTS, A LEGACY OF THE SIXTIES, WERE STILL COMMONPLACE AT THE BEGINNING OF THE 1970S. MARY QUANT OFFERED A SET OF CRAYONS STYLED AFTER THE CARAN D'ACHE PENCILS THAT WERE USED BY MODELS. THEY WERE APPLIED OVER FOUNDATION AND BLENDED WITH THE FINGERS. THEY CONTAINED HUES THAT ENABLED MODELS IN *HARPER'S BAZAAR* AND *QUEEN* TO USE DARK BLUE, YELLOW, AND LILAC AROUND THE EYES, BROWN AND PINK ON THE LIPS, AND BROWN, RED, AND WHITE ON THE CHEEKS.

BIBA INTRODUCED PURPLE NAIL VARNISH, MAHOGANY LIPSTICK, BLACK FACE GLOSS, YELLOW FOUNDATION, AND A PAINT BOX CONTAINING SIX SHADES OF POWDER, TWO WATERCOLORS, TEN SHADES OF FACE GLOSS, FIVE BRUSHES, AND AN APPLICATOR.

COVER GIRL AND BONNE BELL BOTH SOLD TRANSPARENT GELS THAT IMITATED A NATURAL SUNTAN EFFECT. TUBE BLUSHERS WERE ALL THE RAGE, WITH ULTIMA II GELSTICK AND ELIZABETH ARDEN'S COLOR CONTROL THE MOST NOTABLE. SAINT LAURENT ALSO PRODUCED A LIGHTER, PURE-PINK-TONED FOUNDATION BASE THAT COMPLEMENTED A MATCHING LINE OF BLUSHERS AND LIPSTICK.

LIPS

TRENDS IN THE SEVENTIES WERE TOWARD LIPSTICKS THAT WERE EITHER COLOR OR GLOSS. DEEP PINKS, PURPLES, AND RASPBERRY WERE PREVALENT, FOR EXAMPLE, YARDLEY'S DAMSON LUSTRE AND SUGAR PLUM LUSTRE; MARY QUANT'S PRUNE CRUSH AND GRAPE CRUSH; REVLON'S GRAPEVINE; AND ESTÉE LAUDER'S CRANBERRY AND MULBERRY. REVLON INVITED DESIGNERS BILL BLASS AND NORMAN NORELL TO CREATE TWO REDS FOR THEIR ULTIMA II LIPSTICK. THEY ALSO CONTINUED TO PRODUCE FROSTED LIPSTICKS—LUMINESQUE LIPFROSTS—IN SEVENTEEN SHADES. SAINT LAURENT INTRODUCED LIPSTICKS IDENTIFIED BY NUMBERS; THE MOST FAMOUS WAS NO. 19, A PURE FUCHSIA.

EYES

FOR YEARS MASCARA FORMULAS HAD CONSISTED OF WATER, BEESWAX, AND CARNAUBA WAX. WATERPROOF MASCARAS BECAME POSSIBLE WITH THE EVOLUTION OF CERTAIN SOLVENTS IN THE SEVENTIES, FOLLOWED BY LASH LENGTHENERS AND THICKENERS THAT USED INFINITESIMAL FIBERS OF NYLON AND RAYON TO CREATE EXTENSIONS. BECAUSE THESE CAUSED PROBLEMS TO THOSE WITH CONTACTS OR SENSITIVE EYES, IMPROVEMENTS EVENTUALLY TOOK THEIR PLACE. MAYBELLINE'S GREAT LASH MASCARA WAS THE NUMBER-ONE SELLER WORLDWIDE IN 1971 (AND VIRTUALLY EVER SINCE THEN).

INTERNATIONAL COSMETIC COMPANIES SUCH AS SHISEIDO, SAINT LAURENT, REVLON, ESTÉE LAUDER, AND CHANEL PROMOTED BLACK-GRAY "SMOKY" COLORS FOR EYES TO COMPLEMENT THE ERA'S HIGHLY COLORED CHEEKS AND LIPS. A MODERN VERSION OF KOHL EYELINER WAS POPULAR, AND LANCÔME INTRODUCED ITS OWN LINE, CALLED THE KOHLS. MATTE COLORS WERE ESSENTIAL AND IRIDESCENCE—SO POPULAR IN THE SIXTIES— FADED AWAY. THE NATURAL-LOOK COMPANIES OFFERED A VERY DIFFERENT VISION OF BEAUTY WITH TRANSLUCENT SHADOWS IN BROWNS, BEIGES, AND PALE GRAYS, GIVING AN ILLUSION OF DEPTH TO THE EYE.

Future

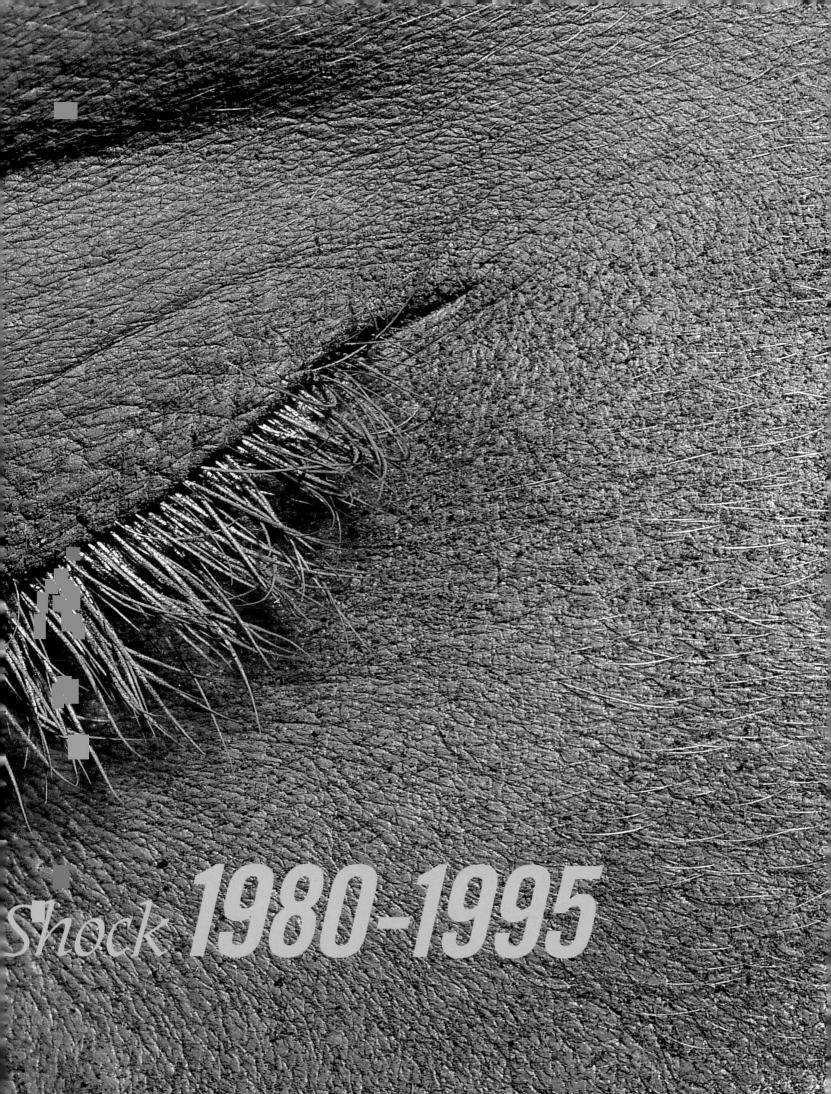

Shock 1980-1995

THE RAPID ACCELERATION OF CULTURAL CHANGE THAT HAD INFORMED THE TWENTIETH CENTURY CREATED AN AESTHETIC ATMOSPHERE THAT, BY THE 1980s, COULD BE TERMED "FUTURE SHOCK." STYLE, CULTURE, AND TRADITION HOVERED AT A STANDSTILL, FROZEN IN AN APPARENT INABILITY TO MOVE BEYOND THE FRONTIERS EXPLORED IN THE EARLIER PART OF THE CENTURY. BEAUTY CULTURE, WHICH ONCE STAKED ITS IDENTITY AND ITS ECONOMY ON THE ABILITY TO INVENT NEW AESTHETIC NORMS EACH DECADE, NOW FOUND ITSELF TRAVELING BACKWARD IN TIME, LOOKING FOR A ROAD THAT WOULD CARRY THE VISION OF BEAUTY INTO THE TWENTY-FIRST CENTURY.

Preceding pages: **MAKEUP RETURNED TO ITS ROOTS IN THE 90s, WITH EARTH TONES AND ETHNIC REFERENCES.** *Photograph by Michael Thompson.*

Opposite: **THE TIMELESS, AGELESS, FULMINATING BEAUTY FAYE DUNAWAY, 1990.** *Photograph by Matthew Rolston. Courtesy Fahey/Klein Gallery, Los Angeles.*

Right: **FIRST BEAUTY COMPOSITE, COMPUTER MERGING OF BETTE DAVIS, AUDREY HEPBURN, GRACE KELLY, SOPHIA LOREN, AND MARILYN MONROE, 1984.** *Photograph by Nancy Burson.*

Oldies, reruns, revivals: from movies to graphics, paintings to plays, flashbacks dominated the public experience during the eighties and early nineties. Art nouveau, Art Deco, forties streamline, fifties boogie, sixties slick, seventies glam rock: all styles, all genres were deftly combined with the burgeoning international influences of Japanese, African, and Eastern design to create a polymorphism with the appeal of novelty—the zest of "postmodernism." Yet as the excitement of eclecticism faded, this immersion in the past induced a panic—and spurred a wholesale questioning of values and fundamental ideas. Was western culture condemning itself to an aesthetic and social life of endless replay?

The face of the end of the century is now a place where images from the past and future come crashing together in a mixture of progress and tradition, memory, and hope. It manifests the fact that we are always echoes of earlier voices, walking catalogs of aphorisms, snapshots, songs, and recipes, composites not only of stories heard in childhood but also of the reverberations of ideas throughout cultural history. In this time of multifariousness, fashion and makeup have risen in cultural significance uniquely because the ephemeral is fundamental to their nature. The laws of fashion are also the laws of change. They regulate how, within the limited objective of adorning four limbs, a head, and a torso, changes both gradual and radical occur from year to year, season to season, and, microcosmically, each morning. Fashion has never had more to teach us about the tempo of culture itself.

The made-up face of the eighties and nineties suggests nostalgia for a time when we could rely on tradition to supply an endless dream of better tomorrows. In truth, Western culture has had little experience living in present time: Eden was great before the fall, Paradise will be swell come Judgment Day; childhood was rosy; therapy will lead to blissful maturity. The belief that we cannot change the future without coming to terms with the past (thereby seizing control of the present) is lodged deeply in the post-Freudian Western ethos. All these have their referents in makeup, both as escape and expression.

As the millennium draws to a close, beauty culture is caught up in formidable economic, scientific, and social upheavals in the international world. The dissolution of many nations' traditional geographic boundaries, the opening of the Soviet bloc, and the widening of the international marketplace (characterized by a proliferation of multinational conglomerates), first led in the early 1980s to burgeoning productivity and then to a lively world economy. Japan and the Far East became particularly significant, and the eighties spiraled into a frenzy of dealmaking and conspicuous consumption on a previously unknown scale. When this fragile economy collapsed in 1987, the values of capitalism were called into question. Other, even more sober reflections accompanied it, as the AIDS epidemic altered sexual behavior, suddenly returning it to a pre-birth control austerity in some quarters, and shrouding sexual attraction in a veil of danger. Women and men who previously made up to attract suitors now gave a second thought to appearing overtly sexual.

Makeup artist Kevyn Aucoin (who helped define the polished, evolving image of the 90s) saw the look in the early 1980s, as "a real white male view of women as Barbie dolls—very glamorous and voluptuous. There was a lot of *big* hair, *big* makeup, *big* breasts." Later in the eighties, neutral, nonspecific colors in cosmetics were ascendant. Andrea Robinson, now president of Ultima II, introduced Revlon's line The Nakeds in 1988 "for nineties women comfortable with who they are, in control of their destiny." The healthy-looking robust allure of well-rounded, gym-toned bodies replaced the waif-like proportions of the sixties and seventies, as the fear of being considered "ill" entered society's subconscious.

Aerobics-primed women were ubiquitous in the

ALY WITH CLAW HAND, THE
SURREAL THING SERIES,
NEW YORK, 1987.
Photograph by Matthew Rolston.
Courtesy Fahey/Klein Gallery,
Los Angeles.

workplace. Their somewhat improved access to higher education, to career opportunities, and to increased pay engendered a backlash against the feminist arguments espoused in the 1970s. Susan Faludi's 1991 best-selling book, *Backlash,* summed up the cost to a new generation of women who had accepted the hard-fought gains of the seventies as a given. Yet women continued to feel the pressure to live schizophrenic lives that required businesslike austerity in the workplace and unthreatening sensuality in the home. The difficulties of resolving the dual and contradictory demands on the feminine personality remained significant, and the image of Superwoman, who tried to be all things to all people in her life, was the subject of numerous articles in the feminine press.

In fashion and beauty the 1980s was a time of expansion into lucrative markets. Yves Saint Laurent went public, Christian Lacroix became the first new couture house in twenty years, Azzedine Alaïa offered his homage to the body, and Japanese, Italian, and American designers confirmed their presence in Paris. The "luxury goods market" developed at an alarming rate, feeding the frenzied appetite of the newly successful business class.

Japanese influence was ascendant, and designers such as Issey Miyake, Yohji Yamamoto, and Rei Kawakubo dominated the international scene. Although Miyake had been shown in Paris since the early seventies, he reached his apogee in 1980, when he was given a retrospective at the Musée des Arts Décoratifs in Paris—one of the first foreign designers to be awarded such an honor. The exhibition catalog (photographed by Irving Penn, with makeup by Tyen) became a reference for the 1980s new hybrid beauty. The image of the oriental face was rendered universal by Tyen's choice of neutral, almost tan foundation to give the skin a healthy glow, black liner to lend the eyes exotic depth, and pale lipstick to give the lips a warm roundness. This was a great departure from the traditional vision of oriental beauty as geisha-like, with white skin, red lips, and rouged cheeks.

Ethnicity, so strictly defined in the 1970s, was now free to wear an "international face." As the Japanese designers overtook the runways, black, white, and Asian women all appeared wearing their clothes. In a memorable collection designed by Rei Kawakubo in 1981 under the name Comme des Garçons, strategically torn clothing was worn by pale-faced models with underlined eyes, unrouged lips, and black smudges artfully placed on the cheeks and forehead. The fashion press immediately dubbed the look "battered child" and denounced the makeup (by English makeup artist Linda Mason) as denigrating to women. Mason defended her work, arguing its artistic relevance to the clothing, but the event ushered in an entirely new view of the fashion show

spectacle, acknowledging its distance from the streets and stressing its evocative, rather than pragmatic, function.

The work of Tunisian-born Azzedine Alaïa became a signal counterpoint to the voluminous folds of Japanese fashions. Reviving the sixties miniskirt (but conceived this time for a woman's body, not a girl's) in stretch-tube materials, Alaïa eulogized the curvaceous female body in motion. He featured distinctly multiracial models with sensual proportions, and his clothing depended on structure more than material. His makeup characteristically recommended a heightened "natural" look, one of oiled surfaces and glossy lips.

Jean-Paul Gaultier also charted new territories, using pornography, film, and the stage as inspiration, and he often showed women's bodies more than the clothes to be worn on them. Gaultier's look was essential 1980s: postmodern confusion. His fashion shows had a Las Vegas feel, with their parading animals, transvestites, female impersonators, men and women wearing androgynous costumes, and models of all ages, shapes, and nationalities. His ads featured theatrical makeup, as well as gray-haired women dressed in fashion usually seen on teenage girls.

Christian Lacroix opened his couture house with his signature "pouf" fashion of 1987, heralded as "a circus of astonishment and innovation." Paul Audrain, a former Lacroix president, explained the appetite for Lacroix's heated color and elaborate ornament: "New social and cultural trends have put the 70s into reverse. There is a new emphasis on sexual values and individuality." Elite was chic again, and debutantes were once more in the news. The Princess of Wales was the world's most photographed bride, along with the Duchess of York and Princess Gloria von Thurn und Taxis. Personifications of the eighties image of conspicuous luxury, they became the poster girls of consumerism.

Karl Lagerfeld, who had been restructuring the Chanel image since 1983, transformed the classic Chanel suit into an original, modern, ultra-chic look. Working with makeup artists Heidi Morawetz and Dominique Moncourtois, he defined the glamour that would color the end of the decade. It was that of a pampered young ingénue with white skin, wearing matte makeup, soft neutral colors, and bright red lips. The look—subtly altered "bourgeois classical"—became as popular as Chanel's monogrammed, chain-link accessories.

As the 1980s drew to a close, personal style gained new value over the ready-made. More visually sophisticated than any previous generation, and in every country balancing extraordinary new pressures, women surprised designers by turning to clothes they felt at home in. Interest in high fashion waned as the world

economy fell into a recession, and "accessible" fashion, incorpo-
rating makeup as *de rigueur*, advanced. In the 1990s, international
cosmetics conglomerates required a well-defined corporate image.
Multitalented artist Serge Lutens, for example, had been hired by
Shiseido (in 1980) to restructure their corporate look and streamline control of both advertising and product.

Lutens was a precursor of the exotic aesthetic that
informed the Japanese movement. Formerly at Dior's cosmetics
division, Lutens had been a leader in cosmetic design and color
conception since the late 1960s. At Shiseido, Lutens's vision was
given free rein with makeup, perfume, and choice of models.
Lutens discussed his philosophy in a 1992 interview with the
author: "I invent personages outside time, outside fashion. I don't
believe that it is wise to show a dream face which all women want
to imitate (but could never attain), but rather a suggestion of a
mood, a texture, a color. I don't care to sell virility or sensuality in
a bottle, but rather the suggestion of eternity." Lutens imagined a
fantastic dreamscape of costumes, accessories, and jewels, creating in his ads scenes inspired by Malevich, by the black-eyed
women of Modigliani, and by the forms and colors of nature.
Lutens claimed that the function of makeup in the 1980s was not
to rejuvenate or to camouflage but to "make evident the expression
of a face, to design it more than to color it." He added, "Makeup is
a decor with two sides—one, the everyday, is a makeup of polite-
ness, quickly done, clean, sober, matte, transparent, and absolutely
natural. The other (which I prefer) is a makeup of expression, with
high heels, red lips, and the comedy of seduction. For this makeup, one should not hesitate to exaggerate, even to shock."

The use of ethnically diverse models really only became
widespread in the decade of the 1980s. Once the exclusive proper-
ty of fashion houses, supermodels like Naomi Campbell, Cindy
Crawford, Paulina Porizkova, Christy Turlington, Linda Evangelista
and others became arbiters of beauty themselves, promoting a
host of products. The emotional, often primitive thinking that
yields a cultural moment's assessment of what beauty is certainly
underwent a profound change as a generation brought up on television came of age in the satellite-dish era. Eighties television
made Bill Cosby an American star, brought images of middle-class
black families into millions of homes, and made athletes such as
Florence Griffith-Joyner and Debby Thomas symbols of racial
pride and of a new female sensibility. Two extraordinarily successful series, *Dallas* and *Dynasty*, featured powerful older women as
seductresses. The actresses who played these roles—Joan Collins,
Linda Evans, and Linda Gray—immediately became beauty icons.

In advertising, minorities (perhaps because they appeared

Above: A RETRO LOOK TO
MAKEUP'S PAST. BOOTS NO.
7 LIPSTICK "THAT WON'T
COME OFF" ADVERTISE-
MENT, 1988.
Photograph by Tony McGee.
Courtesy Boots Cosmetics.

more interesting, more exotic, or more recognizable) were in
increased demand. The pervading trend toward minimalism in
makeup encouraged this tendency, as one of the reservations
about using dark-skinned models had been that it was difficult to
see blush or eye shadow on dark skin. Non-Caucasian models
were first widely seen in the mid-1960s, when the American Flori
Roberts launched the first major cosmetics line for black skin.
Other companies followed, like Gazelle with their 1987 line containing skin-care products specifically designed to capture the
enormous black market. In the 1980s, multinational companies
conversely decided that women of color and older women did not
want to be singled out and thenceforth included all skin colors in
standard color lines.

Reinvention had
become a way of life in the
eighties, especially for those
in the public eye, and the
quest for a perfect beauty,
whether achieved through

I DON'T CARE TO SELL VIRILITY OR SENSUALITY IN A BOTTLE, BUT RATHER THE SUGGESTION OF ETERNITY

total image, makeup, or plastic surgery, was unending. Actress and
solo artist Cher transformed herself from the original sixties hippie
songstress into the forty-something siren she is today—with a little
help from the surgeon's knife and a killer exercise routine. The
accessibility of a rebuilt image stemmed from sheer consumerism:
every individual now had the opportunity to *buy* an identity, via
new jeans, cars, rock and roll records—or a different face.

Pop singers Michael Jackson and Madonna, model Linda
Evangelista, and artist Cindy Sherman were all important references in these trends. The myriad transformations of Michael
Jackson, from child star to megastar, freely mixed influences and
images from many genres and traditions—science fiction, horror,
soul, and male and female impersonation. From his Liz Taylor
eyebrows and Mediterranean spitfire eyeliner to the altered nose
and the skin that eased its way from cocoa brown to café au lait,
Jackson's media-savvy persona was, and is, one of a master
manipulator. Using makeup, plastic surgery, and clothing, Jackson
calls on adulthood and childhood at the same time, offers decadence in the guise of innocence, and plays endlessly with poly-
morphously perverse fancies. Madonna, too, shuffled images as
cannily as a poker player (from punk to glam to futurist to fifties
vixen), with virtually every new record marking a shift. Boy George
had also made cross-dressing hip in the early eighties with his
carefully cultivated image. But after the highs and lows of club
culture, he rejected the material world, shaved off his dreadlocks,
and reemerged as the ultimate karma chameleon—a Hare Krishna.

Right: **ZOMBIE MAKEUP: A DARK-RIMMED, HOLLOW-EYED VIEW OF THE FASHION FUTURE. UNTITLED, SHOT FOR ITALIAN** *VOGUE,* **GERMANY, 1984.**
Photograph by Peter Lindbergh.

Above left: **CONSULTATION
BEFORE THE KNIFE, THE
NEEDLE, THE SAW AND THE
SANDER: PLASTIC SURGERY,
1993.**
Photograph by Raymond Meier.

Right: **HYDRATING MASK, 1993.**
Photograph by Raymond Meier.

The model Linda Evangelista (with the help of photographer Steven Meisel) played with more cosmetic aspects of the art of transformation. Her remarkable physical conversions were demystified when Meisel described the process in a 1987 article in *Allure*: "I saw her wide nose, full cheeks, and weak chin and knew I had to light her from the side of her face so it looked thinner. Then we went in the makeup room, and began the surgery." By surgery, Meisel meant pruning the eyebrows, arranging the long, straggly hair into a "Park Avenue Bouffant, like Baby Jane Holzer, or Jacqueline Kennedy," and outlining her lips to make her mouth look larger. During each successive photo session, Meisel further manipulated Evangelista's image. Changing her hair color from brown to platinum blonde and then to flaming red, the evolution became her signature, celebrating her ability to manipulate her own image without touching the personality underneath. At first criticized as artificial, the process threw Evangelista herself, who complained, after cutting her hair: "I lost all of my confidence...I was canceled from all of the shows in Italy." She had to admit, "It took a while to catch on."

The model as changeling challenged the unwritten rules of beauty. Most women, models especially, searched long and hard for what they considered their most attractive makeup and coiffure—and kept that look as long as possible. "You wouldn't have Cheryl Tiegs putting on a black wig and doing weird things," remarked Meisel. Transformation, as interpreted by Meisel, presents possibility and promise. "There is no perfect beauty," he explained. "I prefer humanness."

The artist Cindy Sherman has dedicated much of her postmodern artistic career to the art of transformation. Since the late 1970s, she has taken pictures of herself in multiple poses, all of which summon up scenes or images from old movies, magazines, TV shows, fairy tales, or nightmares. At first, her "characters" were all women, both female stereotypes and archetypes: the all-American minx, the mysterious film noir heroine, the dark European vamp. She then began to play with more androgynous figures, evoking samurai warriors, sheiks, clowns, and freaks—each time creating a brand-new personage with makeup and costumes. Her images became increasingly powerful—especially as a statement about the ceaseless game of image manipulation so prevalent in the feminine perception of self.

As an augury of our culture's embracing of "Image World," MTV (Music Television), launched in 1981, underscored the domination of the prepared, orchestrated, and transforming visual icon in public consciousness. MTV permanently changed the way music was marketed and perceived, awarding a uniquely powerful role to modern pop figures. By fusing three of the most compelling new media of the twentieth century—television, radio, and recorded music—into a new kind of communication monster, MTV packaged information as sensation. Lionizing beauty over talent, surface over substance, it launched a whole new slate of colorful performers pushing a very different aesthetic—androgynous, proudly fashion-savvy, and bank-book serious about their own pop image. They used makeup as art, constantly staging their various metamorphoses to keep up interest and selling power.

MTV's cultural effect was immediate, influencing media from film to TV to advertising, and by mid-1983, the hegemony of quick cuts, brutally fractured story lines, and dreamlike visions was established. James Farber in *Rolling Stone* magazine noted: "MTV is the ultimate argument against logic; images are simply thrown at you without regard for consequence. The only point is to be aroused and, of course, to avoid boredom."

As image power crested, the allure of transformation rose. The proliferation of surgically altered faces suddenly made the "man-made" face desirable: "That face has such reassuring aspects—whether or not it looks natural, its features are tailored to fall within accepted norms and it eschews any lines or wrinkles that remind us of suffering, aging, and death," said an article in *Mirabella* in 1992. Between 1981 and 1988 there was a 63 percent rise in cosmetic surgery in the United States, according to the American Society of Plastic and Reconstructive Surgeons. Dr. Michael Pertschuk, one of the founders of the University of Pennsylvania's Center for Human Appearance, concurred: "The more people do it, the more it becomes socially acceptable." From sunspots to saddlebags, surgeons began rearranging skin and bones as casually as furniture. Even the nomenclature became cosmetized: "skin resurfacing," or "peels," were mild-sounding terms for a bloody, painful process involving the removal of a layer of the face.

Tattooing (used to reshape lips, eyebrows, and even the aureole that surrounds the nipple) was increasingly used during the 1980s to permanently correct irregularities that cosmetics and makeup only temporarily disguised. Tattoos could ultimately replace all need for shadow, eyeliner, and lipstick. Rarefied techniques claiming to derive from Buddhist religious practice, like implanting five layers of gold wires under the skin to prevent wrinkles were reported in Singapore. In another advance, computer images could now act as windows through which plastic surgeons could clearly see their patients' tissues, muscles, and bone structure. Based on these electronic images, blueprints could be developed for appropriate surgical procedures, virtually eliminating hazard.

Dr. Darrick Antel and Dr. James W. Smith, plastic surgeons at St. Luke's-Roosevelt Hospital Center, researched what Antel called "today's ideal standard of beauty." Their study combined computer imaging with age-old rules of aesthetics to calibrate the "perfect" human face. Overlaying drawing paper on a patient's photograph and using an armory of "ideal" micromeasurements (obtained by measuring a battery of Ford models and referring to L. G. Farhas's canon *The Anthropometry of Head and Face in Medicine*) they produced a computer image of the possible alterations. Changes could be made if the patient was deficient in the cheek area, or had too much bulk in the jaw. The adjustments were often minor, subtle, but from the patient's viewpoint, profound. This pursuit of perfection, Smith pointed out, was uniquely relevant in the fast-moving world of the 1980s: "Now women of every age want to improve their appearance, and more and more plastic surgeons are working to discover what can be done to change them from average to exceptional. You could say it's cosmetic surgery coming of age." (One telling statistic emerged from the craze: 90 percent of plastic surgery patients are women; 90 percent of plastic surgeons are men.)

While the face is the focus of most surgery, conceptions of the body underwent reconsideration in the eighties and nineties. The shift from the tubular, adolescent-boy shape that dominated fashion since Twiggy came on the scene, to the latter-day Junos flaunting breasts and hips that are now current, is just a new round in an age-old cycle regarding the female form. Art historian Kenneth Clark wrote in his classic work, *The Nude,* that "Prehistoric images of women are of two kinds; the bulging statuette from Paleolithic caves which emphasize female attributes till they are little more than symbols of fertility, and the marble dolls of the Cyclades in which the unruly human body has already undergone a geometric discipline." The reblooming of the female figure coincides with the largest baby boom since the postwar period (the era of Jayne Mansfield and Marilyn Monroe). And even if Madonna's armored breastplates scarcely radiate procreative fertility, they do say "health." Fran Weiss, a New York psychotherapist, pointed out: "People are leery of thin; thin could be sick, it could be *the* sickness." So the reign of svelte has given way again to a new body image in which *plump* may still be a four-letter word, but if a full figure is firm, then it is the nineties ideal.

Beauty companies, while long dedicated to preventive measures designed to keep skin looking younger longer, are now

Left: **PALOMA PICASSO, LIPS, NEW YORK, 1989.**
Photograph by Matthew Rolston.
Courtesy Fahey/Klein Gallery,
Los Angeles.

Above: **LIPSTICK STILL-LIFE, 1994.**
Photograph by Raymond Meier.

THE MORE PEOPLE DO IT, THE MORE IT BECOMES SOCIALLY ACCEPTABLE

devising products specifically for older women. By the year 2000, the ranks of those over fifty will swell by millions, and their annual spending power by more than $200 billion. Delaying or counteracting the effects of aging has become a priority for these consumers, the first real generation of sun-worshippers whose chronic skin damage is in evidence. Indeed, in the last decade, aging has come to be seen as a disease, treatable by drugs or surgery. Retin A, invented by Albert Kligman and once used to fight acne, is now regularly prescribed for wrinkles.

But despite the seeming flurry of new cosmetics, a plateau has been reached. An article in *Forbes* in 1989 flatly announced that "The growth in this $16 billion business had practically vanished, and costs of advertising and promotion were escalating." By 1989 sales were rising at a sluggish 6 percent, and the outlook for beauty as a business wasn't good. Consolidations swept the industry worldwide. Fabergé and Elizabeth Arden were acquired by Unilever at a cost of $2 billion. Proctor and Gamble bought Noxell, the maker of both the Cover Girl and Clarion makeup lines. Multinational companies became a significant force at an unprecedented level. An article in *Marketing Cosmetics and Toiletries* in 1993 stated: "It's not so much acquisitions that has agitated the cosmetics industry as the companies doing the acquiring: P&G and Unilever bring with them great experience with mundane products like soap and toilet paper, sparking disdain in the glitzy cosmetics trade: but they also bring mammoth marketing clout, sparking fear....In contrast to the glitzy, intuitive world of cosmetics, Unilever and P&G are the habitats of organization men in gray-flannel suits." The effect on small and midsize cosmetics companies was substantial. Industry watchers predicted that smaller brands, which heretofore could differentiate themselves, would now simply disappear.

Consumer trends were also experiencing a watershed change, as women bought a smaller and smaller percentage of their cosmetics at department stores such as Bloomingdale's, Nordstrom, Harrods, or the Bon Marché. In 1985, big, upscale stores had accounted for almost 18 percent of cosmetics sales, but by 1989, the number descended to 15 percent. Mass-market product lines such as Revlon, Boots, Maybelline, and Cover Girl redrafted themselves with a more sophisticated, upscale image. In 1988, 28 percent of all makeup was sold through supermarkets, while drugstores sold another 27 percent.

How did this sales revolution happen? It was attributed in part to social realities, as women got out in the business world and thus took a more businesslike attitude toward expenditures. In fact, the quality and quantity of products available in drug-

stores and supermarkets had increased dramatically during the 1980s. The choices in the low-and medium-price product lines expanded and improved so that moving down from department store offerings was no longer a severe compromise. A hypoallergenic, ophthalmologist-tested mascara from Maybelline sold for $3.65, raising, for many women, a question about the intelligence of paying $17 for the Yves Saint Laurent version. The eighties customer was more confident, more independent—and much less likely to need the reassurance of buying a product for its image without regard to its quality.

The shift paradoxically reflected a total acceptance of cosmetics; once viewed as luxury items, they had become necessities. The distinction affected spending attitudes, as one Los Angeles beautician explained: "Drive up in a BMW and you make a statement about your purse and your taste—but no one knows whether you are made up with a $3 lipstick or a $17 lipstick."

"One touch of nature makes the whole world kin," wrote Shakespeare in *Troilus and Cressida*, and finally the "three Green Rs"—reduce, reuse, recycle—took hold of the cosmetics world. "By the mid-eighties, we realized something was happening in the market," Leonard Lauder noted in a 1994 interview with the author, "with consumer preferences shifting toward simplicity, toward more natural products and overtones of oriental thinking." Lauder recognized the concept that Anita Roddick, originator of the Body Shop, had embraced since 1976. One of the first successful companies specializing in earth-friendly products, the Body Shop was known for its biodegradable fruit- and vegetable-based treatments, based on age-old recipes and remedies whose formulation openly decried animal testing of cosmetics. Its packaging was recyclable, its "Trade Not Aid" program sponsored indigenous projects like papermaking in Nepal and blue-corn harvesting in New Mexico, and its sales staff (as a condition of employment that emphasized the company's own ethos and social responsibility) was required to donate time to community service. Other British companies went even farther. Beauty Without Cruelty, the first to create a complete line of cosmetics not tested on animals, reserves 48 percent of its profits for animal welfare. Aveda, another early advocate of plant-derived compounds, opened in Minnesota in the eighties, while old pharmacies like Kiehl's (founded in 1851 in New York), long known among actors and models for their organic products, enjoyed a renaissance.

Origins, an affiliate of Estée Lauder, was launched in 1990 as Lauder's own "be kind to nature" brand. William Lauder, grandson of the founder, noted in a *Women's Wear Daily* article in 1991: "There was a consumer revolution going on. We were dealing with

things that were 5,000 years old, marrying the very best of nature with the best of science." Origins's philosophy corresponded to the ideology, with 120 items in the line all organized according to natural skin tones in three ranges: beige to tan, peach to russet, and ivory to pink. The line also included environmental fragrances and sensory therapy products in recycled containers, and customers were invited to return empties. Based on the idea that color derives from nature and that too much artificial help violates a woman's natural beauty, Origins was, as one buyer said succinctly, "anti-makeup makeup." Nevertheless, the popular no-makeup look of 1990s models Kate Moss and Kristen McMenamy did little to disguise the ubiquity of cosmetics: in 1991 twenty billion dollars were spent worldwide on the beauty business.

But by mid-decade the no-makeup look had been once again painted over. "Heavily shaded lips and eyes are back," pronounced influential British makeup artist Mary Greenwell (known in the 80s for her delicate and feminine makeup style) in French *Vogue*, reflecting the fact that the only predictable thing about change in beauty, as in life, is change itself.

During the last decade the really new technical advances in makeup were spearheaded by the Japanese. Fundamental to Japanese cosmetics is the implicit belief that makeup plays an important part in the way a woman regards and projects herself. Marrying this attitude with innovation, Japanese chemists have transformed the industry. Shiseido's offerings have been especially impressive, including their compact foundation that can be used wet or dry. Its formula depends on one magic ingredient, a pigment with a double lipid layer, and utilizes a process that allows UV filters and moisturizers to be incorporated into powders. Shiseido's products are packaged in streamlined black, biomorphic shapes that

REFLECTING THE FACT THAT THE ONLY PREDICTABLE THING ABOUT CHANGE IN BEAUTY, AS IN LIFE, IS CHANGE ITSELF

feel good in the hand and have a classic yet futuristic elegance. Shiseido's inorganic photochromic pigments that change color according to the amount of light they are exposed to, increasing UV protection accordingly, are a similar breakthrough. Kanebo and Shu Uemura also developed independent yet international images and marketing strategies that put them at the forefront of the cosmetics industry.

But between the language of science and the look of art, what does the future hold in store for cosmetics? The possibilities defy the imagination: a sunscreen tablet to protect against UVA, UVB, and any still to-be-discovered damaging rays? A way to

Preceding page:
FRUIT COCKTAIL, 1993.
Photograph by Raymond Meier.

Left: **BEAUTY MAKEOVER, 1994.**
*Photograph by Wayne Maser/
A & C Anthology.*

Top left: **SKIN DERMABRA-SION, 1989.**
Photograph by Marlin Minks.

Center left: UNTITLED (YOUR BODY IS A BATTLEGROUND), **1989, BARBARA KRUGER.**
Photographic/silkscreen/vinyl 112 x 112", Courtesy Mary Boone Gallery, New York.

Below left: **DOUBLE EXPOSURE SHOWING PLACEMENTS FOR SILICONE FACIAL IMPLANTS, 1991.**
Photograph by Marlin Minks.

Right: **CAT EYES, 1993.**
Photograph by Raymond Meier.

prevent hair from graying, not just to camouflage it? Or, more elaborately, a scanner to identify exact skin tone and match foundations to it instantly? An all-in-one foundation that adjusts on the face for every complexion...a purse-size laser that zaps blemishes and wrinkles...a lotion that dissolves cellulite in the sun...a heat-sensor manicure machine into which you just slide your hand while watching your room-size 3-D HD-TV? The first two scenarios, according to Nicholas T. Love, professor of dermatology at UCLA, are already in the realm of possibility, not fantasy.

Part science, part sci-fi, part theater and whimsy, one thing about the face of the next millennium is certain: beauty in the twenty-first century, whatever fantastic form it chooses to take, will certainly be as sought-after as it has proved to be in the past.

PRODUCTS

THE BIG NEWS OF THE EIGHTIES WAS POLYMERS, RESULTING IN VARIOUS FILM FORMS TO COAT LASHES AND INCREASE MASCARA'S LONGEVITY. SHISEIDO'S WATERPROOF MASCARA, ELIZABETH ARDEN'S TWICE AS THICK, AND ESTÉE LAUDER'S MORE THAN MASCARA WERE POPULAR EXAMPLES. IN THE NINETIES MASCARA FORMULAS ADDED KERATINS, A STRENGTHENING PROTEIN. THERE WERE EVEN GREATER REFINEMENTS LIKE PRINCESS MARCELLA BORGHESE'S MAXIMUM MASCARA FOR SENSITIVE EYES, WHICH INCORPORATED SOOTHING BOTANICALS, AS DID LANCÔME'S AQUACILS AND STENDAHL'S MASCARA SOYEUX AU KSF.

BOUTIQUE COMPANIES SPRANG UP, SUCH AS BOBBI BROWN'S NATURAL, BROWN-BASED, SUBTLE SHADINGS, OR M.A.C (MAKE-UP ART COSMETICS), THE BRAINCHILD OF CANADIAN MAKEUP ARTIST FRANK R. TOSCAN, CREATED IN 1984 TO DEVELOP PROFESSIONAL MAKEUP PRODUCTS. WITHIN WEEKS OF ITS ARRIVAL AT HENRI BENDEL, NEW YORK, M.A.C. WAS OUTSELLING EVERY OTHER LINE. WITH NO RECOGNIZABLE FACE AS ITS CORPORATE IDENTITY (UNTIL IT SIGNED DRAG QUEEN RUPAUL IN 1995), NO FREE GIFTS, AND NO ADVERTISING, M.A.C. REFUSES TO PLAY THE BEAUTY GAME. THEIR STUDIO LINE, COLOR CORRECTED FOR FILM AND TV, IS THE FIRST TO CONTAIN SUNBLOCKS AGAINST THE HEAT OF STUDIO LIGHTS.

PART SCIENCE, PART SCI-FI, PART THEATER AND WHIMSY

COMPANIES IN THE FUTURE WILL INVEST MILLIONS IN COMPUTERS FOR PREDICTING PERSONAL BEAUTY CHANGES AND IN SKIN ANALYZERS FOR COLOR, TEXTURE, AND BALANCE. YVES SAINT LAURENT ESTABLISHED A BEAUTY CENTER JUST OUTSIDE PARIS, WITH A SATELLITE DISH ON THE ROOF TO PULL IN INFORMATION DAILY ABOUT RAW MATERIALS, FORMULAS, AND SKIN FROM AROUND THE WORLD. INCREASINGLY, FIRMS SHUN ANIMAL TESTING.

"BEAUTY IS NOT ABOUT LOOKING YOUNG," CLINIQUE POSTERS PROCLAIMED IN A REVOLUTIONARY AD CAMPAIGN. VICTORIA WOODINGER IN *MODERN SALON*, APRIL 1994, NOTED THAT THE FIFTY-YEAR-OLD CUSTOMER CONTROLS 70 PERCENT OF THE AVERAGE U.S. HOUSEHOLD'S NET WORTH, ADVISING BEAUTY SALONS TO SHIFT THEIR FOCUS. THEODORE

Top: UNTITLED, **1984,**
FRANCESCO CLEMENTE.
Woodcut, 22 1/2 x 16 3/4".
Edition 200.
Published by Crown Point Press.

Above: UNTITLED #153. SELF
PORTRAIT, **1985, CINDY**
SHERMAN. *Courtesy Metro*
Pictures Gallery, New York.

Right: **MAKEUP QUOTIDIAN :**
POCKETBOOK CONTENTS,
1993.
Photograph by Raymond Meier.

FITZPATRICK OF HARVARD UNIVERSITY DISCOVERED PSAORALENES, WHICH ENHANCE THE ABILITY OF WHITE SKIN TO WITHSTAND SUN SAFELY. PHOSPHOLIDS ADDED TO MOISTURIZERS FOR OLDER SKIN MADE CELL MEMBRANES STRONGER AND MORE WATERTIGHT. ALPHA-HYDROXY ACIDS TO SLOUGH OFF OLD CELLS BECAME COMMON (CHANEL'S DAY LIFT, ESTÉE LAUDER'S FRUITION, AND LA PRAIRIE'S AGE MANAGEMENT SYSTEMS ARE THREE EXAMPLES). BY 1990 COSMETICS HAD TRULY COME FULL CIRCLE FROM THE MORTAR AND PESTLE PREPARATIONS OF CUCUMBER, MINT, AND VERBENA IN GREAT-GRANDMOTHER'S KITCHEN TO COMMERCIAL PRODUCTS MADE WITHOUT PRESERVATIVES, LIKE ICE BY GERMAINE MONTEIL. IN 1980 TWO FRENCH FIRMS LED THE VANGUARD WITH ANTI-FREE-RADICAL PRODUCTS, LIKE OENAGRALES BY ROCHAS AND GUERLAIN'S EVOLUTION. IN 1981 CHR OF ULTIMA II FINALLY EMERGED WITH A STABLE WATER-SOLUBLE COLLAGEN SKIN-COMPATIBLE CREAM. ANOTHER INNOVATION IN 1981 WAS THE FIRST DRY OIL FOR THE SKIN, CALLED PEAU D'ANGE, BY JEANNE PIAUBERT. ESTÉE LAUDER'S CONCENTRATED HYDRATED CREAM, NIGHT REPAIR, OFFERED YET ANOTHER BIOTECHNOLOGICAL ADVANCE (WHICH SHISEIDO ALSO USED TWO YEARS LATER) IN THE FORM OF THE INGREDIENT HIALURONIC ACID. NINETEEN EIGHTY WAS ALSO THE YEAR OF LIPOSOMES, WHOSE ABILITY TO PENETRATE THE DERMIS MORE DEEPLY OFFERED THE PROMISE OF EXTRA EFFECTIVENESS. ROSE-MARIE HANDJANI OF LANCÔME CREATED NIOSÔME PLUS, WHILE DIOR, IN COLLABORATION WITH THE FAMOUS PARIS HOSPITAL, INSTITUT PASTEUR, MARKETED ITS NEW LIPOSOME PRODUCT, CAPTURE, WHILE LANCASTER LAUNCHED THERAPY. DOMINIQUE SZABO OF GUERLAIN CREATED ARGUABLY THE MOST BEAUTIFUL MAKEUP PRODUCT OF THE DECADE, MÉTÉORITES (1987), TINY BALLS OF SPACE-AGE COLORED POWDERS. IN THE SAME YEAR PACO RABANNE LAUNCHED THE FIRST ANTI-WRINKLE PRODUCT FOR MEN, CALLED CONCENTRÉ ACTIF RESTRUCTURANT.

1900 Paris hosts the first Olympic games in which women may participate.

Face enameling, worn by Queen Alexandra, gains acceptance among the rich, while the natural look of rouge is still preferred by the *demi-monde*.

The virtues of soap and hygiene begin to be extolled everywhere; English actress Lillie Langtry endorses Pear's soap.

Dorothy Gray opens a salon in New York.

1901 Exposition Universale des Arts Décoratifs opens in Paris.

Death of Queen Victoria, at 82 years old, Queen of England and Ireland since 1837.

1902 The Chinese Imperatrice, Tseu Hi (1835–1908), outlaws the bandaging of women's feet.

Helena Rubinstein, a young Pole, opens her first beauty salon in Melbourne, Australia, calling it Valaze.

Dr. Theodor Koller publishes a technical book on cosmetics.

1903 Marie Curie receives the Nobel prize in physics.

Léon Bakst designs Nijinsky's body paint for *L'Après-midi d'un faune*.

Russian dancer Anna Pavlova conquers the western world with her rendition of *Giselle*.

1904 Guerlain's *Crème Secret de Bonne Femme* is created: the oldest existing cream.

1905 Psychoanalysis begins with treatment of women—Freud publishes *Three Essays*, introducing his theory on penis envy.

1906 Sidonie Gabrielle Colette makes a scandal on the Paris stage as a music-hall mime.

Charles Nestle invents the permanent wave machine in London.

Suffragette movements are active in England, France, and USA; 250,000 suffragettes protest in the streets of London.

USA: Pure Food and Drug Act establishes controls on promotion, yet leaves cosmetic producers free to mix any ingredients into makeup.

1907 Liquid nail polish replaces the nail buffer.

The Marcel Wave is invented.

Eugene Schueller creates the first synthetic hair color, baptized Aureole, and soon creates his company called L'Oréal.

Baroness d'Orchamps publishes *Tous les Secrets de la Femme*.

1908 Helena Rubinstein opens her first institute of beauty in London.

1909 Elizabeth Arden establishes her first institute of beauty in New York.

1910 Paul Poiret's revolutionary line *Libérateur* frees women of corsets and introduces oriental style costumes of turbans and hobbie skirts.

Guerlain's Shalimar replaces weak lavender scents with strong musks, marketing them to the liberated 'New Woman'.

1911 Vitagraph produces silent films in Hollywood, launching actresses such as Clara Kimball Young, Norma Talmage, and Mabel Normand.

1912 Madeleine Vionnet opens her Paris fashion house.

Elizabeth Cady Stanton, Charlotte Perkins Gilman, and Inez Milholland lead the New York Suffragette Rally, wearing makeup!

Sherley Amendment to Pure Food and Drug Act (1906) tightens the ban on mislabeling.

Vitamins are synthesized.

1913 Baron Adolf de Meyer is employed by *Vogue* magazine.

1914 Max Factor develops "flexible greasepaint," a thin colored base, for films.

First World War begins.

Actress Theda Bara, also known as 'the vamp', is introduced as the first Hollywood sex symbol in *A Fool There Was*.

1915 Maurice Levy designs the first American made lipsticks and eyebrow pencils in metal slide tubes: the first metal containers for makeup.

T. L. Williams sees Mabel, his sister, using petroleum jelly on her eye-lashes and markets the concept; he later names his company Maybelline.

1916 New York: Helena Rubinstein opens her first American salon.

First edition of British *Vogue* is published.

1917 The bobbed coiffure emerges as a true international fashion trend.

Mary Pickford, consecrated the "small fiancée of the world," becomes the most famous actress in cinema when *Rebecca of Sunnybrook Farm* is released.

Nail polish is commercialized by Cutex.

George Westmore becomes a permanent makeup force in Hollywood.

The February Revolution is launched by women workers in Petrograd, beginning the Russian Revolution.

1918 End of First World War.

1919 Lillian Gish and Mary Pickford become the ideal—vestal virgin "sweethearts"—in silent films such as David W. Griffith's *Le Lys Brisé*.

Beginning of *Toilette Requisites*, trade journal.

1920 Caron introduces Peau Fines, the first perfumed powder.

US Congress ratifies the 19th Amendment, giving women of the United States the right to vote on August 26.

Victor Margueritte's *La Garçonne* is published, creating the ideal of the short-haired, cigarette-smoking, sexually liberated young woman dressed in men's attire.

Aziza cosmetic company originates in Paris when Nina Sussman mixes a batch of mascara in her kitchen.

Death of the Empress Eugénie (94 yrs. old)—the woman for whom mascara was created.

Coco Chanel's simple classic suits and dresses of restricted color replace Poiret's exotic styles of the previous decade.

1921 Yardley opens its first salon in New York.

Launching of fragrances Chanel #5 and Chanel #22.

The first Miss America Pageant is held in Absecon Beach, Atlantic City, New Jersey.

1923 Invention of Kurlash, a tool for curling eyelashes.

John Robert Powers founds the first modeling agency in New York.

Poucher's *Encyclopedia of Cosmetics and Perfumery* is published.

1924 The vogue for African or Oceanic images invades France, sparking controversy.

1925 First true liquid nail lacquer is made available to the public.

Paris is crowned the center of artistic creation at the Exposition Universale des Arts Décoratifs.

USA: a government study is conducted to determine the necessity of a jewel tax on "makeup purses."

Guerlain launches the fragrance Shalimar.

1926 Josephine Baker performs her notorious *Revue Nègre*, and in the *Folies Bergère* at the Casino of Paris; she is consecrated the "Vénus d'Ebene."

Edouard Pinaud launches Mascara 612.

1927 Creation of the lipstick Rouge Baiser, which according to its publicity "permits a kiss."

Minnie Mouse appears with long eyelashes, a small skirt, and high heels.

Julius Penner AG, introduces an effective makeup preservative, paraben.

Caustic Poison Act and the Food, Drug, and Insecticide Administration are founded.

Greta Garbo stars in the silent film *Flesh and the Devil*.

1928 Jean Patou creates Huile de Caldée, the first sun lotion.

A beauty parlor is established as part of treatment for the patients of an Essex County, New Jersey insane asylum.

Max Factor develops Panchromatic Makeup, which was highly sensitive to light and shadow.

Clara Bow, Mae Murray, and Louise Brooks become the flappers of the twenties, starring in movies such as Clarence Badger's *It*.

1929 Reported cases of skin disease increases fifty percent in three years in the US, resulting from unsafe cosmetics ingredients.

Introduction of talking movies changes Hollywood.

Louise Brooks makes *Lulu*.

Jean Patou introduces a fashion collection with natural waistlines and longer dress hemlines.

Wall Street crashes and the Depression begins.

1930 New York: Charles and Martin Revson and Charles Lachman begin Revlon.

Elizabeth Arden invents the Eight Hour Cream.

Marlene Dietrich stars in Josef Von Sternberg's *Der blaue Engel* (The Blue Angel).

1931 Platinum tips are all the rage—an application of opaque silver polish to the tips of red enameled nails.

"Ethical" cosmetics are introduced by Schieffelin and Co., under the name Almay.

Jack Pierce's horror classic *Frankenstein* is released.

Food, Drug, and Insecticide Administration renamed Food and Drug Administration.

Jean Harlow stars in Frank Capra's *The Platinum Blond*.

1932 Betty Boop—animated sex pot—is drawn into the public eye.

USA: Cosmetic Tax Law levied on all products of "luxury definition."

Paris: Colette creates a salon of cosmetics where she sells her own beauty products.

1933 Lucien Lelong introduces a ready-made department, robes d'édition.

1934 The Hayes Production Code of Ethics, spurred by outrage at one Hollywood actress, Mae West, bars open sexuality in Hollywood films—the overtly sexual look of the twenties fades.

Elizabeth Arden opens her Maine Chance spa retreat.

1935 The House of Westmore is opened in Los Angeles.

Max Factor opens a salon in Los Angeles.

1936 Lancôme opens a salon in Paris.

Maquillage Dictionnaire de la Beauté is written by Nadia Grégoire Payot.

Abdication of the King of England in order to marry Wallis Simpson, future Duchess of Windsor.

Eugène Schüeller, founder of L'Oréal, invents the first line of suntan products, Ambre Solaire.

1937 Launching of a new feminine magazine *Marie Claire*, in France.

Schiaparelli launches her perfume Shocking, using a bottle inspired by Mae West's buxom figure.

Dr. Nadia Grégoire Payot, a dermatologist, opens her institute of beauty on the rue Castiglione, Paris.

Max Factor's Pan-Cake water-soluble foundation makes its appearance in film.

1938 Volupté introduces the first lip liner pencils.

Guerlain opens a salon, designed by artist Christian Bérard, on the Champs Elysées.

Food, Drug and Cosmetics Act first imposes penalties for products that were adulterated—containing dangerous or impure substances—or carried a deceptive label.

The Wheeler-Lea Amendment is passed, prohibiting misleading advertising.

Fabrication of the first pair of stockings out of the newly invented material, nylon.

1939 Declaration of Second World War.

1940 Helena Rubinstein launches her perfume, Heaven Scent.

Britain: Limitations of Supplies Order, makes petroleum and alcohol unavailable.

Mae West stars in *My Little*

Chickadee.

1941 Charles Moulton creates Wonder Woman comics.

1942 USA, July: War Production Board issues a classification of cosmetics as an inessential commodity, therefore limiting its production.

Peggy Sage, a French company famous for its nail polish, is launched.

A decree orders the recovery of America's cut hair for use as thread.

USA, October: War Production Board revokes order, realizing the importance cosmetics play for forces at home.

1943 A young American of Austrian origin launches her company: Estée Lauder.

Camouflage creams and anti-sunburn lipsticks are used on the battlefields.

Helena Rubinstein launches the first men's line in cosmetics, called Gourielli.

1945 French women gain the right to vote.

Ebony magazine is founded by John H. Johnson.

Elle magazine is started by Hélène Gordon-Lazareff.

End of Second World War.

1946 Bikini bathing suit invented.

$30 million a year spent on red lipstick in the USA.

The Breck Girl is introduced on the back cover of *Ladies' Home Journal.*

1947 Rita Hayworth stars in Charles Vidor's *Gilda.*

Paris: Christian Dior launches the "New Look;" women protest outside of Neiman Marcus department store waving placards which read 'DOWN WITH THE NEW LOOK', condemning the confining qualities of these new clothes.

Princess Elizabeth marries the Duke of Edinburgh.

1948 Helena Rubinstein invents Silk Film and Silk Tone, two new foundations made with pulverized silk filaments.

1949 Simone de Beauvoir publishes *The Second Sex.*

The Oeil de Biche (Doe Eye) look in eye-lining reigns, created by Etienne Aubrey.

1950 ROC becomes the first cosmetic company to define its product as hypoallergenic.

Audrey Hepburn introduces the gamine image.

Clairol creates the first one-step lightener and hair color and rocks the industry with the advertising campaign Does She...Or Doesn't She?

1951 Hubert and Michel d'Ornano create the new cosmetic company called Orlane.

1952 Simone Signoret stars in *Casque D'Or.*

Revlon launches its Fire and Ice campaign.

1953 Marilyn Monroe appears in *Gentlemen Prefer Blondes.*

Elizabeth II is crowned Queen of England.

Max Factor's Cream Puff (the first compact powder) is introduced with Ava Gardner as spokeswoman.

Youth gains its own identity with a label: "teenager."

1954 Max Factor invents Erase, to be used for hiding dark circles under the eyes.

Juvena, the first Swiss makeup company, is created.

1955 Playboy launches the nude centerfold.

Man-Tan, a self-tanning cosmetic for men, is invented.

1956 Aerosol containers revolutionize cosmetics application.

1957 ROC launches the first sun blocks for different skin types.

Brigitte Bardot stars in *And God Created Woman* (*Et Dieu Créa la Femme*).

Helena Rubinstein invents Mascaramatic, the first liquid mascara in a tube with a wand applicator.

1958 The Delaney Clause is added to Food, Drug and Cosmetics Act of 1938, which forbids the use of any substance found to produce cancer in laboratory animals.

1959 The Barbie doll is created.

1960 Enovid, the first birth control pill, is commercialized.

Hairspray is invented.

1961 Jacqueline Kennedy becomes First Lady.

Sophia Loren wins an Academy Award for her role in *Two Women.*

1962 The first modern bust cream, Tensur Bust, is released by Clarins.

The Twist arrives from France.

Helena Rubinstein creates her $35 Day of Beauty.

1963 Crème Abricot is developed by Christian Dior, to strengthen nails.

Cosmopolitan magazine is started by Helen Gurley Brown.

1964 Helena Rubinstein develops Long Lash Waterproof mascara.

Biba, London Mod shop, begins a mail-order business.

1965 The miniskirt is launched by Mary Quant and André Courrèges.

Flori Roberts launches the first major cosmetics line for black skin.

Jean Shrimpton becomes the Yardley "London Look" girl.

1966 Mary Quant introduces her own cosmetics line, produced by Gala.

New York: National Organization of Women—NOW—is established.

Twiggy, a.k.a. Lesley Hornby, is discovered.

1968 Naomi Sims is the first black woman to appear on the cover of *Life* magazine.

Clinique is started.

1969 Bienfait du Matin, the first protective hydrating cream with color, is developed by Lancôme.

Hand-held blow dryers are invented.

Large Biba store opens in London.

1970 Publication of Germaine Greer's *The Female Eunuch*

1971 *Klute, The Godfather,* and *A Clockwork Orange* are released.

1972 Equal Rights Amendment goes before the US Congress for ratification (where it subsequently fails).

David Bowie's *Ziggy Stardust* is released.

Squibb purchases Charles of the Ritz.

1973 Roe vs. Wade decision passes in US Supreme Court.

Revlon launches "plan cosmo," introducing *Charlie* perfume, the scent for the independent woman.

Publication of Betty Friedan's *The Feminine Mystique.*

1974 Rudi Gernreich produces the first thong bikini.

Steve Rubell opens the Studio 54 disco in New York.

Elizabeth Arden launches Visible Difference.

Beverly Johnson becomes American *Vogue's* first black cover girl.

1975 Chanel introduces its beauty line.

Sex Discrimination Act passed.

Margaux Hemingway signs $1 million contract to represent Babe Cosmetics.

Dolly Parton becomes an American icon when she hits #1 on the charts with three separate singles.

1976 Anita Roddick creates the Body Shop.

Hubert and Isabelle d'Ornano launch Sisley skin care products created with natural plant extracts.

Shere Hite publishes *The Hite Report,* reporting 3,000 women's blunt views on sex.

1977 First celebrity scent is marketed: Candice Bergen's Cie.

Way Bandy publishes *Designing Your Face.*

Clinique launches skin care line for men.

1978 La Prairie—Swiss makeup line using formulas created with a cell-extract base—is founded.

Shiseido funds Harvard physician, Dr. Daniel C. Tostesen, with $85 million, to conduct cosmetic research.

1979 Estée Lauder launches Prescriptives line.

1980 Niosome is created by Rose-Marie Handjani.

Serge Lutens is hired by Shiseido to restructure the corporation's image.

First annual Pharmaceuticals & Cosmetics Manufacturing Expo held in Chicago.

Azzedine Alaïa debuts his body hugging clothing.

1981 Ultima II emerges with a stable water-soluble collagen skin cream.

Peau d'Ange, the first dry oil for the skin, is invented by Jeanne Piaubert.

Sandra Day O'Connor appointed to the Supreme Court.

MTV (Music Television) is launched.

1982 Comme des Garçons shows in Paris for the first time.

Tootsie, starring Dustin Hoffman, explores the power of makeup.

Madonna becomes a star with her self-titled album.

1983 Karl Lagerfeld becomes chief designer for Chanel.

Sally Ride is the first woman astronaut.

Elizabeth Arden Lip Fix is biggest seller in company history

Calvin Klein and Jockey produce men's-style underwear for women.

1984 M.A.C. (Make-up Art Cosmetics) is created by Frank R. Toscan.

Vanessa Williams is crowned the second black Miss America.

Joan Benoit wins the gold medal at the first Olympic women's marathon in Los Angeles.

1985 Paulina Porizkova, 20, signs $6 million endorsement deal with Estée Lauder.

Procter & Gamble buys Richardson-Vicks, maker of Oil of Olay skin-care creams and lotions.

1986 Annual skin cream sales up to $1.9 billion.

1987 Gazelle makeup line for black skin is introduced.

Christian Lacroix opens his couture house.

Paco Rabanne launches first anti-wrinkle product for men, Concentré Actif Restructurant.

Food and Drug Administration objects to false claims of age retardation products: Revlon's Anti-Aging Firmagel, and Night Repair.

1988 A sixty-three percent rise in cosmetic surgery is reported.

Helena Rubinstein company is bought by L'Oréal.

Frances Lear publishes *Lear's:* the first fashion magazine targeted for women over forty.

1989 Li'l Miss Makeup doll targets five and six year olds for makeup sales and use.

Berlin Wall comes down.

British Department of Trade and Industry object to false claims of anti-aging products.

Cindy Crawford signs a $4 million, four year deal with Revlon.

Procter & Gamble purchases Noxell, whose products include Cover Girl and Clarion cosmetics.

1990 Estée Lauder launches Origins, a "kind to nature" brand.

Allure magazine begins publication.

1991 Naomi Wolf publishes *The Beauty Myth.*

Susan Faludi publishes *Backlash.*

Madonna begins her *Blonde Ambition Tour.*

1992 Revlon, Maybelline, and Estée Lauder's Prescriptives, create cosmetic lines aimed exclusively at women of color.

1993 Max Factor and Betrix, a German makeup and fragrance manufacturer, are bought from Revlon by Proctor & Gamble for $1.14 billion in cash.

1995 M.A.C. makeup puts drag queen RuPaul under contract as their spokesperson.

BIBLIOGRAPHY

BOOKS AND ARTICLES

Abbe, James. *Stars des Années 20*. Text by Mary Dawn Earley; introduction by Lillian Gish. Paris: Éditions du Chêne, 1978.

Abdel-Al Sania. *The Makeup Kits of Ancient Egypt*. Washington, D.C.: Cultural and Educational Bureau of the Embassy of Egypt in the U.S.A., 1985.

Ackerman, Diane. *A Natural History of the Senses*. New York: Vintage Books, 1990.

Alleres, Danielle. *Industrie Cosmetique*. Paris: Économica, 1986.

Angeloglou, Maggie. *A History of Make-Up*. New York: Macmillan, 1970.

Aperture 85. New York: Aperture, 1981.

Appell, Louis. *Cosmetics, Fragrances and Flavors*. Whiting, N.J.: Novox, Inc., 1982.

Aretz, Gertrude. *The Elegant Woman from the Rococo Period to Modern Times*. New York: Harcourt, Brace & Co., 1932.

Ash, Mary Kay. *Mary Kay*. New York: Harper & Row, 1981.

Ash, Michael, and Irene Ash. *A Formulary of Cosmetics Preparations*. New York: Chemical Pub. Co., 1977.

Auclair, Marcelle, and Menie Gregoire. *Femmes*. Paris: Librairie Plon, 1967.

Badescu, Mario. *Mario Badescu's Skin Care Program for Men*. New York: Everest House, 1981.

Baily, Margaret J. *Those Glorious Glamour Years: Classic Hollywood Costume Design of the 1930s*. Secaucus, N.J.: Citadel Press, 1982.

Balmain, Pierre. *40 Années de Création*. Bellegarde: Musée de la Mode et du Costume, Palais Galliera, SADAG, 1985.

Balsam, M. S., ed. *Cosmetics: Science and Technology*. 3 vols. 2nd ed. New York: Wiley-Interscience, 1972–1974.

Bandy, Way. *Designing Your Face*. New York: Random House, 1977.

—. *Styling Your Face*. New York: Random House, 1981.

Banner, Lois W. *American Beauty*. New York: Knopf, 1983.

Banta, Mattha. *Imaging American Women: Idea and Ideals in Cultural History*. New York: Columbia University Press, 1987.

Barthes, Roland. *Système de la Mode*. Paris: Éditions du Seuil, 1967.

Batterberry, Michael and Ariane. *Mirror, Mirror: A Social History of Fashion*. New York: Holt, Rinehart & Winston, 1977.

Beaton, Cecil. *The Royal Portraits*. Text by Roy Strong. London: Thames & Hudson, 1988.

Beauvoir, Simone de. *The Second Sex*. New York: Penguin Books, 1972.

Benaïm, Lawrence. *L'Année de la Mode 87–88 and 88–89*. Lyon: La Manufacture, 1988.

Bender, Marilyn. *The Beautiful People*. New York: Coward-McCann, 1967.

—. *At the Top*. Garden City, N.Y.: Doubleday, 1975

Betterton, Rosemary. *Looking On: Images of Femininity in the Visual Arts and Media*. London; New York: Pandora, 1987.

Bitterlin, A. *L'Art du Maquillage*. Paris: Éditions de la Coiffure Française, 1937.

The Body Shop Book. London: Macdonald Orbis, 1985.

Bogoun, Paula. *Blue Eyeshadow Should Still Be Illegal: The World After Retin-A: What Do You Do Now?* Seattle, Wash.: Beginning Press, 1988.

Bony, Anne. *Les Années 30*. Paris: Éditions du Regard, 1987.

—. *Les Années 20*. Paris: Éditions du Regard, 1991.

—. *Les Années 40*. Introduction by Eric Deschodt. Paris: Éditions du Regard, 1985.

—. *Les Années 50*. Introduction by René-Jean Clot. Paris: Éditions du Regard, 1982.

—. *Les Années 60*. Introduction by François Olivier Rousseau. Paris: Éditions du Regard, 1983.

Boone, Sylvia Ardyn. *Radiance from the Waters*. New Haven, Conn.; London: Yale University Press, 1986.

Bore, P. *Cosmetic Analysis, Selective Methods and Techniques*. New York: Marcel Dekker, 1985.

Borel, France. *Le Vêtement Incarné*. Paris: Calmann-Levy, 1992.

Bornay, Alfred. *Bornay's Guide to Skin Care and Makeup for Women of Color*. New York: Simon & Schuster, 1989.

Boucher, François. *Histoire du Costume en Occident de l'Antiquité à Nos Jours*. Paris: Flammarion, 1983.

Boughton, Patricia, and Martha Ellen Hughes. *The Buyer's Guide to Cosmetics*. New York: Random House, 1981.

Bourin, Jeanne. *La Dame de Beauté*. Paris: La Table Ronde, 1982.

Breton, André. *Manifestes du Surréalisme*. Paris: Société Nouvelle des Éditions Pauvert, 1979.

Brownmiller, Susan. *Femininity*. New York: Fawcett Columbine, 1984.

Brumberg, Elaine. *Save Your Money, Save Your Face*. New York: Harper & Row, 1986.

Buonaventura, Wendy. *Les Mille et Une Danses D'Orient*. Paris: Les Éditions Arthaud, 1989.

Cabane, Dr. J. *Le Guide des Vitamines*. Paris: Édition Menges, 1985.

Cameron, Myra. *Mother Nature's Guide to Vibrant Beauty and Health*. Englewood Cliffs, N.J.: Prentice Hall, 1990.

Carmen. *Staying Beautiful: Beauty Secrets and Attitudes from My Forty Years as a Model*. New York: Harper & Row, 1985.

Carr, Larry. *Four Fabulous Faces*. New York: Galahad Books, 1970.

—. *More Fabulous Faces*. New York: Doubleday, 1979.

Castagnoli, Gianni. *80s*. Foreword by Umberto Eco. Milan: Franco-Maria Ricci, 1979.

Chafe, William H. *The Paradox of Change: American Women in the 20th Century*. New York: Oxford University Press, 1991.

Chapkins, Wendy. *Beauty Secrets: Women and the Politics of Appearance*. Boston: South End Press, 1986.

Chapsal, Madeleine, Hélène Cixous, and Sonia Rykiel. *Sonia Rykiel*. Paris: Éditions Herscher, 1985.

Chase, Deborah. *The New Medically Based No-Nonsense Beauty Book*. New York: Henry Holt, 1989.

Chorlton, Penny. *Cover Up: Taking the Lid Off the Cosmetics Industry*. Wellingborough, Northamptonshire, England: Grapevine, 1988.

Chronicle of the 20th Century. Mount Kisco, N.Y.: Chronicle Publications, 1987.

Clark, Kenneth. *Feminine Beauty*. London: Weidenfeld & Nicolson, 1980.

Coleridge, Nicholas, and Stephen Quinn. *The 60s in Queen*. Introduction by Jocelyn Stevens. London: Ebony Press, 1987.

Colette. *Les Héroes Longues*. Transl. Antonia White. New York: Penguin Books, 1917.

—. *The Innocent Libertine*. Transl. Antonia White. New York: Penguin Books, 1987.

Cooley, Arnold J. *The Toilet in Ancient and Modern Times*. London, 1866; rpt. New York: Burt Franklin, 1970.

Corson, Richard. *Fashions in Makeup: From Ancient to Modern Times*. New York: Universe Books, 1972.

Cosmetic, Toiletry and Fragrance Association. *CTFA Cosmetic Ingredient Dictionary*. 3rd ed. Washington, D.C.: CTFA, 1982.

—. *CTFA International Color Handbook*. Washington, D.C.: CTFA, 1985.

Créations Publicitaires et Artistiques de Shiseido. Tokyo: Kyuryodo Art Pub. Co., 1986.

Croutier, Alev Lytle. *Harems le Monde Derrière la Voile*. Paris: Éditions Belfond, 1989.

Da, Lottie, and Jan Alexander. *Bad Girls of the Silver Screen*. New York: Carroll & Graf, 1989.

De Haas, Cherie. *Natural Skin Care*. Garden City, N.Y.: Avery, 1987.

Demornex, Jacqueline. *Lancôme*. Paris: Éditions du Regard, 1985.

DeNavarre, Maison G. *The Chemistry and Manufacture of Cosmetics*. vols. 3 & 4. 2nd ed. Orlando, Fla.: Continental Press, 1975.

Deslandres, Yvonne, and Florence Müller. *Histoire de la Mode au XXe Siècle*. Paris: Éditions Somogy, 1986.

Devlin, Polly. *Vogue Book of Fashion Photography*. Introduction by Alexander Liberman. New York: Condé-Nast Publications, 1979.

Dictionnaire des Produits de Soins de Beauté. 3rd ed. Paris: Éditions Sermadiras, 1986–1987.

Doisneau, Robert. *Robert Doisneau*. Paris: Éditions Contrejour, 1979.

Dormann, Geneviève. *Amoureuse Colette*. Paris: Éditions Herscher, 1984.

Dorsey, Hebe. *The Belle Époque in the Paris Herald*. London: Thames & Hudson, 1986.

Eco, Umberto. *Art and Beauty in the Middle Ages*. Transl. Hugh Bredin. London: Yale University Press, 1986.

Elvinger, Beatrice. *Guide des Produits de Beauté*. Paris: Éditions Albin Michel, 1986.

Erro. *Erro catalogue*. Paris: Éditions du Chêne, 1976.

Esten, John. *Man Ray/Bazaar Years*. Introduction by Willis Hartshorn. New York: Rizzoli, 1988.

Etherington-Smith, Meredith. *Patou*. Paris: Éditions Denöel, 1984.

Europe, Hollywood & Retour. No. 79-avril. Paris: Autrement, 1986.

Fatale Beauté: Une Évidence, Une Énigme. No. 91-juin. Paris: Autrement, 1987.

Faucigny-Lucinge, Jean Louis de. *Fêtes Memorables Bals Costumes 1922–72*. Paris: Éditions Herscher, 1986.

Feinberg, Hilda. *Cosmetics-Perfumery Thesaurus*. New York: CCM Information Corp., 1972.

The Feminine Image: Women of Japan. Honolulu, Hawaii: Honolulu Academy of Arts, 1985.

Finch, Christopher, and Linda Rosenkrantz. *Gone Hollywood*. New York: Doubleday & Co., 1979.

Fletcher, Jefferson Butler. *The Religion of Beauty in Women: And Other Essays on Platonic Love in Poetry and Society*. New York: Haskell House, 1966.

Ford, Eileen. *Eileen Ford's Beauty Now and Forever: Secrets of Beauty After 35*. New York: Simon & Schuster, 1977.

Fraser, Kennedy. *Scenes from the Fashionable World*. New York: Alfred A. Knopf, 1987.

Freedman, Rita Jackaway. *Beauty Bound*. Lexington, Mass.: Lexington Books, 1986.

Friedan, Betty. *The Feminine Mystique*. New York: Dell Publishing, 1983.

Garland, Madge. *The Changing Face of Beauty: Four Thousand Years of Beautiful Women*. New York: M. Barrows, 1957.

Garber, Marjorie. *Vested Interests: Cross Dressing and Cultural Anxiety*. New York: Routledge, 1992.

Ghozland, F. *Cosmétiques Être et Paraître*. Toulouse: Éditions Milan, 1987.

Gill, Michel. *Image of the Body*. London: The Bodley Head, 1989.

Griffin, Roger C., and Stanley Sacharow. *Drug and Cosmetic Packaging*. Park Ridge, N.J.: Noyes Data Corp., 1975.

Grun, Bernard. *The Timetables of History*. New York: Simon & Schuster, 1982.

Gutch, Marian H. [George W. Owens]. *Cosmetics, Toiletries, and Health Care Products: Recent Developments*. Park Ridge, N.J.: Noyes Data Corp., 1978.

Häger, Bengt. *Ballets Suédois*. Paris: Éditions Denöel, 1989.

Hall-Duncan, Nancy. *Histoire de la Photographie de Mode*. Preface by Yves Saint Laurent. Paris: Éditions du Chêne, 1978.

Hammond, Bryan, and Patrick O'Connor. *Josephine Baker*. London: Jonathan Cape, 1988.

Hansen, Joseph, and Evelyn Reed. *Cosmetics, Fashions and the Exploitation of Women*. New York: Pathfinder Press, 1986.

Harrison, Martin. *Appearances: Fashion Photography Since 1945*. New York: Rizzoli, 1991.

Hawes, Elizabeth. *Anything But Love*. New York: Rinehart & Co., 1948.

Hennessy, Val. *In the Gutter*. London: Quartet Books, 1978.

Higham, Charles. *La Scandaleuse Duchesse de Windsor*. Paris: Éditions Jean-Claude Latte, 1989.

Hite, Shere. *The Hite Report*. New York: Dell Publishing, 1976.

Hollander, Anne. *Seeing Through Clothes*. New York: Penguin Books, 1988.

Homer, William Innes. *Alfred Stieglitz and the American Avant-Garde*. London: Secker & Warburg, 1977.

Horst. *Six Decennies de Photographies*. Text by Marten Kanzmater. Munich; Paris: Schirmer/Mosel, 1991.

Howard, George. *The Principles and Practice Of Perfumery and Cosmetics*. Cheltenham, England: Stanley Thornes, 1987.

Hoyningen-Huene, George. *Salute to the Thirties—Horst*. Foreword by Janet Flanner; notes on plates by Valerie Lawford. New York: Viking Press, 1971.

Hubbard, Elizabeth. *Helpful Advice to Women Who Would be Beautiful, an Essay on Beauty with Simple Instructions and Information Concerning Beauty Culture*. New York City; Paris; London: Mrs. Hubbard's Salon, 595 Fifth Avenue, 1910.

Hubbard, Harriet. *Harriet Hubbard Ayer's Book*. New York: Arno Press Books, 1974.

Humeur de Mode. No. 62-septembre. Paris: Autrement, 1984.

Hurlock, Elizabeth B. *The Psychology of Dress: An Analysis of Fashion and Its Motives*. New York: Ronald Press, 1929.

L'Intime. No. 81-juin. Paris: Autrement, 1986.

Israel, Lee. *Estée Lauder: Beyond the Magic*. New York: Macmillan, 1985.

Jackson, Carole. *Color Me Beautiful Makeup Book*. New York: Ballantine, 1987.

Jackson, Judith. *Scentual Touch, A Personal Guide to Aromatherapy*. New York: Henry Holt & Co., 1986.

Javna, John and Gordon. *60s!*. New York: St. Martin's Press, 1988.

Jean Charles de Castelbajac, *Anti-Körper Mode 1970–1988*. Vienna: Osterreichisches Museum für angewandte Kunst, 1988.

Jellinek, J. Stephen. *Formulation and Function of Cosmetics*. New York: Wiley-Interscience, 1970.

Jones, Landon Y. *Great Expectations: America and the Baby Boom Generation*. New York: Ballantine Books, 1986.

Kanin, Ruth. *The Manufacture of Beauty*. Boston: Branden, 1990.

Kertész, André. *Sixty Years of Photography*. Edited by Nicolas Ducrot. New York: Penguin Books, 1972.

Kobal, John. *The Art of the Great Hollywood Portrait: Photographs 1925–1940*. New York: Alfred A. Knopf, 1980.

Köhler, Carl. *A History of Costume*. New York: David McKay, 1963.

Kybalova, Ludmila, Olga Hervenova, and Milena Lamarova. *Encyclopédie Illustrée du Costume et de la Mode*. Paris: Grü, 1970.

Landau, Terry. *About Faces*. New York: Anchor Books, Doubleday, 1989.

Laqueur, Thomas. *Making Sex*. Boston: Harvard University Press, 1990.
Lartigue, Florette. *Jacques-Henri Lartigue: La Traversée du Siècle*. Paris: Bordas, 1990.
Lauder, Estée. *Estée: A Success Story*. New York: Random House, 1985.
Laver, James. *The Age of Illusion*. New York: David McKay, 1972.
—. *The Concise History of Costume and Fashion*. New York: Harry N. Abrams, 1969.
—. *Costume in the Theater*. New York: Hill and Wang, 1965.
—. *Manners and Morals in the Age of Optimism*. New York: Harper & Row, 1966.
Leroy, Geneviève, and Vivian Muguette. *Histoire de la Beauté Féminine à Travers les Ages*. Paris: Acropole, 1989.
Lewis, Alfred Allan, and Constance Woodworth. *Miss Elizabeth Arden*. New York: Coward, McCann & Geoghegan, 1972.
Liggett, Arline, and John. *The Tyranny of Beauty*. London: Victor Gollantz, 1989.
Lloyd, Valerie. *The Art of Vogue: Photographic Covers*. New York: Harmony Books, 1986.
Locantro, Tony. *Some Girls Do and Some Girls Don't (Sheet Music Covers)*. London: Quartet Books, 1985.
London, Liz E., and Anne H. Adams. *Color Right, Dress Right: The Total Look*. New York: Crown, 1985.
Loos, Adolf. *Spoken Into the Void: Collected Essays 1897–1901*. Cambridge, Mass.: MIT Press, 1982.
Lyon, Josette. *Beauté Jeunesse*. Paris: Librarie Hachette, 1970.
Mac Chesney, James C. *Packaging of Cosmetics and Toiletries*. London: Mewnes-Butterworths, 1974.
MacNeil, Robert. *The Way We Were*. New York: Carroll & Graf, 1988.
Man, Ray. *Man Ray 1890–1976*. Preface by Fritz L. Gruber. Berlin: Benedikt Taschen, 1990.
Manzoni, Pablo. *Instant Beauty: The Complete Way to Perfect Makeup*. New York: Simon & Schuster, 1978.
Marcus, Greil. *Lipstick Traces: A Secret History of the Twentieth Century*. London: Secker & Warburg, 1989.
Margueritte, Victor. *La Garçonne*. Paris: Flammarion, 1978.
Maron, Michael. *Instant Makeover Magic*. New York: Rawson, 1983.
Martin, Richard. *Fashion and Surrealism*. New York: Rizzoli, 1987.
Marwick, Arthur. *Beauty in History*. London: Thames & Hudson, 1988.
Marty, Michel. *La Beauté du Diable*. Paris: Éditions Phébus, 1991.
Masters, George, and Norma Lee Browning. *The Masters Way to Beauty*. New York: E. P. Dutton, 1977.
McDermott, Catherine. *Street Style: British Design in the 80s*. New York: Rizzoli, 1987.
McLean, Helen Hall. *Behind the Scenes: The Most Comprehensive Illustrated Guide to Professional Makeup Artistry*. Vancouver, B.C.: Evergreen Press, 1979.
McNair, Barbara, and Stephen Lewis. *The Complete Book of Beauty for the Black Woman*. Englewood Cliffs, N.J.: Prentice-Hall, 1981.
Milinaire, Catherine, and Carol Troy. *Cheap Chic*. New York: Harmony Books, Crown, 1975.
Mills, Joey. *New Classic Beauty: A Step-by-Step Guide to Naturally Glamorous Makeup*. 1st ed. New York: Villard Books, 1987.
Le Monde Selon Ses Créateurs. Paris: Musée de la Mode et du Couture, 1991.
Montez, Lola. *The Arts & Secrets of Beauty*. New York: Chelsea House, 1969.
Montreynaud, Florence. *Le XX'e Siècle des Femmes*. Paris: Éditions Nathan, 1989.
Morris, Desmond. *Body Watching*. New York: Crown, 1985.
—. *La Clé des Gestes*. Paris: Bernard Grasset, 1977.
—. *Manwatching*. New York: Harry N. Abrams, 1977.
Moskowitz, Howard R. *Cosmetics Product Testing: A Modern Psychophysical Approach*. New York: M. Dekker, 1984.
Muray, Nicholas. *Muray's Celebrity Portraits of the 20s and 30s*. New York: Dover Publications, 1970.
Nater, Johan P., and Anton C. de Groot. *Unwanted Effects of Cosmetics and Drugs Used in Dermatology*. New York: Elsevier, 1985.
N'Diaye, Catherine. *La Coquetterie*. Paris: Éditions Autrement, 1987.
Odeurs. No. 92-septembre. Paris: Autrement, 1987.
O'Higgins, Patrick. *Madame: An Intimate Biography of Helena Rubinstein*. New York: Viking, 1971.
Parrot, Nicole. *Mannequins*. New York: Academy Editions, St. Martin's Press, 1982.
Parsons, Frank Alvah. *Psychology of Dress*. New York: Doubleday, Page and Co., 1920.
Pomey-Rey, Daniele. *Bien Dans Sa Peau*. Paris: Éditions du Centurion, 1989.
Post, Laurens van der. *A Portrait of All the Russians*. New York: William Morrow, 1967.
Poucher, W. A. *Perfumes, Cosmetics and Soaps*. Vols. 1–3. Revised by George Howard. 7th ed. London: Chapman and Hall, 1974.
Quant, Mary, and Felicity Green. *Color by Quant*. New York: McGraw-Hill, 1984.
Rejaunier, Jeanne. *The Beauty Trap*. London: New English Library, 1970.
Revlon Art of Beauty. Garden City, N.Y.: Dolphin Books, 1982.
Rinzler, Carol Ann. *Cosmetics: What the Ads Don't Tell You*. New York: Crowell, 1977.
Roberts, Nancy. *Breaking All the Rules*. New York: Viking, 1985.
Rogol, Susi. *Makeup for Redheads*. New York: Villard Books, 1984.
—. *Makeup for Blondes*. New York: Villard Books, 1984.
Roth, Sanford. *Portraits Années 50*. Paris: Éditions Albin Michel, 1989.
Rubinstein, Helena. *My Life for Beauty*. New York: Simon & Schuster, 1964.
Rudofsky, Bernard. *The Unfashionable Human Body*. New York: Doubleday, 1971.
Rykiel, Sonia. *Et Je la Voudrais Nue...*. Paris: Éditions Grasset et Fasquelle, 1979.
Searight, Susan. *The Use and Function of Tattooing on Moroccan Women*. New Haven, Conn.: Human Relations Area Files, 1984.
Sembach, K. J. *Into the Thirties*. London: Thames & Hudson, 1972.
Scavullo, Francesco, and Sean Byrnes. *Scavullo Women*. New York: Harper & Row, 1982.
Shrimpton, Jean. *The Truth About Modeling*. London: W. H. Allen, 1964.
Sims, Naomi. *All About Health and Beauty for the Black Woman*. Garden City, N.Y.: Doubleday, 1976.
Sobieszek, Robert A. *The Art of Persuasion*. New York: Harry N. Abrams, 1988.
Soyer, Gérard-Lovis. *Jean-Gabriel Domergue: L'Art et à la Mode*. Paris: Les Éditions Sous le Vent, 1984.
Spada, James. *Grace*. Paris: Éditions Jean-Claude Latte, 1988.
Spiegel, Dr. Leo A. "The Child's Concept of Beauty: A Study in Concept Formation" *Journal of Genetic Psychology*. No. 77 (1950).
Springs, Alice. *Portraits*. Introduction by Christian Caujolle; transl. Anne-Marie Deschodt. Paris: Éditions du Regard, 1983.
Squire, Geoffrey. *Dress and Society 1560–1970*. New York: Viking Press, 1974.
Stabile, Toni. *Everything You Want to Know About Cosmetics*. New York: Dodd, Mead, 1984.
Stallings, Penny. *Flesh & Fantasy*. New York: St. Martin's Press, 1978.
Stanley, Louis. *The Beauty of Women*. London: W. H. Allen & Co., 1955.
Statler, Oliver. *All-Japan: the Catalogue of Everything Japanese*. New York: William Morrow, 1984.
Steele, Valerie. *Fashion and Eroticism: Ideals of Feminine Beauty from the Victorian Era to the Jazz Age*. New York: Oxford University Press, 1985.
Steichen, Edward. *The Master Prints 1895–1914*. Text by Dennis Longwell. New York: Museum of Modern Art, 1978.
Suleiman, Susan Rabin. *The Female Body in Western Culture: Contemporary Perspectives*. Cambridge, Mass.: Harvard University Press, 1986.
Swanson, Gloria. *Swanson on Swanson*. New York: Random House, 1980.
Taylor, G. Rattray. *Sex in History*. New York: Vanguard Press, 1954.
Thevoz, Michel. *The Painted Body*. New York: Rizzoli, 1984.
Tiger, Lionl. *The Pursuit of Pleasure*. Boston: Little, Brown, 1992.
Tisserand, Robert B. *The Art of Aromatherapy*. Rochester, Vt.: Healing Arts Press, 1977.
Tobias, Andrew. *Fire and Ice: The Story of Charles Revson, the Man Who Built the Revlon Empire*. New York: William Morrow, 1976.
Toiletries, Beauty Aids, Cosmetics and Fragrances. Fairchild Fact File. New York: Fairchild Publications, 1982.
Tolstoi, Tatiana. *De l'Élégance Masculine*. Paris: Acropole, 1987.
Toussaint-Samat, Maguelonne. *Histoire Technique et Morale du Vêtement*. Paris: Bordas, 1990.
Trent, Paul. *The Image Makers: 60 Years of Hollywood Glamour*. New York: Harmony Books, 1982.
Turbeville, Deborah. *Wallflower*. New York: Congreve, 1978.
Vieira, Mark. *Les Dieux D'Hollywood: Scènes et Portraits Immortel*. Paris: Éditions Atlas, 1989.
Viguie, Liane. *Mannequin Haute Couture*. Paris: Éditions Robert Laffont, 1977.
Wald, Carol. *Myth America*. New York: Pantheon Books, 1975.
Wand, Betty. *Secrets from Women in Their Prime*. Glendale, Cal.: Barr Publishing, 1988.
Warner, Marina. *Monuments & Maidens: The Allegory of the Female Form*. London: Weidenfeld & Nicolson, 1985.
Weill, Alain. *Les Réclames des Années 50*. Paris: Le Dernier Terrain Vague, 1983.
Wells, F. V. *Cosmetics and The Skin*. New York: Reinhold, 1964.
Wendkos-La Torre, Carryl. *The Make-Up Center Book*. New York: St. Martin's Press, 1979.
Westmore, Frank, and Muriel Davidson. *The Westmores of Hollywood*. New York: J. B. Lippincott, 1976.
Whittick, Arnold. *Symbols, Signs and Their Meaning and Uses in Design*. London: Leonard Hill Books, International Textbook Co., 1971.
Williams, Jay. *Jeanne d'Art*. Paris: Éditions R.S.T., 1967.
Winter, Ruth. *A Consumer's Dictionary of Cosmetic Ingredients*. Rev. ed. New York: Crown, 1976.
Wolf, Naomi. *The Beauty Myth*. New York: William Morrow, 1991.
Wykes-Joyce, Max. *Cosmetics and Adornment: Ancient and Contemporary Usage*. London: Peter Owen, 1961.

PERIODICALS

Allure. New York: Condé Nast Publications, Ltd., 1990–1995.
American Elle. New York: Hachette/Filipacchi, 1985–1995.
American Vogue. New York: Condé Nast Publications, Ltd., 1892–1995.
Art, goût, beauté. Paris: 1922–1933.
Beauty Fashion. New York: Beauty Fashion, 1977–1995.
British Elle. London; New York: Hachette/Filipacchi, 1985–1995.
British Vogue. London; New York: Condé Nast Publications, Ltd., 1916–1995.
Business Week. New York: McGraw Hill, 1929–1995.
Cosmetic World. The Ledes Group, 1967–1995.
Colliers. New York: Harper, 1898–1957.
Cosmopolitan. New York: The Hearst Corporation, 1875–1995.
Ebony. Chicago: John H. Johnson Publications, 1945–1995.
FDC-The Rose Sheet. Chevy Chase, MD: FDC Reports Inc., 1980–1995.
Flash Art International. Volume xxiii, No. 155, Nov/Dec 1990. Milano: Giancarlo Politi Editore, 1990.
Forbes. New York: Forbes, Inc., 1917–1995.
French Elle. Paris; New York: Hachette/Filipacchi, 1945–1995.
French Vogue. Paris; New York: Condé Nast Publications, Ltd., 1920–1940; 1945–1995.
German Vogue. Frankfurt; New York: Condé Nast Publications, Ltd., 1928–1995.
Glamour. New York: Condé Nast Publications, Ltd., 1939–1995.
Good Housekeeping. New York: The Hearst Corporation, 1885–1995.
Harper's Bazaar. New York: The Hearst Corporation, 1867–1995.
Harper's & Queen. London: The National Magazine Company, 1862–1995.
Hygeia. Chicago: American Medical Association, 1923–1950.
Interview. New York: Brant Publications, 1969–1995.
Italian Vogue. Milan; New York: Condé Nast Publications, Ltd., 1971–1995.
Ladies Home Journal. New York: The Meredith Corporation, 1883–1995.
Life. New York: Time Inc., 1936–1995.
Mademoiselle. New York: Condé Nast Publications, Ltd., 1935–1995.
Marie-Claire. New York: The Hearst Corporation, 1937–1995.
Mirabella. New York: Hachette/Filipacchi, 1989–1995.
Motion Picture. Brooklyn, N.Y.: 1911–1954.
Ms.. New York: Lang Communications, 1972–1995.
New York World. New York: 1860–1931.
Newsweek. New York: Newsweek Inc., 1933–1995.
Point de Vue. No. 2276, March 1992. Paris: Europa Press-Mantel/Sipa Press, 1992.
La Revue Mondiale. Paris: La Rennaisance Latine, 1895–1935.
Rolling Stone. New York: Wenner Media, 1967–1995.
Self. New York: Condé Nast Publications, Ltd., 1979–1995.
Seventeen. New York: K-3 Magazines, 1950–1995.
Stage. Evanston, Ill.: American Educational Theatre, 1965–1977.
The Nation. New York: The Nation Company, 1865–1995.
The New York Times. New York: New York Times, 1851–1995.
The Wall Street Journal. Dow Jones, 1889–1995.
Time. New York: Time Inc., 1923–1995.
Toilet Requisites. New York: Beauty Fashion, 1920–1977.
Votre Beauté. Paris: Votre Beauté SA, 1935–1995.
W. New York: Fairchild Publications, 1972–1995.
Women's Wear Daily. New York: Fairchild Publications, 1910–1995.

COMPANY HISTORIES

ELIZABETH ARDEN

Elizabeth Arden was founded in 1910 by Florence Graham Nightingale. Nightingale took the name from a novel by Elizabeth von Arnim called *Elisabeth and Her German Garden*. Beginning in the 1920s Elizabeth Arden emerged into a cosmetics empire based primarily upon the concept of combining beauty parlors and hair salons, with the color pink as their theme. In 1910, Nightingale opened the now-famous salon on New York's Fifth Avenue. In 1914 she met A. F. Swanson, a chemist, who over a half-century helped transform her cosmetic dreams into a reality of products and profit. In 1921 the Place Vendôme salon in Paris was opened (it closed in 1974), and by 1938 nineteen American salons and seventeen overseas licenses were running. Arden helped gain acceptance for eye makeup around the world, which at the time existed solely in Paris. The Arden skin-care system consisted of four essential steps—cleanse, tone, hydrate, and nourish. Nightingale rigorously tested her products' effectiveness; Arden products like 8-Hour Cream, Visible Difference, Millennium, and Ceramide were all enormous successes. Arden as a company disappeared in 1966 in a legal morass, but reemerged in 1971, owned by the Eli Lilly company. In 1986 Fabergé purchased the name, only to be bought out by Unilever in 1989.

AVON

Avon products began in 1886 as the California Perfume Co.. Founder David H. McConnell, a door-to-door book salesman, developed the idea of offering vials of scent with his bibles, and found that customers were more interested in the perfume. Avon Products began in 1950 when McConnell gave a sample case to the first Avon lady. With over 1.5 million representatives selling door-to-door in one hundred countries, Avon is one of the world's largest-selling brands of cosmetics. Principal lines include Avon Color, Daily Revival skin care, Skin So-Soft bath line, Undeniable, Imari, Giorgio, and Red.

BOURJOIS

Bourjois, a French cosmetics house founded in 1863 by Alexandre-Napoleon Bourjois, was initially dedicated to theater makeup. Sarah Bernhardt wore Bourjois rouge on the stage as well as Bourjois Java rice powder (1863), which became Bourjois's first worldwide makeup success, with two million boxes sold per year. Bourjois created the first powder compact in 1890, calling it Manon Lescaut, and in 1912 opened a new era in makeup with Les Pastels Joues, whose round, flower-printed container appeared in every home. By 1913, Bourjois products were being sold in New York, London, Barcelona, Sydney, Brussels, Buenos Aires, and Vienna, among other cities. Still a leading brand in one hundred countries, Bourjois's headquarters share a building with Chanel in Neuilly, a suburb of Paris.

CARON

Ernest Daltroff (c. 1870–1941) chose the name of famous acrobat Caron for his small perfumery, founded in 1904. Caron's fragrances became known, especially Daltroff's Tabac Blond, created in 1919. Caron shunned door-to-door sales, advertising, and credit, preferring to concentrate on an elite approach to marketing. Peau Fine, one of the first makeup compacts, became an immediate success around the world. World War II forced Daltroff to emigrate to Canada; his longtime collaborator, Felicie Vanpouille, known as "Madame," took over his 10 Place Vendôme premises in Paris. In 1962, Madame's successor, J. P. Elkann, abolished all salon distribution, although Caron is still found in perfumeries and department stores. In 1966 it was bought by Robbins, an American pharmaceutical firm, and again in 1987 by Cora-Revillon.

CHARLES OF THE RITZ

After World War I, a young French hairdresser sailed to America and opened an elegant salon in New York's Ritz Hotel. "Charles of the Ritz" became an instant success, and by 1926 had launched the cosmetics company that still bears his name. Now grown enormously, the company merged with Lanvin/U.S. in 1964, and in 1965 Yves Saint Laurent became its majority shareholder. In 1972 Squibb purchased Charles of the Ritz, and in 1986, Yves Saint Laurent again bought the company in order to control their perfume line. The rest of their activities were relinquished to Merloz. Charles of the Ritz products are sold both in the U.S. and in Europe.

CLARINS

Based in Neuilly-sur-Seine, France, Clarins was founded in 1954 by Jacques Courtin (now chairman and CEO). Clarins leads the European treatment market with its skin-care and makeup products, and original Thierry Mugler fragrances. Eighty percent of Clarins's sales occur in foreign markets (110 countries) and are especially strong in Southeast Asia. Its eighty-three products are concentrated in three lines: facial skin care, body care, and suntanning. Clarins's focus on research to discover new principles to reinvigorate established products is the hallmark of the corporation and has helped it to remain a leading name with its international clientele. Questionnaires packaged in each product that ask for consumer feedback led, in 1991, to the first anti-pollution makeup. Clarins's innovations have become classics; among them L'eau Dynamisante, Eye Contour Treatment, Maquillage Anti-pollution, Gel Multi-Minceur Anti-Capiton, and Le Double Serum Phyto-Concentre.

COTY

Coty, originally a French perfume company, was created in 1904 by Corsican, François-Joseph-Marie Spoturno (1874–1934), who took as his pseudonym the name of his mother, Marie Coti. With his friend Raymond Goery, he developed a perfume called La Rose Jacqueminot in 1904; in a few months it had made a fortune. In 1905 l'Origan, the first perfume containing ivalia, was created. Spoturno was a clever businessman with a nose for self-promotion. His signature was written across Coty's black delivery vans in gold; he also collaborated with Baccarat and Lalique in making beautiful flasks and boxes for his products. He developed and trademarked names for his products and commissioned Léon Bakst to design white-gold metal containers to encase Coty pressed powder, which accompanied each Coty perfume purchase. In twenty-five years he produced twenty-one fragrances, and Coty was everywhere: the Soviet Union, the U.S. (where 60 percent of sales were made), in the Orient. Spoturno called himself, on his calling card, "artist, industrialist, technician, economist, financier, sociologist." It was this hubris that contributed to his downfall. The house of Coty never fully recovered from bankruptcy caused by the crash of 1929; Spoturno died in 1934. In 1966 Coty was bought by Pfizer, a U.S. pharmaceutical firm and in 1991 by the Benkisser group, and is now primarily a mass-market fragrance and cosmetic specialist in the U.S.. The Coty award is still a symbol of prestige.

MAX FACTOR

Born in Lodz, Poland, Max Factor was the first makeup artist of the Imperial Theater of the tsar. He emigrated in 1904 to Hollywood where he developed products for the cinema industry. He founded his own brand of cosmetics in Los Angeles in 1909. The Society line was launched in 1916, and the Colour Harmony line was launched in 1918; with powder, rouge, eye shadow, and lipstick harmonized to create a natural look. In 1927, the brand was distributed throughout the U.S.. By 1930, it was exported in eighty-one countries under the slogan "Max Factor, the makeup of the stars." In 1928, he received an Academy Award for his Panchromatic Makeup. In 1938 he invented Pan Cake Makeup for use with Technicolor stock. For twenty years, Max Factor used a marketing campaign that proposed that women use makeup like the stars. Joan Crawford, Hedy Lamarr, Mae West, Lana Turner, Jean Harlow, Gloria Swanson, and Elizabeth Taylor were just some of the clients on whom he worked his makeup magic. Between 1932 and 1946, his products were perfected for television. In a new innovation in 1972, a model was signed to an exclusive contract; in 1986, Jane Seymour for perfume Le Jardin d'Amour and Jaclyn Smith were the spokespersons. In 1988 No Color Mascara was elected product of the year by *Fortune* magazine, who gave it the Rex Award. From its creation, Max Factor was driven by creativity. Its laboratories worked with exceptional effectiveness to maintain quality control. The company is a member of four worldwide cosmetic societies. Since 1973, its ownership has passed from group to group, each successively more important than the last: after the Norton Simon Group came Orlane, then Halston, then Playtex, then Beatrice. Distributed by Revlon until 1993, it was then bought by Proctor and Gamble.

GUERLAIN

This classic French makeup and cosmetics company was started by Pierre-François-Pascal Guerlain, a perfumer in the Hotel Meurice, rue de Rivoli, Paris, in 1828. The young chemist met acclaim as the perfumer to King Charles X in 1853–55, when he created his famous Eau de Cologne Impériale, with its bee-shaped bottle. Other society commissions followed: Balzac even asked him to make a perfume for him before writing César Birotteau. In 1864 his children Gabriel and Aimé joined the firm, creating the famous Jicky 1889; L'Heure Bleue, 1912; Mitsouko, 1919; and Shalimar, 1925. Each scent ranked highly among those of their time. Liu, created in 1929, was the scent of the 1930s along with Vol de Nuit (1933), which was dedicated to aviator Antoine de Saint Exupéry. Guerlain expanded into providing services when it opened its Beauty Institute on the Champs-Élysées in 1938. Guerlain was a true pioneer in cosmetics, and among their innovations are the introduction of expiration dates for beauty products; replacing homemade recipes with scientific formulas; and creating one of the first schools of beauty. Since the newest factory was built at Chartres in 1973, new lines like Issima (1980) and Evolution (1986) have been introduced along with revolutionary makeup such as Terracotta (1984), Météorites (1987), and l'Or de Guerlain (1991), popular in Asia. Since 1828, its eight Parisian stores have seen 321 perfumes come and go. In 1994, the Groupe LVMH bought a share of Guerlain, ending the 166-year family hegemony of this extraordinary company.

ESTÉE LAUDER

Estée Lauder was founded in 1946 by Estée Lauder when she introduced the "Lauder Girls" to the glamour scene of New York's Saks Fifth Avenue. Estée Lauder trained sales women to give advice to customers and gave a gift with each purchase to new customers, a breakthrough marketing strategy. Lauder had repeated success, driven by her sense of refinement, her obsession with quality, and the flair with which she delivered her ideas, many of which were long before their time. She gave rouge colors evocative names like Rose Flirt and created the first seasonal colors. Because of Ms. Lauder's belief in research and development, the company counted new breakthroughs, like Night Repair Serum in 1981, Eyezone, and Re-Nutriv. Youth Dew was a successful perfume first launched in 1952, and its fragrance appeared in bath oil, body powder, and body lotion. This was followed by other perfumes: Aramis for men, 1966; Estée, 1968; Alliage, 1972; Beautiful, 1985; Knowing, 1988; and Spellbound, 1992. She has received many prizes and distinctions, many of which have been from financial and scientific organizations. The company today has five brands: Aramis, Origins, Clinique, Prescriptives, and Estée Lauder. Represented in hundreds of countries, with 50 percent of its business in the US, Estée Lauder is one of the most powerful cosmetics companies in the world still owned and controlled by the original family.

LANCÔME

Lancôme was created in 1935 in the House of François Coty, father of the modern perfumery, by Armand Petitjean. He launched five luxuriously bottled perfumes and established a business with three divisions: perfume, makeup, and well-being. In 1936, it launched Nutrix, a nourishing night cream. During World War II, Petitjean set up a school for technicians where young women learned to become perfect ambassadresses of the brand. In the 1950s, the company's catalog included products that were before their time, intended to promote well-being. For example, the Oceae line, a precursor of today's thalassotherapy. In the late fifties, the brand encountered difficulties. Petitjean had dreams of conquering the U.S. but recognized that it would consume his fortune. The company was sold to L'Oréal in 1964. The new Lancôme aggressively sought new world markets: Europe, the U.S. in the seventies, and finally Asia. In the nineties Lancôme began to make inroads to Japan. Lancôme's packaging is becoming increasingly simplified: white and gray for skin-care products, black and gold for makeup. Sold in 143 countries and represented by Isabella Rossellini until 1995, Lancôme is one of the worldwide leaders in cosmetics.

L'ORÉAL

Founded in 1907 by chemical engineer Eugène Schueller to sell one of his inventions—the first synthetic hair tints—today L'Oréal's business is the largest in the world. Beauty and hair care products each represent 30% of the empire, and color and treatment cosmetics make 40%. L'Oréal's subsidiaries include Lancôme, Helena Rubinstein, Vichy, Laboratoires Garnier, and Cacharel. Among the principal lines are Pléntitude, Studio Line, Elsève (L'Oréal); Niosôme, Hydrative (Lancôme); Ambre Solaire (Garnier); and Rouge Forever (Helena Rubinstein). The founder's daughter Liliane Bettencourt still holds a first option on shares if they are sold. The current CEO is Welshman Lindsay Owen-Jones.

ORLANE

Orlane was created as a perfume company in France in 1946 by Count Guillaume d'Ornano with his sons Hubert and Michel, and Jean d'Albret. By 1947 the company had expanded into beauty products. Orlane created a new concept: a single face cream was not enough. Instead, they said, day and night creams were required. In 1948–50, Orlane launched Le Crème Astrale, Le Crème à l'Orange (enriched with vitamin C), Le Crème Intégrale, and Le Crème Active. In 1966 Orlane opened its Institute of Beauty on the Avenue Victor Hugo, an education center for estheticians. In 1968 they launched Crème B21, the first cream with amino acids, and in the eighties, they launched three important products: Extrait Vitall (1983), B21-Bio-energic (1985), and Hydro-Climat (1986). When Orlane was acquired in 1970 by the American group Morton Norwich and then by Max Factor, Hubert d'Ornano created his own brand, Sisley, and opened an ultra-modern factory in Orléans. An Italian company, Kelemata, acquired Orlane in 1985. Orlane is sold in one hundred countries throughout the world.

PINAUD

Eduard Pinaud was one of the five great perfumers of the nineteenth century, furnishing all the courts of Europe with his royal concoctions: Royale de l'Imperatrice, Royale de l'Empereur, Royale de la reine Victoria, and Le Bouquet Imperial Russe. His fame helped bring his skin-care products to the masses: La Graisse d'Ours du Nord ("Cream of the Northern Bear") and La Crème de Limaçon. In 1875 he presented his first line of makeup, a streamlined assembly of soap, toilet water, and fragrance. Pinaud won an award in 1889 at the Exposition Universelle for his products made with ixora, a flower from Madagascar. His fame was assured after World War II when his 612, the first mascara, made Pinaud a household name. His successors, Emile Meyer, M. M. Victor, and Henri and George Klotz, spread the Pinaud fame to five continents and constructed the Pinaud Gallery on Fifth Avenue. Success spawned imitators: G. E. Pinaud, Pinaux, and Pineau. France-Parfums bought the distinguished house in 1987.

L. T. PIVER

This French cosmetics and perfumes company was founded in 1774 by Pierre-Guillaume Dissey and had its premises at 111 rue Saint Martin, Paris. In 1813, Louis-Toussaint Piver took control, creating Véritable Eau de Cologne, Triple Eau de Cologne, and Eau de Cologne des Princes. Le Trèfle Incarnat (1900), Floramye (1903), and Pompeïa (1907), were real innovations, using salicylate d'amyle (discovered in 1898) as an active ingredient, and thus joining art with chemistry. In 1914, Piver invented Cuir de Russie (which Chanel copied in 1924); his Rêve d'Or (1926) still sells in Arab countries today. Before World War II Piver had forty-four factories worldwide, but the "designer perfume" trend that began in the 1950s seriously crimped Piver's traditional market, so the company began to develop hair products as well. Bought in 1972 by Sogemaric, and in 1979 by Rhône-Poulenc, it was relaunched in the U.S. in 1991.

MARY QUANT

English ready-to-wear designer Mary Quant, born in England in 1934, studied at Goldsmith's College of Art where she met her husband, Alexander Plunket Greene. In 1956 she opened her first boutique, Bazaar, in London's King's Road. In 1961 Quant began to export to the U.S. and in 1963 started her famous Ginger Group line. The name Quant quickly became synonymous with the Swinging Sixties. Quant style championed the miniskirt and the Vidal Sassoon geometric haircut; she won an OBE (Order of the British Empire) in 1966, the same year she founded her makeup line with its famous daisy logo. Soon a flurry of other Quant products were developed: linens, stationery, carpets, and wallpaper. By the late 1970s her catalyzing influence had waned, though Mary Quant, Ltd., remains an important company with sales figures well into the millions of pounds annually.

REVLON

In 1932 Charles Revson decided to found a company to manufacture cosmetics products with his brother, Joseph, and a chemist, Charles Lachman. (He created the name Revlon by substituting an L from the name of his chemist for the S in his own name.) His empire was based on an opaque nail polish that used pigments instead of dyes for their colors. His intuition and dynamism enabled him to anticipate women's desires in cosmetics. In the middle of an economic recession, he offered gaiety, colors, diversity in selection, and a feel for luxury and quality. In 1939, implementing the idea of coordinating lipstick and nail colors catapulted Revlon into a multimillion-dollar business. He associated his products with the image of stars by having them pose for publicity shots as they toured the world. The company was responsible for a record number of innovations, as many for attention to detail as for cosmetics. In 1955 they invented a replaceable lipstick cartridge, calling it Futurama, and in 1958 they produced Touch & Glow, the first liquid makeup with a stable emulsion. Their research laboratories studied almost five hundred products at the same time. Since 1960, the brand has been diversified into various lines: Natural Wonder, Ultima II, Charles Revson, Princess Marcella Borghese and Norell. With each new line came a fragrance: Intimate, 1955; Charlie, 1973, from Revlon; Aquamarine from Natural Wonder; Ultima and Ciara from Charles Revson; Fiamma and Andiamo from Borghese. Ronald Perelman, CEO since 1985, is looking to expand the company; currently it ranks as the seventh largest cosmetics company in the world.

HELENA RUBINSTEIN

This brand of cosmetics was founded in 1902 by Helena Rubinstein, nicknamed by Jean Cocteau the "empress of beauty." She opened the Valaze House of Beauty in Australia in 1902. She then conquered London, Paris, and New York. The 1930s were important in terms of the number of salons she opened, and in other developments, especially waterproof mascara. After World War II, the company created products that were at the avant-garde of technology: a makeup remover called Deep Cleanser; the first vitamin-enriched product, Lanolin Vitamin Formula; the first hydrating product, Skin Dew; the first biological skin cream with scientifically proven effectiveness, Skin Life; and the first automatic mascara. This accomplished businesswoman was immortalized by the painters of her time, from Marie Laurencin to Dali. In 1988, the company was bought by L'Oréal.

SANOFI (ELF-SANOFI)

This French pharmaceutical group was created in 1973 by Rene Sautier and Jean-François Dechecq; it is now twenty-first among pharmaceutical groups in the world. Sanofi was born of the diversification of Elf-Aquitaine (a corporation with a petroleum division), and contains three manufacturing divisions: health, beauty, and food. The pharmacy branch represents more than 50 percent of sales, due to its alliances with Sanofi, Winthrop, and its development agreements with Bristol-Meyers-Squibb. The beauty branch became, after the acquisition of Yves Saint Laurent in January 1993, the world's third largest perfume and beauty corporation after L'Oréal and Estée Lauder. Besides Yves Saint Laurent, the group owns Roger & Gallet, Van Cleef & Arpels perfume, Stendhal, Oscar de la Renta, Geoffrey Beene, Perry Ellis, Krizia, and Fendi, 55 percent of Nina Ricci, and 63 percent of Yves Rocher.

SHISEIDO

Founded in 1872 by Yushin Fukuhara, grandfather of the present CEO, Shiseido was the first Western-style pharmacy in Japan and became the leading cosmetics manufacturer of the region. Shiseido translates as "Elegy of earthly virtues, bringing new life and engendering values." Pioneer of the oriental aesthetic in science and commerce, Shiseido's research showed a special dedication to the science of beauty and well-being. Its policy is corporate evidence of this concern: Shiseido puts part of its huge revenues into cultural events, opening in 1919 the first occidental art gallery in Japan and in 1937 publishing a popular magazine introducing Western culture to Japan. Now sold in forty countries, with its strategy for the year 2000 called "Grand Design," Shiseido produces cosmetics, toiletries, perfumes, pharmaceuticals, and food. In Europe and Japan their artistic director is Serge Lutens.

YARDLEY

William Yardley, son of the aristocratic family of the lords of Essex, founded this English perfume company in 1770 to make soap, floral waters, and hair wax. William's grandson, Charles Yardley, Jr., developed Yardley into a world-renowned firm. The company won prizes in 1851 and 1865 expositions and formed affiliates in Australia in 1910, in the U.S. in 1920, in Canada in 1923, and in France in 1924. Since 1921, Yardley has furnished soap to the Prince of Wales, thus enhancing the company's image as a symbol of British quality and style. In 1966, Yardley's look was updated by the sixties icon, Jean Shrimpton. Her natural beauty became its emblem, and demand for its products escalated to new heights—one thousand products were produced each week. English Lavender, invented in 1910, is still known the world over. In 1970 British American Tobacco acquired Yardley, which was bought again in 1986 by Beecham, and in 1990 by the U.S. concern Wasserstein, Perella & Co.

Library of Congress Cataloging-in-Publication Data
de Castelbajac, Kate
The face of the century: 100 years of makeup and style / Kate de Castelbajac
p. cm
ISBN 0-8478-1895-0
1. Cosmetics–History–20th century. 2. Fashion–History–20th century. 1. Title
GT2340.D43 1995   95-6718
391'.63'0904–dc20
CIP

Printed in Italy

This book was produced by Umbra Editions under the direction of Nan Richardson and Catherine Chermayeff with Kathy McCarver Mnuchin, Amy Kisch, Eric Rosen, Susan Duca, Tanuja Desai, Lala Herrero-Salas, and Carrie Breitinger. Melissa Pierson copyedited the text.

The book was designed by Roger Gorman of Reiner Design Consultants, Inc. New York, with assistance from Hannah Leider, Rick Patrick, and Stephan Jay-Rayon.

ACKNOWLEDGMENTS

To Guilhelm, Louis Marie, and Jean-Charles de Castelbajac, and to my father, William Chambers and my mother, Lillian Chambers, whose support and encouragement through this long endeavor was deeply appreciated.

I also owe an enormous debt to a large number of individuals who gave generously of their time and expertise on this subject. My grateful thanks especially to the following:

Alexandre; Dawn Baude; Geoffrey Beene; Laurence Benahim; Bettina; Bruno and Christina Bischofberger; Hazel Bishop; Lucy and François Boutin; Pierre Brochet; Catherine Canovas; Madelaine Castagne; May Castleberry; Joseph and Barbara Chambers; May Chan; Jacques Clement; Francesco Clemente; George and Anna Condo; André Courrèges; Lily Dacher; Barbara Daly; Jonathan David; Annabelle D'Huarte; Leslie Dunton Downer; Dominique Heriad Dubreuil; Jean Louis and Rena Dumas; Olivier Echaudmason; Loulou de la Falaise; Eileen Ford; Inès de la Fressange; Yoshiaharu Fukuhara; Naik le Fur; Marceline Gabel; Françoise Gilot; Keith Haring; Alain Jacquet; Dean Anne Jardim; Betsey Johnson; Grace Jones; William Klein; William I. Koch; John Leeds; Jacqueline du Lubac; Jose Luis; Marianne MacEvoy; Malcolm MacLaren; Pablo Manzoni; Karen Marta; Linda Mason; Chantal and Patrick de Maupou; Sue Mengers; Grace Mirabella; Issey Miyake; Heidi Morawetz; Suzanne Moncur; Thierry Mugler; Lindsay Owen Jones; Claude and Sydney Picasso; Richard Prince; Colombe Pringle; Paco Rabanne; Henri Racamier; Dr. Pomey Rey; Maurice Roger; Chantal Roos; Rex; Dominique de St. Mars; Kenny Scharf; Mary Secord; Antoinette Seilliere; Paul Sinclair; Catherine Stern; Robyn Peterson Surprenant; Lynn Sutherland; Deborah Turbeville; Tyen; Maria Jose Valadao; Guilhen de Vibraye; Kristen, Cynthia and Jack Vogel; Vivienne Westwood; Kansai Yamamoto; Yohji Yamamoto.

The following individuals provided the endless support, information, encouragement and sheer stamina necessary to bring this project to a satisfying conclusion.

Susannah Appelbaum, Testino Studio; Beth Balsam, Revlon; Lillian Bassman; Susan Bernard; Susan Biehn, Lancôme; Billy Boy; Kathleen Blumenfeld; Richard Brunning; Nancy Burson; Mikki Carpenter, MOMA; May Castleberry; Sasha Chermayeff; Mari Chihaya, Shiseido; Veronique Damagnez; Jonathan David; Diana Edkins, Condé Nast; David Fahey, Fahey/Klein Gallery; Daniela Ferro; Amy Fischer, Procter & Gamble; Raymond Foye; Monah Gettner; Dana Glazer; Guerlain; Angela Hart, Yardley of London; Susan Arnot Heany, Elizabeth Arden; Andy Karsch; Yasushi Kunii, Shiseido; Keith de Lellis; Peter Lindbergh; Davide Manfredi; Karen Marta, Rebecca McGreevy, Estée Lauder; Marlin Minks; Raymond Meier; Sarah Moon; Leah Nicole, Matthew Rolston Studio; Carolyn O'Connor, Revlon; Bill Orcutt; Lauren Purcell, Harper's Bazaar; Matthew Rolston; Irving Salero, F.I.T.; Manuela Salgo; Beth Savage, The Andy Warhol Foundation; Marina Schinz; Michael Shulman, Archive Pictures; Leslie Simitch; Giovanni Testino; Mario Testino; Deborah Turbeville; Astrid Vargas-Conte; Tom Walker; Mark Wanamaker, Bison Archive; Ron Warren, Mary Boone Gallery; Marvin Westmore; Taki Wise, Staley Wise Gallery, Tim Zach.

ILLUSTRATION CREDITS